VOLUNTARISM AND SOCIAL WORK PRACTICE

A Growing Collaboration

Edited by

Florence S. Schwartz
Hunter College of the
City University of New York

UNIVERSITY
PRESS OF
AMERICA

LANHAM • NEW YORK • LONDON

Copyright © 1984 by

University Press of America,™ Inc.

4720 Boston Way
Lanham, MD 20706

3 Henrietta Street
London WC2E 8LU England

Produced with funding from the
Lois and Samuel Silberman Fund and
The Association of Junior Leagues.

Co-Published by arrangement with
The Association of Junior Leagues.

Library of Congress Cataloging in Publication Data
Main entry under title:

Voluntarism and social work practice.

   1. Social service–United States–Addresses, essays,
lectures. 2. Voluntarism–United States–Addresses,
essays, lectures. 3. Volunteer workers in social service –
United States–Addresses, essays, lectures. 4. Social
service–Addresses, essays, lectures. 5. Voluntarism –
Addresses, essays, lectures. 6. Volunteer workers in social
service–Addresses, essays, lectures. I. Schwartz, Florence
S. (Florence Shisko), 1921–   .
HV91.V62   1984   361.3'7'0973   83–21749
ISBN 0–8191–3677–8 (alk. paper)
ISBN 0–8191–3678–6 (pbk. : alk. paper)

TABLE OF CONTENTS

PREFACE

These are watershed times for volunteering in America. As a
result of a variety of social, economic and political factors,
the "who, what, where, when, why and how" of volunteering have
all been subjected to scrutiny and have all undergone change.

Today's volunteers are young, old and in-between. They are male
and female, urban, suburban and rural, from every socioeconomic
group and every educational level. They still work in hospitals,
museums and religious institutions, but they also are advocates
for children in the courts, hospice workers, counsellors in shelters for battered women and career advisers for youth in prison.
Many are available 24 hours a day; many take time away from paid
careers to devote themselves to their volunteer commitments. They
volunteer for a variety of reasons. Certainly altruism remains
an important motivating factor for some volunteers. There are
many others, however, who, while not lacking a desire to help
others, are drawn to volunteering by an interest in learning new
skills, testing new career directions, meeting interesting people
or filling other gaps in their lives.

How people volunteer--the interaction between the volunteers themselves and the agencies with which they work--has been the area in
which change has been the hardest to identify. New patterns, new
ways of operating, while clearly necessary in the eyes of many,
have been slow to develop. It was to help meet this critical need,
particularly as it involved the relationship between social workers
and volunteers, that the Association of Junior Leagues convened an

an interagency task force whose members developed a project called
Voluntarism and Social Work Practice. The effort, supported by
the Lois and Samuel Silberman Fund and directed by Florence S.
Schwartz, was an attempt to build increased understanding of volunteers and their role in social agencies, and to encourage the
inclusion of material on volunteers in the social work curriculum.

This volume is only one of the outcomes of that program. It contains the scholarly work of many outstanding social work professionals and volunteers and can be used in both course work and
field work. Because of its breadth and quality, the material
presented here should lead to an enhanced understanding of voluntarism and its potential for improving the social service
delivery systems.

As an international organization with 150,000 members in the
United States, Canada, and Mexico, committed to promoting the
solution of community problems through the involvement of trained
volunteers, the Association of Junior Leagues is proud to have
played a part in this important effort.

Voluntarism and Social Work Practice fills a major gap in the
literature on voluntarism and it is our hope that, as it is used
to increase the social work profession's understanding of volunteers, it will ultimately help us all develop a more responsive
and productive social service system.

                              Deborah L. Seidel
                              Executive Director
                    The Association of Junior Leagues, Inc.

New York
August 1983

ACKNOWLEDGMENTS

Many people helped make this book a reality. Most of all, the volunteers and staff members who demonstrated the effectiveness of a working partnership.

Jon Van Til, as Editor-on-Chief of the Journal of Voluntary Action Research, provided the opportunity to publish most of these articles in the special issue on which this book is based. I am grateful to the Editor and Board of the Association of Voluntary Action Scholars for permission to reprint the articles. Special thanks to Dr. Van Til for his continued support and encouragement.

Stella Sanua shepherded the manuscript from beginning to end. Betty Anne Friedman did much of the editing. Ruby Fulk typed the manuscript.

Many readers provided professional expertise by commenting on the submissions.

Generous support was provided by the Association of Junior Leagues and the Lois and Samuel Silberman Fund.

My deep appreciation to them all.

                                        Florence S. Schwartz

VOLUNTARISM AND SOCIAL WORK PRACTICE
INTRODUCTION

Growing out of the project "Voluntarism and Social Work
Practice" directed by Florence S. Schwartz and supported by
the Association of Junior Leagues and the Lois and Samuel
Silberman Fund, this book responds to a gap identified by
project participants as - "a dearth of well researched and
well prepared professional writings that can be used as part of
curricula in courses, field work and special projects that will
help expand the education of social workers regarding the broad
range of volunteer programs, the history and role of voluntarism in our society, and the special techniques and guidelines professionals need to learn to deal with voluntarism."
Indeed, the need to make knowledge about voluntarism and the
important role of volunteers an integral part of professional
social work education has long been recognized by those working
with volunteers. The official if belated recognition given to
this problem by the Delegate Assemblies of NASW in 1977 and the
Council on Social Work Education in 1980 gave impetus to the
undertaking of the project from which this book comes.

This book edited by Florence S. Schwartz with its scholarly,
informative and provocative articles provides an excellent base
for meeting the expressed need. It should be useful not only to
students of social work, but also to accredited practitioners
whose professional education omitted knowledge about volunteers.
In my experience, attempts to introduce social work students
through field work to the roles of agency board members and
volunteers was thwarted because supervisors of social casework
students themselves often had no access to people carrying these
roles.

Except for the excellent article by Kramer which provides a
conceptual framework for the analysis of the relationship between
boards and their executive directors, the content of this book
does not cover the more familiar volunteer programs in traditional
agencies such as hospitals and familiar volunteer programs in
traditional agencies such as hospitals and family and children.
Rather it challenges social workers and their helping organizations to develop and expand volunteer programs to meet new and
changing ways of delivering service. Background articles provide
insights on current volunteer program practice problems by
placing them in the context of socio-economic and political
developments affecting voluntarism. For example, Reisch and
Wenocur examine the historical background of professional-

volunteer relationships as reflected in the development of voluntarism, and analyze the changing relationship between professionals and volunteers in the social services in the context of the changing role of social services in the United States' political economy. The authors urge the voluntary sector to help volunteers "move beyond their direct service roles" to community development activities such as need assessments in local communities, and through social action initiatives to promote new or changed services, to assist in finding funds and other necessary resources. This development, it is predicted, would change the professional-volunteer relationships into a partnership for social change, thus taking the voluntary agency back to its initial functions of pioneer, gadfly, and social reformer.

In his excellent well documented article, Guzzetta explores the issue of Volunteerism and Professionalism in terms of questions of identity and relationships as these have emerged and changed throughout the history of social services. He gives attention to the evolving meaning of "public" and "voluntary" agencies and the implications of these changes to volunteer-professional relationships, thus coming to the heart of a major problem for volunteer programs that has existed for many years.

The articles in this book are well researched, and tend to challenge the volunteer role in the present system of social service delivery by suggesting imaginative solutions to today's problems through the involvement of volunteers in new roles, and changed relationships between the volunteer and professional staff. This is accomplished by historical and analytical articles based on case examples.

Attention is given to the newer forms of human service delivery to meet more recently recognized needs such as child and spouse abuse, and alcoholism. These less bureaucratised organizations and self help groups offer a wide latitude for volunteer responsibility as did the early stages in the development of family and child welfare and other more traditional social service agencies. (Articles by Raiff and Shore, Weil, and Pincus and Keeling address volunteer roles in such settings.)

As reported in the article by Pincus and Keeling, the volunteer role experience of professionals acting as consultants to self help groups has important implications for both professional social workers and their agencies. Insights gained about the negative impact of behavior dictated by the professional role in a formal organization becomes clear to the professional experiencing a new growth experience when free to use knowledge without having to "wear the professional mask" in an informal, self help setting.

x

Indeed, Sequin notes the ability of older volunteers to take charge of programs for the aging by identifying tasks, recruiting and inducting older volunteers. Such programs have the dual goal of meeting the needs of the volunteers and of those served by the organization. These goals are not competing but complimentary. This excellent article takes into account both formal and informal communications of paid staff and volunteer staff, with specific reference as to how the volunteer structure is articulated with the organizational structure. It is helpful in giving both conditions for success and in recognizing limiting conditions.

The Weil article also concerns the aging, by reporting and analyzing a successful project in which seniors planned and lobbied for needed services after undertaking a major needs assessment. They developed a model for comprehensive services for the aging which they then advocated and for which they won success.

An article by Perlmutter argues the advantages of having a professional social worker serve as administrator of volunteer programs because through professional sanctions there is easier access to the executive director, board, staff, and organizational supports. Another article by Cynthia Pincus urges that the advocacy function of volunteers be structurally separated from the responsibility of the agency's volunteer department. An advocacy department should report directly to the Executive Director and the board and be agency wide in its relationships. Perlmutter also recognized the need for specialized training programs for coordinators of volunteers and advocates that such training be provided by schools of social work which offer a concentration in administration.

A number of articles suggest content for professional training, particularly the one by Herrington who indicates how knowledge and practice can be integrated in the current curriculum through various courses, or be given as a separate course or courses. There is general support for a practicum through a field work experience which involves working with volunteers in direct service, on committees and boards. This training presumably covers professional roles vis-a-vis volunteer roles in direct service, advocacy, training and administration.

An informative and provocative article analyzes the variables affecting volunteer participation by minorities. This piece by King Davis should be required reading for social work students. Several articles explore changing concepts of volunteer motivation and take into account self fulfillment and self actualization. The final article by Eva Schindler-Rainman projects the future of volunteers in a changing society and

predicts the use of new technologies in accomplishing these
tasks.

This book offers valuable information for human service agency
boards, administrators and staffs who should be encouraged to
redesign their volunteer programs so as to make them an integral
part of the administration of the programs, and more responsive
to the needs of volunteers and constituents.

It is to be hoped that sequels to the articles in this book will
address organizational structures which facilitate professional
and volunteer staff relationships. Another area insufficiently
addressed here is the unique contribution made by the volunteer
by virtue of the volunteer status not possible to the paid
professional.

Two articles address the need for collaboration among volunteers,
professional social workers and schools of social work in order
to break stereotypes about volunteers held by professional
social workers. The article by Lowy reports on an experiment
in Germany while Schwartz reports on the project in the United
States of which this book is a product.

May this project encourage social agencies, professional associations, organizations promoting volunteer work, and schools of
social work actively to promote the inclusion in professional
social work education of knowledge about voluntarism and the
knowledge and skills needed to work with volunteers and to
administer volunteer programs. It would be appropriate for the
coalition of organizations that worked together to sponsor the
project which gave birth to this book, Voluntarism and Social
Work Practice, to carry forward to fruition a long overdue
development in social work education.

Violet M. Sieder, PhD
Professor Emerita
Brandeis University

PROFESSIONALIZATION AND VOLUNTARISM IN SOCIAL WELFARE: CHANGING ROLES AND FUNCTIONS

Michael Reisch

Stanley Wenocur

University of Maryland at Baltimore
Baltimore, Maryland

INTRODUCTION

This paper explores the relationship between voluntarism and the professionalization of the helping function by social work within the voluntary social welfare system. Our thesis is that this relationship has been one of tension as a result of changes in the political economy with regard to the provision of social protection and social welfare services. This tension has led to role differentiation, specialization, and functional loss by volunteers and social workers. The essence of this tension has been the efforts of social workers historically to move the provision of social work services from the sphere of voluntary activities into the arena of paid occupational roles that carry with them the status, opportunities and rewards of professionalism. This ongoing transformation also needs to be viewed in the broader context of social welfare in industrial and post-industrial capitalism.

If the lessons of history are meaningful, the voluntary sector would be misguided to interpret recent events as an opportunity to reassert its former dominance in the social services field. Nor should the voluntary sector confuse its traditional devotion to de-centralized decision making and service delivery with the Reagan Administration's sweeping reductions in public social services and benefits carried out under the rubric of returning control to localities. The prior failure of the voluntary sector to alleviate the social costs of industrial capitalism occurred, not for lack of effort or will, but for lack of resources and an insufficient analysis of the roots of the problems with which it was confronted. The failure of the social work profession to make a greater impact on the alleviation of social distress relates similarly to a faulty analysis which has led to a willingness to sacrifice its reformist ideals for much more narrow technocratic solutions.

1

DEFINITIONS

As defined in this paper, voluntary social welfare organizations, in contrast to public or private-for-profit social welfare enterprises, are characterized by (a) incorporation on a non-profit basis, currently with 501 c(3) status; (b) a group of private citizens organized to pursue their particular social welfare-related values of interests, with (c) no legal responsibility for the general welfare or for continuation beyond the extent of their own interests, and (d) funded heavily, though not exclusively, through voluntary contributions (Levin, 1977). These organizations include those which provide direct services to individuals and families, social planning, community development, and social reform activities. For our purposes, the sum total of these organizations in American society constitutes the voluntary social welfare sector.

Professional social work, in this paper, refers to the occupational activities of persons credentialed by social work educational programs at the Bachelors, Masters, or Doctoral degree level. In this paper, "volunteers are individuals who freely contribute their services, without remuneration, to public or voluntary organizations engaged in all types of social welfare activities" (Sieder and Kirshbaum, 1977). Finally, by political economic analysis, we mean the study of both the economic and the political systems, with specific attention to the interrelationships between them.

HISTORICAL BACKGROUND

The same political and socio-economic forces which led to the creation of voluntary social service organizations ultimately produced the phenomenon of professionalization that subsequently altered and, to some extent, jeopardized the status of voluntarism. Initially, voluntary societies developed both to serve humanitarian ends and to increase the strength of organized churches in American social life (Banner, 1973: 23-31; de Tocqueville, 1945 ed.).

Yet, motives beyond benevolence spurred the growth of voluntarism in the United States during the first half of the nineteenth century. For women, voluntary activity provided a means to do social good and enhanced their awareness of social inequality. Many women volunteers in "social welfare" organizations formed the core of the emerging feminist movement (Banner, 1973: 33). For religious humanitarians, the voluntary association constituted "the third major ingredient of a 'Christian Republicanism', a potential deterrent to the excessive accumulation of power by the federal government and a means for "involving citizens with their government and thus insuring that democracy would actually function in a republican framework" (Banner, 1973: 40; Gutman, 1976). Others saw the voluntary organization as a means to create a "harmonious community" to protect traditional social values and social relationships. Some observers were skeptical, however, that the democratic vision they desired could be produced in the microcosm of the association.

These doubts were justified. Upper class men quickly dominated these voluntary organizations and shaped them to their values and interests. This paralleled the spread of upper class dominance in other parts of the U.S. political economy. The creation of endowed cultural and service institutions by wealthy individuals and families reflected efforts by the emerging commercial class to gain an additional means of economic control. Such institutions freed businesses from familial and community demands and served as a device for the concentration of diffuse investment capital (Hall, 1974: 4). A significant consequence of this development was that the upper class strengthened its hold on the capital resources of the nation and extended this power to all areas of cultural and social life. This included the administration of major social welfare organizations and the credential-granting apparatuses for the emerging professions. The impact of this far-reaching control became apparent at the end of the nineteenth century when a new form of voluntary service association--the Charities Organization Society--arose.

Most sources agree that the rapid growth of the COS--more than 150 appeared between 1877-1904--reflected more than a widespread effort to reform existing practices in "charities and corrections." The participants in the COS also sought to heal the wounds of social life which industrial growth and urbanization had wrought and to recreate a semi-mythic vision of an "organic community" (Bender, 1972). The notion of an "organic community" rested on a pathological view of urban life and the urban working classes, particularly the foreign born. The COS, therefore, sought to produce its version of "a more complete democracy" by emulating "the virtues of the small town in the settings of an urban, industrial system" (Kusmer, 1973: 666-67; Gettleman, 1963: 327; Wiebe, 1967; for a later example see Mills, 1943). This approach did not fundamentally alter the economic, social and political status quo.

In fact, many businessmen and professionals were attracted to this new form of voluntary organization because it aimed to alleviate social ills without jeopardizing the privileges of the upper class. Supporters of the COS agreed with the Reverend D. O. Kellogg that organized charity represented "the real answer to the Socialistic and Communistic theories now being energetically taught to the people" (Quoted in Gettleman, 1963: 318). Indeed, the COS became an instrument in the establishment of control by the corporate class over all aspects of social and institutional life (Kolko, 1967).

The critical feature of the COS was its use of volunteers--friendly visitors-- to establish personal relationships with the poor. Volunteers were to use their influence and practical suggestions, rather than alms, to alleviate the plight of the needy. Friendly visitors were usually upper or middle class women, who were attracted to social activism by the influence of feminist ideas, a sense of noblesse oblige, and a view of charity work as an extension of their domestic role (Kusmer, 1973: 669-71; Becker, 1964: 59). COS literature stressed the paramount importance of the friendly visitors, assumed that volunteer work was superior to paid work, and that voluntary service was, in many ways, unique. Indeed, friendly visitors combined both expressive and instrumental functions in their work--a combination of moralism and scientific analysis (Becker, 1964: 62-63).

Experience tempered the initial moralism of the COS with a broader understanding of socio-economic issues. Nevertheless, the COS failed to engage in a rigorous analysis of the roots of poverty and chose to avoid rather than confront the issue of class conflict. This stance enabled the COS movement to retain the support of the business community throughout the heyday of organized charities (Kusmer, 1973: 668, 672-76; Gettleman, 1975: 57; Gettleman, 1963: 325; Becker, 1964: 71). There was a congruence between COS activities and the interests of sponsors. Yet, the expansion of COS activities promoted specialization within the volunteer role and led to the emergence of social work as a profession. Such specialization, however, coincided with the needs of the broader political economy (Leiby, 1978: 356).

At the outset, professional charity workers comprised the smallest component of the staffs of the COS and were regarded as the "handmaidens" of the friendly visitors. Their functions included program development, fund raising and supervision. By the late 1890's, however, social needs increased to the extent that it became clear volunteers could not handle them adequately. They could not meet either the intellectual demands or the need for efficiency in operation. By the turn of the century, the tenets of scientific charity were more consistently applied through the medium of professional expertise (Kusmer, 1973: 662; Levin, 1969: 86). For example, in the aftermath of the depression of the 1890's, the New York City COS increased its professional staff by one-third and the call went out in the voluntary sector for the creation of professional training schools for charity workers (Becker, 1964).[1]

The advent of professional training soon thereafter accelerated the demise of the friendly visitors. By 1907, more than half of the major COS had abandoned their use entirely (Jones and Herrick, 1976: 4). Ten years later, the roles of professionals and volunteers in the COS were reversed. Volunteers were restricted to carefully defined and supervised roles and, in many cities, did little more than routine office work. Their members had declined to a level as low as 25% of the peak years of voluntary activity in the 1890's (Kusmer, 1973: 671-72; Becker, 1964: 67-69). This decline in numbers may also have been exacerbated by the shift in interest among potential women volunteers from the "social question" to issues involving women's suffrage, temperance and pacifism.[2]

After a temporary resurgence of voluntarism during World War I, the demise of volunteers in social welfare organizations continued in the 1920's. Although statistics on volunteer activity in the 1920's are difficult to find, available evidence indicates that social service agencies continued to make less frequent use of volunteers as the professional social work enterprise spread. Difficulties in training and supervising volunteers and the absence of clear definitions of appropriate volunteer roles were frequently cited as factors which compounded the problem (Jones and Herrick, 1976: 12-16).

The tremendous increase in social and individual needs produced by the Great Depression of the 1930's led to massive public sector intervention in the social services to prevent social upheaval and revive the shattered U. S. economy. This stimulated the demand for personnel - a demand which professional social work lacked the resources to meet. Volunteers provided an obvious solution, but integrating volunteers into social service organizations was complicated. The development of a large public welfare bureaucracy, the emergence of group work as a method of professional social work and the growing thrust towards psychological treatment in family service agencies raised additional questions about the volunteer-professional relationship in social work.

In the end, staff shortages in the public sector led to an accommodation of sorts in which personnel standards were lowered to facilitate volunteer participation. The absence of clear professional boundaries defining group work allowed greater flexibility in the utilization of volunteer staff in settlement houses and community centers. And, in family agencies, a renewed interest in voluntary activity developed in the late 1930's along with new efforts to devise ways to involve volunteers more successfully (Levin, 1969: 88; Jones and Herrick, 1976: 26-27, 43-44, 62-63). By the end of the New Deal era, a common pattern of staff organization in voluntary agencies appeared, consisting of a lay board, professional staff and volunteer auxiliaries.

After World War II, volunteer agencies concentrated on clarifying further issues of volunteer participation and board-professional relationships. By the 1950's, an uncomfortable compromise had been reached. Professionals were given control over direct service functions, administration and training. Volunteer boards were given policy making duties, while volunteers in direct service were left with nonspecified or clerical responsibilities (Levin, 1969: 89-90).

By the late 1950's, the awareness of social need faded as a consumer-oriented, service dominated economy emerged. Voluntary agencies now served clients who were often from middle or upper income groups. Their needs were more likely to be defined as psycho-social rather than socio-economic. This "disengagement from the poor" served well the professional aspirations of the social work enterprise. No longer were social workers regarded largely as dispensers of charity. With this shift came an acceptance of the volunteer-professional role distinctions that had evolved since the New Deal. The "rediscovery" of poverty and its consequences in the next decade marked a rude awakening for the social service field that challenged and, eventually, overhauled the existing arrangement of volunteer-professional relationships.

THE EXPANSION OF THE SOCIAL SERVICE SECTOR, 1960-1980

The professionalization of social work that began at the turn of the century accelerated rapidly in the 1960's and 1970's with the expansion of government spending for social welfare. But professionalization and the growth of services were not limited to the sphere of social work alone. Rather they have paralleled changes in the larger political-economy characterized by Bell (1973) and others during the 1970's as "the coming of post-industrial society" and "the change from a goods producing to a service economy" (Bell, 1973). The expansion of voluntarism during this same period represents still another service-related facet of "post-industrial" change and, therefore, needs to be interpreted in that context.

The expansion of the welfare state in the last twenty years has been an in-fluential ingredient in the growth of the service sector in the U. S. economy. Between 1960 and 1975 social welfare expenditures, including education, in the public sector grew from $52.3 billion to $286.5 billion and nearly doubled as a percentage of the GNP, increasing from 10.6% to 20.1% (NASW, 1977).

By comparison, the expansion of the voluntary sector has been a much smaller aspect of service sector growth as reflected approximately in private philan-thropic allocations in the fields of health, education and welfare. Between 1960 and 1975 these allocations expanded from $3.8 to $10.1 billion, clearly a growth in absolute dollars, but a significant drop proportionately in relation to public expenditures for the same purposes (NASW, 1977).

Additional data on the size and relative growth rate in the voluntary social welfare sector can be obtained by comparing fund-raising figures for local United Way Organizations (LUWO's) between 1960 and 1975. These agencies, which support some 37,000 member service organizations, form the core of the voluntary social welfare sector by dint of the historical ties between the United Way and its Charity Organization Society counterpart a century ago. Between 1960 and 1975, the total of LUWO fund-raising in the U.S. and Canada increased 110%, from $486 million to $1.023 billion. Considered over a fifteen year span, the annual increase averaged between 2 and 6%, barely able to keep pace with rises in the cost of living (United Way of America, 1971-72, 1976-77).

The import of the figures presented thus far seems fairly clear. We must first look to the public sector to assess the political-economy of social welfare and professional social work. Because of the magnitude of the changes there, the impact of the public sector on professionalization and voluntarism has been profound, as well. With limited space to develop a full picture here, the points we would like to make about the political economy of social services are as follows:

First, the development and growth of major social programs over the past two decades, such as Medicare and Medicaid, SSI, Title XX, and the Community Mental Health Act, seem to have established in the liberal consciousness an acceptance of "the welfare state" as a minimum requirement of modern society to ensure social protection and improve the quality of life. In the 1970's, however, conservatives vigorously debated the definitions and levels of these minimum requirements. As higher wages and increased services (in cash and kind) raised the real income of the working class, conservatives have reaped political capital by focusing on the burden of high taxes and the need for a balanced budget.

Secondly, some economists have treated social service spending as an important "counter-cyclical" tool for stabilizing the economy. Thus, the public social welfare sector, as a massive transfer payment system, has served as (1) a stimulant to the economy; (2) a mechanism for reducing inflation by making higher levels of unemployment more tolerable, and (3) a means for directing the flow of subsidy payments to selected sectors of the economy (e.g., housing, food, health, industry) (Horesji, 1977). From a political perspective, the welfare system has also served as a means to control the marginal work force and to cool civil unrest (Piven and Cloward, 1971).

Thirdly, the flexibility of the social service sector budget as a counter-cyclical mechanism has required the introduction of massive information and accountability systems and planning/managerial expertise--termed the "rationalization of social services" (Hirschhorn, 1978). Thus, in a capitalistic economy subject to upward and downward economic growth cycles, "the size, scope...and timing of social service spending are all determined by the existing conditions of production" (Hirschhorn, 1978: 154). The rationalization of social services refines the capabilities of the public sector as a transfer system.

Fourth, this rationalization has been weighted towards meeting short-term political-economic exigencies rather than long-term investments in creating an educated, technically skilled and physically healthy workforce. The emphasis on cost-benefit formulations has limited the realization of the potential of social services to stimulate continued economic growth through innovation, knowledge development and the creation of new consumer markets including services themselves.[3]

Fifth, social service expansion raises with it the issue of political control over the resulting development (Hirschhorn, 1978). With investment in human capital, newly productive groups compete over ideological definitions, resources and control of different parts of the economy. While innovation may be intellectually desirable, it is also threatening to the existing political economic structure (cf. Toffler, 1980). Ironically, this struggle for control represents a serious contradiction of social service development in post-industrial society. In the words of Hirschhorn (1978: 165),

> To the degree that services do not become developmental,
> to the degree that they do not transform production,
> marketing, and job allocation, then to that degree do
> services become unproductive, wasteful and irrational.
> We face the "development of underdevelopment" at the
> center of late capitalist societies.

PROFESSIONALIZATION AND "VOLUNTARIZATION" OF THE SOCIAL WELFARE SECTOR

THE EXPANSION OF THE SOCIAL SERVICE WORK FORCE

The expansion of the social welfare sector in the last twenty years involved
extensive growth in the social service work force, far beyond comparable growth
in the civilian labor force and other professional, technical and kindred
workers (PTKs). This rapid expansion represents a significant factor by itself
in the political-economy of professional social work and voluntarism. As shown
in Table 1, between 1960 and 1977 the civilian labor force grew by 41%, the PTK
work force by 89%, and the social service work force by 242%.

TABLE 1*

Total Employed Civilian Labor Force, Professional-
Technical and Kindred Workers, and Social Service
Workers (in thousands)

Year	Civilian Labor Force	PTK	Social Service Workers
1960	64,000	7,223	95
1970	77,500	11,351	217
1974	85,900	12,338	300
1977	90,500	13,692	325

*Siegel, 1975. Table augmented by figures from Table 19, Employed Persons by
Detailed Occupation, 1972-77, Handbook of Labor Statistics,
1978, U. S. Department of Labor, June 1979.

When public and voluntary social welfare programs expand, the demand for social
workers and other human service workers goes up correspondingly. When these
programs contract, so does the demand. From a political-economic perspective,
social service workers operate in a competitive market place and are dependent
almost entirely upon the state and private philanthropy to purchase their
services. Professionalization of social work with its concomitant thrust
towards licensing can be viewed as an attempt to regulate market demand and
supply through the development of institutional controls (Hardcastle and Katz,
1979).

THE PROFESSIONALIZATION OF SOCIAL WORK: 1960-1980

In the last twenty years of public and voluntary social service expansion, the
supply of professional social workers could not keep pace with the market
despite federal funding to support social work education. This supply-demand

situation, along with the rejuvenation of voluntarism stimulated by government in the same period, altered the shape of the social work profession and its relationship to voluntarism.

Precise figures on the extent of social work professionalization in the public and voluntary sectors are difficult to obtain. Yet, the data for the period 1963-1978 suggest that

(a) by the late 1970's, the professionalized social work force had increased from 15,400 to 30,800 in the voluntary sector and 92,400 to 123,000 in the public; and

(b) the growth of the professional social work force could not keep pace with the tripling of demand for social service workers (Hardcastle and Katz, 1979; NASW, 1977; Bureau of Labor Statistics, 1981).

In brief, the professionalization of social work in the past twenty years received much direct support from public funds, as the government tried to meet its personnel needs for an expanding social service sector. The government not only gave funds directly for student training, particularly at the MSW level, but it also supported efforts to establish undergraduate and doctoral education as a means for meeting the demands for social service workers. Little of this direct public support promoted the professionalization by social work of the voluntary sector. Professional social workers were attracted to the public sector in much greater numbers than to the voluntary, primarily because of the job opportunities there. NASW members involuntarily unemployed stayed remarkably low at 3% or less (Hardcastle and Katz, 1979). Still the supply of professional social workers could not keep pace with the demand.

Outside of support to professional social work, the efforts of government to expand the social services sector took many different forms responsive to still other pressures in the larger society. Ultimately, these initiatives created a series of political-economic problems for the social work profession. The efforts of social work to resolve these dilemmas bear directly on volunteer-professional role tensions and compatibilities.

In response to its staffing shortages, and out of a desire to respond to and blunt the thrust of community-based social action organizations during the past two decades, the government encouraged and even required the participation of non-professional community residents on the boards of newly formed or re-constituted community agencies (Gilbert, 1970; Moynihan, 1969; Marris and Rein, 1967). Government also promoted the training and utilization of community residents in direct service positions as "paraprofessionals" (Austin, 1978; Pearl and Riessman, 1965; Grosser et al., 1969; Sobey, 1970). Consequently, between 1960-70 the number of non-college educated, non-trained social service workers increased from 11,580 to 41,887, or from 10 to 19% of the total social service work force (Siegel, 1975: 10).

The social work profession acted to ensure that the expansion of the social service component of the labor force would not jeopardize its tenuous monopoly in the human service field. Through the vehicle of professional accreditation, the profession asserted control over new undergraduate training programs by creating standards for BSW education, opening membership in NASW to BSW graduates (1972), and developing a six level classification plan for social service workers with the BSW graduate as the entry level professional for social service employment (1973). Social work also paid increasing attention to

8

licensing procedures and regulations which defined the relationship between paraprofessionals and professionals. The latter ensured the maintenance of professional dominance over the definition of social work functions.[4]

Nevertheless, from a political-economic perspective, the evidence of the past two decades suggests that the social work profession has been only partially successful in its efforts to preserve its dominant position in the human services (Specht, 1972). The emergence and growth of other human service programs such as family and community development, human ecology, educational counselling, marital counselling, etc. and the expansion of other professions like nursing into areas previously limited to social work, have forced the social work profession to redefine its professional function within a changing political economy. One aspect of this redefinition has been the increasing incorporation of business-oriented technologies into social work practice--in the areas of fiscal planning, management and program evaluation, for example--as part of a broad-based attempt to bring the social work enterprise into the mainstream of political-economic developments and ensure its continued viability in the eyes of its sponsors (Lewis, 1978). Another feature of the profession's redefinition has been the expansion of the social work enterprise into relatively uncharted regions of professional practice, such as industrial social work and rural services, where the dominance of one profession has not been established.

A third component of this redefinition has been the reconceptualization of the relationship between the social work profession and the voluntary sector and the relative roles of volunteers and professionals within the service agency. There is evidence that the disaffection of many social workers with employment conditions in the public sector has begun to swell the ranks of private practice, rather than practice within the voluntary sector (Hardcastle and Katz, 1979; Stoesz, 1980). Yet the growth of the voluntary sector as a consequence of Revenue Sharing and Title XX--what Smith (1979) calls the increasing public use of the private sector--has produced an increase in the use of quasi-voluntary service organizations to meet social service needs, and hence more funds for hiring social work professionals. As we enter the 1980's, this trend remains uncertain. The Reagan Administration is moving resolutely towards the use of block grants to state and local governmental units for social service funding, along with a concomitant reduction in monies within the block grants and a philosophical emphasis on market place solutions for service needs. The latter thrust could encourage greater professional entrepreneurship via professional consultation and private practice instead of a growth in voluntary sector-governmental partnership arrangements.

A by-product of the revitalization of the voluntary sector and the reduction in the general level of government social service expenditures in recent years has been the development of new forms of service delivery--the resurgence of self-help groups and the promotion of networking, both of which have their roots in a broadly felt, somewhat amorphous dissatisfaction that antedates the current growth of the voluntary sector partially supported by public funds. Both have been utilized by consumers as alternatives to traditional social service delivery systems. Yet the pressures of political-economic developments are now making these alternative forms attractive to mainstream service providers (Stoesz, 1980; Sarason and Lorentz, 1979). These developments are likely to have considerable impact, not merely on the types of services offered to communities, but also on the relationships between professionals and volunteers within these remodelled service settings, and more broadly on government-voluntary sector relationships. Before making some prognoses regarding these trends and some recommendations about policy formulation in the decade ahead, it will be helpful to complete the last section of our review and analysis, namely, the growth of voluntarism in the last twenty years and the government's role therein.

THE EXPANSION OF VOLUNTARISM, 1960-1980

The expansion of voluntarism in the past two decades is a well-known social phenomenon. Data on this expansion are presented and reviewed briefly below along with a review of government activity to promote voluntarism. But more important for our purposes will be the establishment of a connection between the growth of voluntarism and (1) the post-industrial political-economic milieu in which it occurred, (2) the challenge it has posed for the professionalization of social work, and (3) the ways in which this challenge has been accommodated in voluntary-professional relationships.

Between 1960 and 1980, government efforts to promote voluntarism took many forms including legislative sanction for voluntary activity in the public social services sector through amendments in 1962, 1967 and 1974 to the Social Security Act; the establishment of the federal National Program for Voluntary Action (1969) and an Office of Voluntary Action in the Executive Branch (1969, later abolished); the creation of VISTA, the Peace Corps, and a series of additional volunteer programs such as Foster Grandparents and the Retired Senior Volunteer Program (RSVP) and their consolidation into ACTION (1971) as the federal agency responsible for promoting voluntarism; and the Voluntary Services Act of 1973. The federal government also encouraged, originally with federal dollars and cabinet-level support during the Nixon Administration, the development of a non-governmental structure to promote and coordinate voluntarism--the National Center for Voluntary Action (NCVA). The success of NCVA can be measured by the 350 plus Voluntary Action Centers (VACs) which it established throughout the country, funded largely by United Way Organizations with some additional resources from other voluntary sector organizations and local governmental units. Through the "New Federalism" and the implementation of Title XX (1975) of the Social Security Act, the government further encouraged and stimulated government-voluntary sector arrangements for the delivery of services.

Like professional social work, voluntarism became a thriving enterprise in the nurturant environment provided by government to expand the social service sector. A number of national organizations outside of government were formed to promote and protect voluntarism, such as The Independent Sector; books and articles burgeoned in scholarly circles; and trade journals, such as Volunteer's Digest, Volunteer Leader, the Grantsmanship Center News and the Philanthropy Monthly were created, reflecting a sizable constituency and the need for communication and coordination within an increasingly coherent, revitalized sector of growth in its own right (Langton, 1980; Smith, 1973, 1974).

The statistics on the growth of voluntarism are impressive. In 1974, 24% of the population over age 13, or some 37 million persons, performed voluntary work in an organized setting, an increase of nearly 60% from 1965 (Americans Volunteer, 1969, 1975).[5] In both years, volunteers were more likely to be white women between the ages of 25-54. For convenience these comparative figures are presented in Table 2.

Not shown in Table 2 is the fact that for both survey years voluntarism was clearly associated with education, occupation and income. In other words,

Table 2*

Comparative Data on Voluntarism in the United States for the Years 1965 and 1974

	1965	1974
Number of volunteers	22 million	37 million
Average Hours Worked per Week	5.6	9.0
Number of Paid Workers in Labor Force	71 million	85 million
Work Force Equivalent of Volunteers at 40 Hours per Week for a Year	940,000 persons	3.5 million persons
Percent of Persons Over Age 14 Who Volunteered	18% (16%)**	24% (20%)**
Percent of Male Volunteers in Population	15%	20%
Percent of Female Volunteers in Population	21%	26%
Race		
Black	10%	13%
White & Other	19%	25%
Age Group Participation Rate (% of Civilian Population)		
Age 25-54	21.7%	30%
Age 45-54	18.1%	25%

* Data are based on two national surveys by the United States Bureau of the Census, one in 1965 for the Department of Labor and one in 1975 for ACTION which was designed to be comparable. (See Americans Volunteer, 1969 and 1975.)

** Percent adjusted to exclude volunteers in religious organizations.

voluntarism, not surprisingly, appears to be related to social class such that the higher the class, based on occupation, income and education, the higher the rate of voluntary participation.[6]

Two additional national surveys conducted for the Filer Commission in 1974 (Morgan et al., 1977: 169) also indicated that while volunteering was widely distributed, a relatively small percentage of households accounted for a majority of the volunteer work.

The magnitude of volunteering in human service organizations during the last twenty years suggests that voluntarism has played a significant political-economic role in the post-industrial expansion of the social service sector and may continue to do so in the future. This new role has also posed several challenges to the professionalization of social work. Wolozin calculated that between 1964 and 1974 the dollar value of volunteer services contributed by Americans increased nearly five times to more than $33.9 billion in 1974 (1974: 4). If these figures were included, the services component of the GNP would have risen by more than 6% in 1974.

As a self-contained, growing segment of the U.S. economy, the voluntary sector has created a sizable artificial, non-paid labor market. These data are reflected in Table 2, in the 3.5 million person workforce equivalent provided by volunteers in 1974. This "artificial" workforce has been augmented by the government-sponsored ACTION program in at least two important ways: first, its senior citizen programs, RSVP and Foster Grandparents, which respectively had 269,000 and 17,425 volunteers in 1980, enabled the government to provide a service to the elderly and through them to others, and to encourage the adjustment of the alleged "less-productive" members of the labor force to their retirement from the labor market; secondly, through its programs directed at youth and low income persons, especially VISTA with 4,400 "quasi"-volunteers in 1980, the government provided low-paid personnel for a broad range of voluntary sector organizations to meet social service needs. One economic effect of this expansion of the voluntary sector has been to depress the salaries of social service workers, professional and non-professional.

Another impact suggested by these data has been that with volunteers as a "cushion," it is easier for human services to be cut back, since their presence blunts social conflict that might have been engendered by the reductions in needed services. Since the majority of volunteers are women, a third effect, according to feminists (Heide, 1973; Sherman, 1975; Trefethen, 1975) has been the perpetuation of sex-role stereotypes of women who perform vast quantities of unpaid work, often in direct service functions, as though their time had no economic value.

While some question this, it is through these functions that voluntarism has presented the greatest threats to professional social work. Its role in depressing professional wage levels is fairly apparent. Another source of threat, less apparent, has been that voluntarism itself has begun to become professionalized, just as social welfare did in an earlier era. The professionalization of voluntary action has primarily occurred in the area of volunteer administration, recognized by the Department of Labor in its 1976 Dictionary of Occupational Titles, which specifies a six-step career ladder for volunteer administrators. Through an emphasis on volunteer coordination, training of volunteers, and consultation on the administration of volunteer programs, as stressed by the Voluntary Action Centers (Sieder and Kirshbaum, 1977), the volunteer work force is, in effect, being shaped to meet social service needs efficiently and effectively. Specially trained, and already either well-educated or possessing some unique attribute based on a special knowledge of or relationship to a client population, the volunteer rather directly challenges the value of the specialized competence claimed by the professional social worker.

According to the Bureau of the Census (Americans Volunteer, 1974: 22) and United Way studies (1974), the most prevalent form of volunteer work by far has been the provision of direct service, as opposed to organizational sustaining activities (fund-raising) or board/committee policy and planning work. These latter categories of voluntary activity have presented the least threat to the social work profession because they fundamentally create and support social service organization--the remnant of an historical, philanthropic obligation rooted in class privilege and prerogatives. The threat of the direct service volunteer to social work's claims for professional status and rewards, however, has been well recognized by the social work profession. It has been acknowledged, for example, in NASW's Standards for Social Work Personnel Practices (1975: 23), section 14.0 on "Use of Volunteers":

The primary purpose for the use of volunteers shall be to enrich, extend, or otherwise to supplement the services of agency staff for the benefit of clients. When volunteers are used, the agency shall have a written policy that includes the following points:

1. A clear delineation of the functions and activities appropriate for volunteer and paid staff....

4. Procedures for orienting and training as well as for monitoring the activities and contributions of volunteers to the service or program.

5. A statement of assurance that volunteers will not be utilized in any way that would decrease the use of paid personnel. It should be a fundamental personnel policy of any agency or institution making use of unpaid volunteers that such personnel will not be permitted to supplant regular, paid staff. (emphasis added)

While these policies may make good administrative sense, they also serve to protect the professional domain of social work practice by carefully regulating the role of the volunteer and fitting him/her into the definitions of service controlled by the social work professional.

In a broader sense, the treatment of voluntarism by the social work profession is in keeping with its political-economic requirements for professionalization. In order to sustain and build the professional enterprise, social work must recruit consumers and producers, control entry to the profession, support its claims to specialized competency, and maintain positive relations with political elites who will, in turn, support the professional enterprise. The educated volunteers in social welfare agencies furnish a pool of recruits for further professional training through their experiences in the social service agencies, so long as that experience remains unpaid or underpaid and carefully monitored to prevent encroachment on professional "turf." At the same time, concentration in direct service technologies and rationalization of service delivery can easily be supported by the largely upper-middle and upper class business and professional elites who constitute social agency boards and advisory committees and carry out its organization-sustaining work, also as volunteers. In these ways, voluntarism is accommodated to the political-economy of professionalization and vice-versa. When the helping function was professionalized by social work, the social reform function that was also part of its historic tradition was vitiated. The accommodation of voluntarism to professionalization in social work and the professionalization of voluntary action as a continuing dynamic of "post-industrial" capitalism suggest that this conservative pattern may be repeated in the future.

CONCLUSION

This paper has sought to analyze the changing relationship between professionals and volunteers in the social service sector, in the context of the changing role of social services in the U.S. political-economy. In the late 19th and early 20th century, when industrial capitalism was rapidly expanding, the voluntary sector accepted primary responsibility for addressing the social costs generated by this growth. The social work profession emerged in the efforts to find better ways to manage these responsibilities, thereby creating a tension between voluntarism and professionalization in social welfare.

With the Depression of the 1930's, the voluntary sector was forced to acknowledge that it could no longer manage the burden it had taken on, and the public sector--particularly the federal government--began to take over. For social work, the development of public social services provided new opportunities for professional expansion. Since the Depression, the growth and continued profitability of the corporate sector has been made possible by the shift of the social costs of private enterprise onto the public sector (Kapp, 1947; O'Connor, 1973). During the last twenty years, public sector services burgeoned in the social welfare field as well as in many other new areas. In order to meet staffing needs in the public social services sector, government promoted both the professionalization of social work (and other human service professions) and voluntarism. Government support satisfied the self-interests of both of these groups as well as provided a means for handling other political and economic pressures. Increasingly dependent on federal support, despite misgivings, both professional social work and voluntarism were amenable to rationalization and, hence, a role in counter-cyclical adjustments to the economy. Their new-found prominence also brought to the fore once again the historical tensions between professional social work and voluntarism over the delineation and specialization of function in the service sector.

Ultimately, however, the enormity of the social costs transferred from private enterprise to the public sector in the last twenty years has produced the "fiscal crisis of the state" (O'Connor, 1973). The current policies of the Reagan Administration to reduce the social welfare state to a skeleton can be viewed as an attempt to solve this fiscal crisis without jeopardizing existing political economic arrangements. Therefore, we are about to witness a new phase in the cost-shifting process, namely a partial transfer of the costs of corporate expansion, already borne by the public sector, onto a "resurgent" voluntary sector.

In order for the voluntary sector to survive as a socially beneficial force in American society in the difficult years ahead, it will have to resist any transfer of functions to it from the public sector. Instead, it will have to oppose government reductions in social services and benefits quite vigorously and advocate for increased social responsibility. Otherwise, the voluntary sector may find itself in the unhappy position of assuming a burden it can not carry successfully, or standing by quietly as the social fabric of American society is torn to shreds.

In addition, the voluntary sector should seek to reestablish a developmental role in service innovation and delivery. This means that the voluntary sector should help volunteers move beyond their direct-service roles into the kind of community development activities that characterized at least some voluntary efforts in an earlier era. Such activities might include carrying out social needs assessments in local communities that document the effects of governmental cutbacks, translating those needs assessments into social action initiatives as did the volunteer reformers in the past, and actively searching out incipient service delivery and community development efforts to assist in finding funds and other necessary resources. These new roles may require a radical re-definition of volunteer-professional relationships, such that volunteers spend less time trying to fit their work into the mold of the professional social agency and more time trying to move the social agency into new definitions of its professional function. The outcome could be a new partnership for social change between these two actors.

In the past, the voluntary sector has claimed the functions of pioneer, gadfly and social reformer. These roles will be even more difficult to implement in the future (if ever they were in the past), because of the emerging professionalization of voluntary activity and the growth of the voluntary sector as a discernible component in the U.S. economy. Necessity derived from shrinking financial resources and fewer social service jobs, rather than lofty ideals, however, may prove the stronger force for change in voluntary sector-professional relations. The resulting alliance could also serve as a powerful force for progressive social change in the larger political-economy.

Notes

1. The ranks of professional social workers were swollen further by the reconciliation between COS and settlement house workers which occurred early in the 20th century (Davis, 1967).

2. Gettleman argues, in fact, that the professionalization of social work developed as a solution to the problem created by the growing radicalism of voluntary charity workers. By inculcating charity workers with a professional spirit, their social activism might be blunted by an overriding sense of professional commitment (Gettleman, 1975: 58-59).

3. The productive potential of the social service sector has been further masked by an anti-service bias in the GNP as a measure of national productivity. Because the GNP measures growth in services by expenditures (and for other reasons), it ignores, for example, the multiplier effect of human development involved in health care, education and social services. Thus, by some estimates, the true value of the expansion of the social service sector may be undermeasured by as much as 50% (Gartner and Riessman, 1974: 40-42).

4. In 1964, the NASW Delegate Assembly rejected a proposel to include individuals without professional training in the association (Schorr, 1966). By 1972, NASW had given BSW degree-holders full professional membership status and the Council on Social Work Education (CSWE) had moved formally to accredit undergraduate social work programs. In 1973, NASW's Standards for Social Service Manpower outlined a six-level classification plan for social work employees in which the third level (social worker) was the BSW degree-holder--now at a professional level of entry. By 1977, 207 colleges and universities provided accredited undergraduate social work education. By July 1978, 23 state governments had established some form of licensure or legal registration for social workers, and many more states had similar legislation underway (Hardcastle and Katz, 1979; NASW, 1977).

5. For comparative purposes, the 1965 figures are probably underestimated due to differences in the survey question format and content from which these data are derived.

6. This relationship probably explains the lower volunteer rates of Blacks as compared to other racial groups. Interestingly, however, in 1974, the survey data indicated that volunteer work was higher for Blacks in two

fields of activity--religion (54% vs. 50%) and civic and community action
(21% vs. 14%) (<u>Americans Volunteer</u>, 1975: 7). Fields of voluntary activity
where whites were predominant were health, education, justice, recreation,
social welfare, citizenship and politics.

REFERENCES

Americans Volunteer
   1969   Department of Labor, Bureau of Manpower Statistics, Manpower/
          Automation Research Monograph #10, Washington, D.C.

Americans Volunteer
   1975   1974, ACTION, Washington, D.C. (February).

Austin, Michael J.
   1976   <u>Professionals and Paraprofessionals</u>.   New York: Human Sciences Press.

Axinn, June, and Herman Levin
   1975   <u>Social Welfare: A History of the American Response to Need</u>.
          New York: Dodd, Mead.

Banner, Lois
   1973   "Religious Benevolence as Social Control: A Critique of an Interpre-
          tation," The Journal of American History, Vol. LX (1).

Becker, Dorothy
   1964   "Exit Lady Bountiful: The Volunteer and the Professional Social
          Worker," Social Service Review, Vol. 38 (1): 57-72.

Bell, Daniel
   1973   <u>The Coming of Post-Industrial Society</u>.   New York: Basic Books.

Bender, Thomas
   1972   <u>Toward an Urban Vision</u>. New York: Doubleday. See especially the
          chapter on "The Idea of Community and the Problem of Urban Reform."

Blatchford, Joseph H.
   1974   "Federal Volunteer Programs," in John G. Cull and Richard E. Hardy
          (eds.), <u>Volunteerism: An Emerging Profession</u>. Springfield, Ill.:
          Charles C. Thomas, Publisher.

Bremner, Robert H.
   1956   "Scientific Philanthropy: 1873-1893," Social Service Review, Vol. 30
          (2): 168-173.

Bureau of Labor Statistics
   1981   <u>Occupational Outlook Handbook</u>. Washington, D.C.

Campfens, Hubert
   1980   "Ethnicity as an Organizing Principle of Social Policy and Practice
          in the Modern Welfare State," in <u>Symposium Papers</u>, University of
          Toronto, May.

Davis, Allen F.
  1967   Spearheads for Reform: The Social Settlements and the Progressive
          Movement, 1890-1914. New York: Oxford University Press.

Gartner, Alan and Frank Riessman
  1974   The Service Society and the Consumer Vanguard. New York: Harper and
          Row. See "A Note on the GNP," 39-42.

Gettleman, Marvin
  1963   "Charity and Social Classes in the United States, 1874-1900, I,"
          American Journal of Economics and Sociology, Vol. 22 (3): 313-329.

  1975   "Philanthropy as Social Control in Late Nineteenth Century America:
          Some Hypotheses and Data on the Use of Social Work," Societas,
          Vol. 5, Winter.

Gilbert, Neil
  1970   Clients or Constituents. San Francisco, Ca.: Jossey-Bass.

Ginzberg, Eli
  1979   "The Professionalization of the U.S. Labor Force," Scientific
          American, March, 48-53.

Grosser, Charles, William E. Henry and James G. Kelly
  1969   Non-Professionals in the Human Services, San Francisco, Ca.: Jossey-
          Bass.

Gutman, Herbert
  1976   Work, Culture and Society in Industrializing America. New York:
          Vintage Books.

Hall, Peter Dobkin
  1975   "The Model of Boston Charity: A Theory of Charitable Benevolence and
          Class Development," Science and Society, XXXVIII, Winter 1974-1975,
          464-477.

Hardcastle, David and Arthur J. Katz
  1979   Employment and Unemployment in Social Work: A Study of NASW Members.
          Washington, D.C.: NASW.

Heide, Wilma Scott
  1973   "Trends Affecting Volunteers Today: A Feminist Perspective on Volun-
          teering for a Healthy Society," unpublished paper, delivered at the
          1973 Convention of the National Easter Seal Society for Crippled
          Adults and Children, Washington, D.C., National Organization for Women.

Heilbroner, Robert
  1973   "What is Post-Industrial Society?," Dissent, April 1, 163-176.

Hirschhorn, Larry.
  1979   "The Political Economy of Social Service Rationalization," Contemporary
          Crises 2 (January 1978), 63-81, Elsevier Scientific Publishing Company,
          Amsterdam, The Netherlands. Reprinted in Richard Quinney (ed.),
          Capitalist Society: Readings for a Critical Sociology, Homewood, Ill.:
          Dorsey Press.

Horesji, John E., Thomas Walz and Patrick R. Connolly
   1977   <u>Working in Welfare: Survival Through Positive Action</u>. Iowa City, Iowa: University of Iowa School of Social Work.

Jones, John Finbar and John Middlemist Kerrick
   1976   <u>Citizens in Service: Volunteers in Social Welfare During the Depression, 1929-1941</u>. Ann Arbor, Mich.: Michigan State University Press.

Kapp, Joseph
   1947   <u>The Social Costs of Private Enterprise</u>. New York: Basic Books.

Kolko, Gabriel
   1967   <u>The Triumph of Conservatism: A Reinterpretation of American History, 1900-1916</u>. Chicago: Quadrangle Books.

Kusmer, Kenneth L.
   1973   "The Functions of Organized Charity in the Progressive Era: Chicago as a Case Study," The Journal of American History, Vol. LX (3), December, 657-678.

Langton, Stuart
   1980   "The New Voluntarism," unpublished paper presented at a conference on "Philosophical Issues in Voluntarism," Virginia Polytechnical Institute and State University, Blacksburg, Virginia, November 14-15.

Lieberman, Morton A., and Leonard D. Borman
   1979   <u>Self Help Groups for Coping with Crises</u>. San Francisco, Ca.: Jossey-Bass.

Leiby, James
   1978   <u>A History of Social Welfare and Social Work in the United States</u>. New York: Columbia University Press.

Levin, Herman
   1969   "Volunteers in Social Welfare: The Challenge of Their Future," Social Work, January, 85-94.

   1977   "Voluntary Organizations in Social Welfare," Encyclopedia of Social Work, New York: NASW, Vol. 17.

Lewis, Harold
   1978   "The Management of the Non-Profit Social Service Organization," in Simon Slavin (ed.), <u>Social Administration</u>. New York: Council on Social Work Education.

   1980   "Informal Support Networks and the Welfare State: Some Ethical Considerations," unpublished paper presented to the annual meeting of the Family Service Association of America, Toronto, May.

Lloyd, Gary
   1971   <u>Charities, Settlements and Social Work, 1890-1915: An Inquiry into Philosophy and Methods</u>. New Orleans, La.: Tulane University Press.

Lubove, Roy
    1975   <u>The Professional Altruist: The Emergence of Social Work as a Career,</u>
            <u>1880-1930</u>. New York: Atheneum Press. See especially Chapter 1 on the
            COS.

Marris, Peter and Martin Rein
    1967   <u>Dilemmas of Social Reform</u>. London: Routledge and Kegan Paul, Ltd.

Mills, C. Wright
    1943   "The Professional Ideology of Social Pathologists," American Journal
            of Sociology, Vol. 49 (September): 165-180.

Morgan, James N., Richard F. Dye, and Judith H. Hybels
    1977   "Results from Two National Surveys of Philanthropic Activity," (1974)
            a study conducted for the Commission on Private Philanthropy and Public
            Needs, Vol. I, <u>History, Trends and Current Magnitudes</u>, Washington, D.C.:
            Department of the Treasury.

Moynihan, Daniel P.
    1969   <u>Maximum Feasible Misunderstanding</u>. New York: Free Press.

National Association of Social Workers
    1975   <u>Standards for Social Work Personnel Practices, NASW Policy Statements</u>
            <u>2</u>. Washington, D.C.: NASW.

    1977   <u>Encyclopedia of Social Work</u>, Seventeenth Issue. Washington, D.C.:
            NASW.

O'Connor, James
    1973   <u>The Fiscal Crisis of the State</u>. New York: St. Martin's Press.

Pearl, Arthur and Frank Riessman
    1965   <u>New Careers for the Poor</u>. New York: Free Press.

Perlman, Janice E.
    1979   "Grassroots Empowerment and Government Response," Social Policy,
            September/October, 16-21.

Piven, Frances and Richard Cloward
    1971   <u>Regulating the Poor: The Functions of Public Welfare</u>. New York:
            Random House.

Pumphrey, Ralph and Muriel Pumphrey
    1961   <u>The Heritage of American Social Work: Readings in its Philosophical</u>
            <u>and Institutional Development</u>. New York: Columbia University Press.
            See especially Chapters XXI, XXIV, XXVII and XXX.

Sarason, Seymour B. and Elizabeth Lorentz
    1979   <u>The Challenge of the Resource Exchange Network</u>. San Francisco, Ca.:
            Jossey-Bass.

Schorr, Alvin
    1966   Editorial in Social Work, Vol. 11, October.

Sherman, Wendy
  1975 "Voluntarism?," unpublished paper, University of Maryland, School of
          Social Work and Community Planning, Baltimore, Maryland, July.

Sieder, Violet M. and Doris Kirshbaum
  1977 "Volunteers," Encyclopedia of Social Work, Washington, D.C.: NASW,
          1582-1590.

Siegel, Sheldon
  1975 Social Service Manpower Needs: An Overview to 1980. New York:
          Council on Social Work Education, 1975.

Smith, Bruce L. R.
  1979 "The Public Use of the Private Sector," in Bruce Smith (ed.), The
          New Political Economy: The Public Use of the Private Sector.
          New York: John Wiley and Sons.

Smith, David Horton
  1973 Voluntary Action Research, 1973 and Voluntary Action Research, 1974.
  1974 Lexington, Mass.: Lexington Books, D. C. Heath and Company.

Sobey, Francine
  1970 The Nonprofessional Rcvolution in Mental Health. New York: Columbia
          University Press.

Specht, Harry
  1972 "The De-professionalization of Social Work," Social Work, Vol. 17
          (March): 3-15.

Stevenson, Gelvin
  1978 "Social Relations of Production and Consumption in the Human Service
          Occupations," International Journal of Health Services, Vol. 8 (3),
          as reproduced in Rand Wilson (compiler), Professionals as Workers:
          A Selection of Readings, Policy Training Center, Cambridge, Massachusetts,
          91-103.

Stoesz, David
  1980 "Mental Health Service Delivery in Post-Industrial Society: The Case
          of the Family Life Center," D.S.W. Dissertation, University of
          Maryland, School of Social Work and Community Planning, June.

Tocqueville, Alexis de
  1945 Democracy in America, Phillips Bradley (ed.), 2 vols. New York
          Alfred Knopf.

Toffler, Alvin
  1980 The Third Wave. New York: William Morrow & Company.

Trefethen, Florence Newman
  1975 "The Volunteer: 'Saint or Scab?'," in "Voluntarism: A New Controversy,"
          Alumnae Bulletin, Bryn Mawr University, Spring, 11-14.

Trolander, Judith
  1975 Settlement Houses and the Great Depression. Detroit, Mich.: Wayne
          State University Press.

United Way of America
   1971   1971-1972 Directory, Alexandria, Virginia.

   1977   "1976-1977 Annual Report," Alexandria, Virginia.

   1974   "A Study of the Quantity of Volunteer Activity of United Way and Its
           Member Agencies," Project Director--John Glaser, Alexandria, Virginia,
           December. Prepared for the Commission on Private Philanthropy and
           Public Needs (the Filer Commission).

Wiebe, Robert H.
   1967   The Search for Order, 1877-1920. New York: Hill and Wang.

Wolozin, Harold
   1976   The Value of Volunteer Services in the U.S., ACTION, Washington,
           D.C., pamphlet no. 3530.4, September.

DEVELOPING SOCIAL WORK SKILLS
FOR WORK WITH VOLUNTEERS

Adrienne Ahlgren Haeuser
University of Wisconsin at Milwaukee

and

Florence S. Schwartz
Hunter College of the City University of New York

In contrast with voluntarism, which connotes principles of voluntary participation in human service systems, volunteerism focuses
not on abstract principles, but on the persons who volunteer, the
services they provide, and the professionals to whom they relate.
Volunteers are defined as individuals or groups who contribute
services to human service programs without remuneration. Volunteer tasks range from participation in policymaking to direct
service to clients. Today's volunteer will usually be assuming
one or more of the following roles specified in a recent edition
of the Encyclopedia of Social Work:

(1) identifying conditions or problems that require therapeutic
or rehabilitative services; (2) policy making; (3) providing
direct services; (4) fund raising; (5) acting as spokesmen for
an organization, interpreting its programs and the problems to
which they are directed; (6) reporting and evaluating community
reactions to programs; (7) collaborating in community planning
activities; (8) developing new service delivery systems; (9)
acting as advocates of the poor and disenfranchised; (10) protest
and public action (Sieder and Kirschbaum, 1977).

Historians and social commentators from the time of Tocqueville
have affirmed the value of both voluntarism and volunteerism in
a democratic society. It is assumed that a democratic society in

Reprinted from Social Casework, 61 (December 1980), 595-601,
by permission of the publisher, Family Service Association of
America, New York.

this decade will continue to value voluntarism and volunteerism and that the value of voluntarism or the principle of citizen participation in community affairs does not require substantiation. On the other hand, although volunteerism will continue to be espoused, a persistent obstacle to its further development should be addressed, that is, the covert and overt, conscious and unconscious resistance of professional paid staff. This article addresses that problem and proposes that for social workers this resistance is rooted in misunderstandings and professional training that fails to value volunteerism and therefore fails to teach skill in volunteer use.

DISPELLING THE "LADY BOUNTIFUL" MYTH

In what may ultimately prove to be an historic action, the 1977 National Association of Social Workers (NASW) Delegate Assembly meeting in Portland, Oregon, approved a policy statement on volunteers and social service systems. This statement recognizes that "volunteerism has special significance in social service" because "the profession of social work evolved from the seeds of volunteer involvment" (NASW News 22, July 1977). This early involvement has consistently created problems in two respects for social work use of volunteers. First, the myth persists that volunteers replicate the noblesse oblige tradition of the early "Lady Bountifuls." Second, the profession has been defensive of its professional territoriality.

In the coming years, some volunteers will continue to come from the affluent and middle classes as in the past, but some will also come from lower income groups. It is now estimated that 12 percent of those with family incomes below $4,000 are part of the volunteer force (NASW News 22, July 1977), they come from consumer groups and from all age groups. Men are increasingly joining the volunteer force, as are teenagers, persons preparing for retirement, and members of employee groups. Some people who have had special problems often volunteer in order to use their own experiences productively in self-help groups. Transition volunteers provide short-term service as they prepare to return to independent living. Whereas the Lady Bountiful of the past may have been not only unpaid but perhaps, at times, inept, today's volunteers can be better described as simply "unpaid." Many volunteers are highly skilled or sincerely interested in acquiring new skills. The NASW policy statement points out that "volunteer opportunities for self-realization may be particularly important for women in a time of role transition" (NASW News 22, July 1977). Social workers with their nonjudgmental approach to clients would do well to approach volunteers in the same nonjudgmental way, rather than regarding their status as a criterion for their service or evaluation. In fact, one mission of social work should be to assure equal opportunities for volunteering to the powerless, the poor, and the consumer of services. The essential point is that the volunteer of this decade bears as little resemblance to the stereotype of social work's volunteer forebears as 1980 does to 1900.

SOCIETAL AND PROFESSIONAL ISSUES AFFECTING VOLUNTEERISM

Conditions in this decade that will affect volunteerism are both societal and professional. Increased automation will lead to a changing employment situation, resulting in fewer jobs, more options for earlier retirement, and more job changes, including second and third careers during a lifetime. Volunteering may fill the gaps between jobs, or in the increasing nonwork hours, or represent one way of maintaining self-esteem and active interests in retirement years. Volunteering may also provide stimulation and training leading to job changes.

With respect to employment, this decade will see increased evidence of a sense of social responsibility on the part of both unions and management. Programs to assist employees and their families as well as company or union programs benefiting the larger community can be expected to increase. Tight budgets will probably demand that these programs include volunteer as well as professional manpower. In these and other capacities, well-trained and supervised volunteers can make many important contributions to the functioning of the community and its organizations.

As the world becomes increasingly complex, institutionalized, and bureaucratic, the quest for identity becomes more urgent. In the past few years, awareness has increased that the quest for self-actualization as an individual, requires becoming involved in altruistic endeavors as well as in self-centered activities, and that a sense of belonging to the community as well as to the self is essential for self-esteem and growth as a social person. Volunteering offers an opportunity for self-actualization and personal growth that may or may not include some skills development with the potential for future employment. Whether or not this occurs, the process of involvement as a volunteer may prevent such personal problems as alcoholism, anomie, depression, and spouse or child abuse. Volunteering also mitigates the impersonal relationships between people and the organized agencies and bureaucracies with which all must deal.

Additionally, from a societal perspective, the impact the women's movement will have on volunteerism must be anticipated. Will the National Organization for Women's 1974 resolution discouraging women from volunteering affect the availability of women volunteers? Perhaps not, for many women may concur with Joan Mondale, who said, "I am an ardent, committed believer in the women's movement.... But for me to reject the value of the woman volunteer is for me to repudiate the vast majority of my life's work" (Mondale, 1977). What does seem clear is that all volunteers, but particularly women, will be increasingly seeking volunteer jobs that require skills or promote skills development and that volunteers will be increasingly used in direct service to clients as members of multidisciplinary teams.

The use of volunteers in tasks comparable to those performed by paid paraprofessionals presents problems and opportunities:

During the 60's the social work profession accepted the concept of the paraprofessional in the human relations field in a way they had never accepted the volunteer (though many of the motivations and needs of the paraprofessional and the volunteer are often the same). Since they were paid, the paraprofessionals became part of the bureaucratic hierarchy and therefore could be fitted in, whereas the volunteer does not fit in so clearly and may even be considered a threat (Schwartz, 1977).

On the other hand, the gradually increasing use of volunteer paraprofessionals on multidisciplinary teams suggests that these persons can fulfill a valued and unique function. "Their neutrality and holistic perspective is appreciated by overloaded specialists with limited time for the human touch" (Naylor, 1973). Volunteers on multidisciplinary teams can promote crossdisciplinary communication and prevent a tendency on the part of agencies to pass the buck. In addition, direct service volunteers in authority-based agencies such as protective services may be able to form relationships with hostile clients, relationships that are not always easily established by the caseworker.

The client can readily accept that the volunteer is involved because he or she cares and can identify the volunteer as an ally. The volunteer does not have the apparent authority or control over the client's life inherent in the caseworker's role and therefore is less likely to be perceived in a threatening light. The volunteer can become a safe person to whom the client can express his or her anger and fears about the agency, the workers, and the situation. As both a friend to the client and part of the agency, the volunteer becomes a means by which the client relates to the agency and caseworker in a less threatening atmosphere (U.S. Dept. HEW, 1977).

Professionals are beginning to recognize that among the causes of alienation is the distance between the people served and the institutions serving them. The professional response has been consumer participation in service delivery, decentralization of services, and the development of paraprofessional roles for both paid and volunteer staff.

In addition, the growth of undergraduate social work programs has begun to change the tasks of various social workers. M.S.W.

graduates will be increasingly providing supervision, consultation, staff and program development, planning, and evaluation, while the B.S.W. graduate will be providing direct service to clients and working in more immediate contact with direct service volunteers. It is hoped that M.S.W. programs will develop curricula for the rapidly evolving role of volunteer coordinator or director. The NASW policy statement notes that the volunteer services coordinator position should be encouraged and should be at the supervisory or management level, with job specifications including a training component (NASW News 22, July 1977).

Also, from a professional perspective, the goal of social work is expected to continue to move away from pathology to preventive intervention. This means, for example, more self-help programs, hot lines, and citizen advocacy programs in which professionally screened, trained, and supervised volunteers predominate. Obviously, as the role of administration of volunteer activities assumes increasing importance, social workers in direct services should be increasingly prepared to work in cooperation with volunteers. Social work students need to become aware of the Department of Health and Human Services (HHS) office of volunteer development and with the information in the HHS volunteer development system brochure. This system specifies the discrete responsibilities and activities to be undertaken by the agency executive, the volunteer director, and all line staff in their use of volunteers.

PROFESSIONAL RESISTANCE

Ivan Scheier, president of the National Information Center on Volunteerism, wrote recently: "Volunteer program problems come and go. Only one has persevered near the top of the problem parade for ten years: paid staff and agency non-support of volunteers" (Scheier, 1977). A pilot study of the differential use of volunteers in public welfare settings indicates that the extent to which paid staff use volunteers seems related to their having been volunteers themselves (Stewart, Pollane and Blenkner, 1972).

The 1977 edition of the Encyclopedia of Social Work includes a revision of the prior edition's article on volunteers. Although both articles note the ineffective or inadequate use of volunteers by generally unsympathetic social workers, the 1977 article adds very specifically that "many social workers have not been sufficiently trained to work with citizens' policy making groups or volunteer members of service teams" (Sieder and Kirschbaum, 1977). Furthermore, the 1977 NASW Delegate Assembly policy statement advocates the development of "educational programs for social workers for effective involvement of volunteers in policy making, advocacy, administration and direct service" and "in collaboration with CSWE, encourage development of curriculum on citizen participation." The policy statement also notes that: "Achievement of the implementation of such a policy is dependent on making work with volunteers integral to professional training in both class and field training" (NASW News 22, July 1977).

In The New Volunteerism, the authors report the spectacular success and subsequent demise of a case aide volunteer program in a mental hospital in Massachusetts. From their experience, they generalize that "the use of volunteers raises some ethical issues, both on the current operation of existing social agencies and in social work education. The dearth of relevant uses of volunteer skills is due not to the volunteers themselves but to the professionals who, for the most part, are not equipped or willing to deal with them" (Feinstein and Cavanaugh, 1976).

The Director of HHS's office of volunteer development has said that "no professional education curriculum prepares practitioners adequately for work with volunteers" and that "students in the helping profession ought to recognize the extent to which their understanding of volunteers can affect their professional competence and scope of influence" (Naylor, 1973).

Scheier points out that paid staff and agency resistance to volunteers is often labelled as a lack of staff orientation. However, he claims that this presupposes staff desire to learn (Scheier, 1977). He may be right in describing the problem as a lack of motivation, because social work education does not teach professional-volunteer collaboration in practice as a value nor as a skill to be acquired. This should not be confused with voluntarism as a principle, which is indeed promoted in the social work curriculum.

THE CRITICAL ISSUE

Foremost among the issues that social work education must address in order to elevate volunteerism to an area of expertise is the myth that volunteers represent cheap labor and may, therefore, be used to replace or decrease professional staff. Many professionals, like the general public, believe that the use of volunteers costs nothing, but, in fact, an effective volunteer program is not necessarily cheap. A good volunteer program requires the services of a paid volunteer coordinator, and its purpose is to extend and enrich human services, not to replace professionals. The NASW policy statement is very clear on these points:

Volunteers should not supplant or decrease the need for suitably qualified, regularly employed staff. Written policies of agencies should include the following: (1) a statement of assurance that volunteers will not be used to replace or decrease the use of paid staff; (2) a clear differentiation of the functions and activities appropriate for volunteer and paid staff; (3) job descriptions for each category of volunteers; (4) provision for reimbursement of volunteer expenses as appropriate; (5) procedures for monitoring, evaluating and measuring volunteer activities and contributions (NASW News 22, July 1977).

With a policy that differentiates between the functions of volunteers and of staff, and with the functions specified in job descriptions for both, professional social workers should not feel threatened. Furthermore, professionals should realize that volunteers frequently identify needs and help to develop programs that are subsequently implemented by professionals. By clearly differentiating and describing both professional and volunteer functions, professionals may find that they gain strength and support from the knowledge that they have allies in their efforts. Social work students should learn that even "in situations where professional help is available and being used, a volunteer brings a sense of everyday life and community concern that cannot be supplied in any other way" (Stratton, 1977). Further, with volunteer giving decreasing, it would be impossible, even with the most enthusiastic fundraising efforts to replace the services of volunteers with paid staff (Brieland, 1977).

Professional resistance might be further dissipated if professionals understood more clearly that the volunteer's service to a client or to an agency is not the only benefit of the volunteer's activity. The volunteer often becomes an advocate for the agency, for the client, and for broad-scale social changes in the community. The dedicated and informed volunteer is a citizen advocate whose lack of self-interest permits and gives credibility to public support for programs where professionals would be accused of vested interest. "Volunteers active in a program have a ring of unmistakable authenticity. They also have a network of relationships to other citizens in churches, service clubs, ethnic groups, neighborhoods which can be commandeered for a cause. Paid staff could never muster these people alone; not having volunteers can mean not having friends when you need them!" (Naylor, 1973). Social work students should be taught that good working relationships with volunteers can mean access to power for case or cause advocacy.

SOCIAL WORK SKILLS FOR VOLUNTEER ADMINISTRATORS

Some social work students should have the opportunity to specialize in volunteer administration. It is the volunteer administrators who are the key persons in dealing with the problem of relating volunteers to professionals. They are the links that connect five constituencies: the volunteers, the staff, the agency leadership, the clients, and the community. It is important to be conscious of the needs and functions of all these groups.

First is the volunteer group itself. Volunteers should be provided with opportunities that are satisfying and growth-
producing and that meet individual needs. Second is the agency
staff, professional as well as nonprofessional. A major task is
to deal with the aforementioned resistance and motivation of
professionals and enable staff members to use volunteers in ways
that are productive, nonthreatening, innovative, and distinct
from professional functions. The critical skill here is the
ability to develop explicit job descriptions for volunteers in
relation to the explicit job descriptions of professional staff.

The days when volunteers could supervise volunteers are past.
In differentiating among the preprofessional (technician), the
professional (master), and the advanced professional (expert),
Dean Harold Lewis of the Hunter College School of Social Work
describes the expectations of the professional worker as being
"to operate from principles whose justifications are to be found
in value-related commendations and theory-based propositions,
adhering to professional as well as agency styles and utilizing
various methods of intervention" (Lewis, 1976). Volunteer
administration and coordination clearly falls into Lewis's demand
for the professional degree of skill.

It is important that the volunteer administrator be particularly
alert to the tendency of social work professionals to work more
effectively with older adults and teenagers and less effectively
with adult volunteers. The former can be viewed as clients over
whom the professional has some power. The latter are not
perceived as clients but as successful, competent people, and
staff members often find it difficult to supervise such people.

The volunteer administrator's third constituency is at the highest
power level of the agency, including board members and agency
executives. This constituency needs to be helped to understand
the roles of the volunteer and to be able to differentiate between these and professional functions. Because board members
and executives ultimately control the allocation of financial
and staff resources, their cooperation is essential.

The fourth, but perhaps the most important constituency, is
that of the consumers of agency service. This group should be
the focus of all that occurs in the agency program. It is a
group that needs reassurance that quality service is being
delivered by both professionals and volunteers.

The fifth constituency is the community, the contributors and
supporters of the services.

The volunteer administrator needs to have the counseling skills
of the direct practice social worker and to apply them to the

unique and difficult counseling function of screening, placing, and supervising volunteers. It is important that volunteer administrators understand the needs and motivations of this special constituency in order to help make the work of volunteers useful to the agency and its clients, nor can it be forgotten that the volunteer also needs to be helped to derive satisfaction from volunteering. Research suggests that although most volunteers state altruistic reasons for volunteering, personal self-fulfilling needs must be met in order to provide a satisfying experience. The background useful for directing, programming, and supervising such activities and meeting such needs involves behavioral knowledge and skills, including those of casework and group work.

The volunteer administrator also needs management skills, as he or she works with various groups and individuals in the organizational structure and, in many cases, creates the structure. Volunteer administrators have a management function that can be broken down into four basic processes: planning, organizing, directing, and controlling. Differential skills are needed, according to whether one is dealing with a bureaucracy (for example, a hospital) or the more informal structure of a community center. Volunteer administrators should be knowledgeable regarding political, economic, and social factors affecting the delivery of service and use of volunteers. An understanding of such factors should, therefore, be part of their education.

In addition to being counselor-social worker and administrator, the director of volunteer services needs to be an educator. With respect to the five constituencies mentioned above (volunteers, staff, board, clients, and community), the administrator can perform a significant educational function in respect to enhancing the skills and knowledge of volunteers and other persons associated with the agency. Volunteer administrators must be expert at designing or providing both initial training and orientation programs for volunteers as well as providing ongoing in-service training.

Finally, it is highly desirable that volunteer administrators have public relations skills. The volunteer administrator must be able to interpret the agency program and to recruit appropriate volunteers.

CONCLUSION

For economic and societal reasons, this decade is likely to see more and a wider variety of persons wanting to volunteer. It is also likely that more volunteers will wish to provide direct service to clients. However, the extent to which this additional personpower will be used to extend, enrich, and maximize human service effectiveness depends largely on professional gatekeepers

31

who heretofore have often demonstrated covert and overt resistance to professional-volunteer collaboration. Overcoming this resistance will require professionals who understand and can implement a volunteer development system and professionals who clearly understand the difference between their role and that of the volunteer. Overcoming this resistance will also require adding more knowledge about volunteerism to the social work curriculum at both the B.S.W. and M.S.W. levels; students should learn that professional-volunteer collaboration is a growing trend of the profession and should acquire basic skills in relating to volunteers. Graduate students should have the option of developing a career in volunteer administration by acquiring related skills in counseling, administration, training, and public relations.

With the adoption of a policy statement on volunteers and social service systems by the 1977 NASW Delegate Assembly, the outlook is hopeful. The immediate challenge appears to be to advocate implementation of the final recommendation: "to refer this policy to the NASW-CSWE Task Force to develop standards and guidelines for implementing in social work education" (NASW News 22, July 1977).

In 1980, the House of Delegates of the Council on Social Work Education passed a resolution recommending that a task force made up of persons engaged in social work education, social work practice, and active volunteers be appointed to address the subject of social work education and the maximum involvement of volunteers.

Notes

1. Violet M. Sieder and Doris C. Kirschbaum, "Volunteers," Encyclopedia of Social Work, 17th ed. (Washington, D.C.: National Association of Social Workers, 1977), p. 1582.

2. National Association of Social Workers, 1977 Delegate Assembly Policy Statement, "Volunteers and the Social Service Systems," NASW News 22 (July 1977): 39.

3. Ibid.

4. Ibid.

5. Joan Mondale, quoted in the Edwardsville Intelligencer (Illinois), 15 November 1977.

6. Florence S. Schwartz, "Training a Professional Staff to Work with a Program Volunteer," Volunteer Administration 10 (Spring 1977): 11.

7. Harriet Naylor, Volunteers Today: Finding, Training and Working with Them (Dryden, New York: Dryden Associates, 1973), p. 186.

8. National Center on Child Abuse and Neglect, Volunteers in Child Abuse and Neglect Programs (Washington, D.C.: U.S. Department of Health, Education and Welfare, June 1977), p. 13.

9. National Association of Social Workers, "Volunteers and Systems," p. 39.

10. Ivan Scheier, "Staff Nonsupport of Volunteers," Voluntary Action Leadership (Fall 1977): p. 32.

11. Merrilee L. Stewart, Leonard Pollane, and Margaret Blenkner, Differential Use of Volunteers in Public Welfare Settings (Athens, Georgia: Regional Institute of Social Welfare Research, August 1972).

12. Sieder and Kirschbaum, "Volunteers," p. 1583.

13. National Association of Social Workers, "Volunteers and Systems," p. 39.

14. Barbara Feinstein and Catherine Cavanaugh, The New Volunteerism (Cambridge, Mass.: Schenkman Publishing, 1976), p. 141.

15. Naylor, Volunteers Today, p. 188.

16. Scheier, "Nonsupport of Volunteers," p. 32.

17. National Association of Social Workers, "Volunteers and Systems, p. 39.

18. Ann Stratton, "Letters," Social Work 22 (July 1977): 335.

19. Donald Brieland, "Editorial," Social Work 22 (March 1977): 86.

20. Naylor, Volunteers Today, p. 189.

21. Harold Lewis, "The Structure of Professional Skill," in Social Work in Practice, ed. Bernard Ross and S.K. Khinduka (Washington, D.C.: National Association of Social Workers, 1976), p. 11.

22. National Association of Social Workers, "Volunteers and Systems," p. 40.

REFERENCES

Brieland, Donald
   1977   "Editorial," Social Work 22 (March): 86.

Feinstein, Barbara and Catherine Cavanaugh
   1976   The New Volunteerism. Cambridge, Mass.: Schenkman
         Publishing, p. 141.

Lewis, Harold
   1976   "The Structure of Professional Skill," in Social Work
         in Practice, ed. Bernard Ross and S. K. Khinduka.
         Washington, D.C.: National Association of Social
         Workers, p. 11.

Mondale, Joan
   1977   Quoted in the Edwardsville Intelligencer (Illinois),
         November 15.

Naylor, Harriet
   1973   Volunteers Today: Finding, Training and Working with
         Them. Dryden, New York: Dryden Associates, p. 186.

National Association of Social Workers
   1977   1977 Delegate Assembly Policy Statement, "Volunteers
         and the Social Service Systems," NASW News 22 (July):
         39.

Scheier, Ivan
   1977   "Staff Nonsupport of Volunteers," Voluntary Action
         Leadership (Fall): p. 32.

Schwartz, Florence S.
   1977   "Training a Professional Staff to Work with a Program
         Volunteer," Volunteer Administration 10 (Spring): 11.

Sieder, Violet M. and Doris C. Kirschbaum
   1977   "Volunteers," Encyclopedia of Social Work, 17th ed.
         Washington, D.C.: National Association of Social
         Workers, p- 1582.

Stewart, Merrilee L., Leonard Pollane, and Margaret Blenkner
   1972   Differential Use of Volunteers in Public Welfare
         Settings. Athens, Ga.: Regional Institute of Social
         Welfare Research.

Stratton, Ann
   1977   "Letters," Social Work 22 (July): 335.

COOPERATION OF VOLUNTEERS AND PROFESSIONALS IN SOCIAL SERVICES

Louis Lowy
Boston University

THE ORIGINS OF THE PROJECT

In January 1975, a Project was initiated at the Fachhochschule in Cologne, and in early 1979, the results were evaluated and recommendations made to be implemented subsequently. Seven social service agencies in Nordrhein-Westfalen and four Schools of Social Work participated. Each of those agencies assumed responsibility for a particular social service project that required collaboration between professional social workers and volunteers, such as provisions of rural social services; delivery of health services in a local hospital; initiation of a new social service program in a problem-concentrated area in an industrial town; organization of neighborhood assistance in a low income suburban area of a metropolitan city; recruitment of volunteers to help people with personal and interpersonal problems. Another program focused on recruitment and training of agency board members.

The following kinds of agencies took part in this Project: Caritas organization in the industrial Ruhr district; a Caritas branch agency in a satellite city of a large metropolitan area; a general hospital in a middle-sized city; a social service agency (multi-service center) in a middle-sized city; a social welfare center in a rural town; a family and children's service agency in a metropolitan city; and a day care center of a smaller city in a densely populated industrial area.

The volunteers who participated in the various agency activities were classified according to three categories or levels:

1) Policy-making; e.g., Board members, members of Board committees, etc.

2) Administrative; e.g., Volunteers who performed clerical, fiscal, managerial, public relations tasks, etc. (making use of their expertise).

3) Direct (Personal) Service Provisions; e.g., Home-makers, interviewers, case-managers, recreation workers, group leaders, lobby specialists, etc.

It was found that this tri-level categorization was a useful way to differentiate and assign volunteer workers and to clarify respective functions and status.

In no instance was there a director of volunteers who assumed general responsibility for coordinating volunteer functions as part of regular agency operations.

The Project staff professionals, by virtue of their Project assignments, assumed some of these roles, though they had not become institutionalized upon completion of the Project. And none of the Project staff had come forth to recommend the universal creation of a "director of volunteers." At this point there was quite a bit of hesitation whether such a position would indeed promote the appropriate use of volunteers and lead to a decrease of barriers between them and professional staff. There was fear, indeed, that such a step might lead to the anomaly of the "professionalization of volunteerism."

The objectives of the various agency groups were: to clarify the function of professionals and volunteers; to assess positive and negative experiences which had occurred as a result of such collaboration; to find out some of the presumed causes and to devise mechanisms to improve the collaboration between professionals and volunteers and to make recommendations as to how social service practice could be improved by utilizing volunteers jointly with professionals. Ultimately, answers were to be sought regarding how professional training and continuing education can benefit from the findings of this Project, and how training and supervision of volunteers can be enhanced.

In many countries of Western Europe, and particularly in West Germany, in the not so distant past, social welfare workers were volunteers or paid non-professionals, analogous to practices in the United States during the 19th and early 20th centuries. Since World War II, a major change had occurred: social welfare activities had become increasingly professionalized. Much of this was due to Anglo-Saxon, particularly North American influences. This professionalization movement relegated volunteers to the backstage and created a competition with professionals who had assumed a more dominant role in social service agencies. However, there were questions about the role and status of clients, and socio-political critics questioned fundamental assumptions about the role of social programs and their legitimation. Several mutual aid organizations and citizen initiatives emerged, and many sought the participation of those who were affected by social programs, not unlike what happened during the War on Poverty in the sixties in the USA. Didn't the professionals destroy the spirit of self help, so essential to providing services? Wouldn't volunteers broaden the support base for the delivery of social services? Couldn't volunteers become a less expensive source of service providers than social workers? Wouldn't volunteers be better able to help themselves in the process of helping others? These types of questions led to a new orientation towards the social encounter. No longer were volunteers seen only as supplementary workers (because there were no

professionals around), but they were also seen as a resource to assist people
who could not be reached by professional social workers because of social
class distance or ethnic differences. While various "Welfare States" in
Europe reduced social inequality and achieved greater social justice, they
also created a sizable bureaucracy that spawned a sense of considerable
alienation among beneficiaries of the welfare state. Social work assumed a
personalizing and humanizing role in providing social services which called
for role clarification of social work professionals on the one hand and
volunteer service providers on the other. Finally, the question was posed:
How can both interact with one another to the benefit of all citizens? A
clarification of role differences and similarities was also expected to define
more clearly the role of the professional. Furthermore, a number of implications for the training and for continuing education for social workers became
obvious.

OPERATION AND RESULTS OF PROJECT

The Project consisted of a planning, implementation, and an evaluation phase.
The planning phase in 1975-76 consisted of definition of goals and the design
of seven projects by social agencies. During phases 1 and 2, various study
weeks were arranged to monitor the Project, to compare experiences, to iron
out problems and to analyze data. The implementation period (1976-77) saw the
operationalization of the 7 project designs, the administering of question-
naires to volunteers and professionals that participated in each of these 7
projects. The evaluation phase (1977-78) consisted of an analysis of the
collected data, their review and discussion and spelling out of recommendations.
Subsequently, curricular concepts were developed and in June 1978, the project
design, operation and results were published (Bock et al., 1979).

What were some of the barriers between professionals and volunteers? First,
there were those that related to the structure of organizations. Many organizations, agencies and institutions have a complicated and often quite invisible
organizational structure. The various tasks, competencies and qualifications
of those who maintain positions are frequently unclear. Working contracts with
volunteers about their function, time involvement, etc., have been found to be
non-existent. Many resources, be they fiscal, clerical, spatial, etc., have
not been made available to volunteers though professionals enjoy access to
them. Specific functions of volunteers have rarely been clearly communicated
to professionals and vice versa. Many problems also existed that were related
to the fulfillment of respective roles. The mandate of the social workers is
still quite unclear and job descriptions are not contributing to make clearer
to the volunteer what specific tasks the social workers perform, and why.
Often the role of the social worker is seen as a facilitator, a neighbor, a
well-meaning friend or therapist. The recently enunciated role of advocate
has been unclear to many social workers and volunteers alike. Skills that
have come to be known now as "generic skills" and that are inherent in the
social work role repertoire have not yet found their way into the practice
of many agencies. However, the role descriptions of volunteers have been
found to be even more diffused and confused. Their expectations are often
unclear and their image is hazy. Frequently the practical tasks that they
perform are not seen as worthy or as highly valued as the more professional
tasks of the social worker. Very often there is also social distance between
the professional social worker and his/her clients which many volunteers try

to bridge, but that is often perceived as unprofessional behavior. Many volunteers provide auxiliary services, and they come to feel that many such efforts are undervalued and given low status. Professional judgements and decision-making are generally reserved for the professional and many volunteers are not deemed as having enough competency to participate in making vital decisions. On the other hand, volunteers do not know that many professional social workers are competent in areas in which volunteers are also competent.

In addition to these role problems, there are interpersonal problems; there are anxieties and fears on the part of professionals that which increasing use of volunteers they themselves will become superfluous and in times of limited employment opportunities such fears tend to become more reality-based and threatening. On the other hand, volunteers also have anxieties as to their competence and performance capacities. As a result, negative feelings by both groups are brought to the fore. Sometimes volunteers experience difficulty with terminating contracts and relationships with the people with whom they work, and relationships are continued beyond apparent necessity. Mutual prejudices are formed and if not reduced, they become hardened.

IMPLICATIONS OF PROJECT

In this Project, an attempt was made to look at the various tasks and practice functions by professionals and volunteers, at their respective roles and at interventive repertoires. The success of the activity of the social worker depends appreciably on the extent to which clients are involved in the solution of their problems, and how various resources are mobilized to help solve the defined problems. This means activating self help forces so that the social worker can make him/her self superfluous. How can volunteers complement, if not supplement the activities of social workers? A series of recommendations was made to agencies on how to effect organizational changes, how to clarify respective roles, how to recruit volunteers and conclude contracts between volunteers and professionals, how to clarify communication structures, and how to create opportunities for on-going supervision and training and carry out such efforts.

The Project defined necessary job qualifications for professionals and volunteers. For professionals such qualifications were to include:

1) A quality of appreciation for differential competencies of various categories of volunteers that should be utilized in providing social welfare services to individuals, families, groups, organizations, neighborhoods (communities);

2) Skills in assessing such competencies and an ability to allocate them appropriately for the benefit of service consumers and also for service-providing volunteers and professionals;

3) Skills in recruiting, training, orienting, monitoring and evaluating the contributions of volunteers;

4) Ability in defining respective contributions, tasks, limitations of volunteers, in re-assigning them when desirable and to relate their

work to the work of professionals, i.e., to bring it into as much harmony as possible by striving for complementarity;

5) Capability and grace to convey to volunteers the value of their engagement vis-a-vis the agency, the constituency, the community.

For volunteers such qualifications should call for:

1) A quality of appreciation for tasks performed by professionals and for the educational requisites needed to carry out such tasks, especially when they involve more complex operations, such as psycho-social diagnosis, family-counseling, organizing neighborhood advocacy groups, hospice-counseling, group treatment, etc.;

2) Skills in performing those tasks for which volunteers offer their services and ability to accept assistance, supervision, in-service training etc., in order to improve work performance in the services of goal achievement of the agency;

3) A sense of commitment to regularity and reasonable continuity of service provision (on any of the three levels), as long as the volunteer arrangement is maintained;

4) Demonstrating respect for confidentiality of data and information when so required, because of the nature of the volunteer's activities in relation to overall agency services.

Of major importance was the finding that social workers have to become more skilled in carrying out advocacy functions and engage volunteers accordingly to make them a part of the total advocacy system. Specific competencies, their boundaries and overlaps, have to be understood and mutually recognized. Certain expertise may be more available among volunteers than among professionals. Normal life experiences and continued contact in the community are important resources which volunteers bring to the job. In other words, resources of the volunteers have to be just as much understood, identified, and utilized as the resources that the professional brings. Mutual role expectations need to be clarified not only in the beginning, but continuously as the work proceeds.

What are the rewards for volunteers? How can they obtain recognition in the community for their efforts and achieve status? Though psychic gratification cannot be imposed, it can be achieved if the agency creates a working environment that promotes collegiality and collaboration. Public recognition and the award of certificates and diplomas, properly earned, by an agency (local, state or national) were highly recommended in order to promote visibility of volunteer activities and nurture motivation by those who give of themselves, their time and their efforts.

There are significant implications for the training of social workers. In this Project, a number of curricular elements were identified that should be part of every training endeavor of social workers. Such elements included: specifications of objectives for work with volunteers in organizations and in the community; understanding communication structures and diverse forms of teamwork and cooperation; analysis of respective tasks to be performed by volunteers and by professionals; recruitment and selection of volunteers;

preparation, planning and implementation of a volunteer program; avenues for helping volunteers to become engaged in the work according to individual competencies, personal interests and abilities, etc. It was recommended that social work students have practical experiences in working with volunteers. Therefore, field work should include "working with volunteers" as an assignment. Opportunities for volunteer supervision should be made available to all trainees.

In addition, the Project identified content areas for continuing education for both professionals as well as volunteers. In any effort of this kind, volunteers and professionals have to work together in the planning, design and implementation phase as role-modeling is a key factor in learning.

The hypotheses that social work activities can best be performed when volunteers and professionals work together had become well confirmed in this Project. Differentiation of respective tasks and roles is a continuing process rather than a single activity. Boundaries must be permeable rather than rigidly fixed.

Additional reports will be published that deal with subsequent efforts that have been undertaken since the completion of the Project. The interest in the use of volunteers in German-speaking countries as well as in other countries of Western Europe has been growing in leaps and bounds. The international dialogue is ready to proceed and to pick up the echoes emanating from it.

REFERENCES

Bock Teresa, Louis Lowy, Monika Pankoke und andere
  1979   Kooperation freitätiger und beruflicher Mitarbeiter in Sozialen Diensten. Lambertus-Verlag, Freiburg im Breisgau.

VOLUNTARISM, VOLUNTEERS AND SOCIAL WORK PRACTICE

Florence S. Schwartz
Hunter College of the City University of New York

This report represents the first results of a project in social work which addressed an area of concern that has been largely ignored in the social work profession. It organized the effort, the experience and the wisdom of approximately 150 people who participated in a specially created network. For almost a year, this network focused its attention on the complex relationships among social work institutions, their professional staff, volunteers who render service to them and the schools of social work that train and educate their staff and leadership.

The project had its origins in the concern of a group of people that the lack of clarity in these relationships limited the effectiveness of the various organizations. Resolutions of the Delegate Assemblies of the National Association of Social Work (1977) and the Council on Social Work Education (1980) reflected a growing concern on the part of the profession for the volunteer and social work practice. It was therefore appropriate that the relationships and the weaknesses therein be explored. The project began that exploration by drawing on the experience of practitioners in many areas in order to consider some ideas for change.

The Voluntarism and Social Work Practice project was sponsored and co-ordinated by an Inter-Agency Task Force funded by The Lois and Samuel Silberman Fund and directed by a Project Director.

The Inter-Agency Task Force was organized and convened by the Association of Junior Leagues in the Spring of 1979. It included the Association of Junior Leagues, the Family Service Association of America, the National Assembly of Health and Welfare Organizations, the National Council of Jewish Women, and Volunteer: National Center for Citizen Involvement, with the encouragement of the Council on Social Work Education.

41

The objectives of the project were:

1. To identify the role of the volunteer in social work practice.
2. To identify the issues inherent in the relationship between the involvement of volunteers and social work practice.
3. To develop data on current curriculum content in schools of social work regarding voluntarism.
4. To make recommendations for an approach to curriculum development involving both classroom and field work.

The project involved a collaborative effort among professional staff, volunteers and social work educators.

An issue that the Task Force identified as one they wished to work on was the problem of the social worker and the volunteer -- specifically the resistance of social workers to the more effective involvement of volunteers in social work services.[1]

Another issue was that of many social workers coming into the field showing a lack of understanding of the historical role and significance of the voluntary sector in the development and delivery of social services, particularly evident among social workers going into the growing area of public services.

The Task Force set up a network of six units, each in a different city, and each involving a leading graduate school of social work. Each network unit was asked by the Task Force to explore the status of voluntarism and volunteers in social agencies in the community and in the school of social work, to identify what changes are needed to enhance the effectiveness of volunteers and to suggest ways to better prepare social work students and staff to work with volunteers.

BACKGROUND

Volunteers, according to the Encyclopedia of Social Work, assume one or more of the following roles: (1) identifying conditions or problems that require therapeutic or rehabilitative services; (2) policy making; (3) providing direct services; (4) fund raising; (5) acting as spokesmen for an organization, interpreting its programs and the problems to which they are directed; (6) reporting and evaluating community reactions to programs; (7) collaborating in community planning activities; (8) developing new service delivery systems; (9) acting as advocates of the poor and disenfranchised; (10) protest and public action.[2]

Citizen participation in community affairs has deep roots in the American experience. Eduard C. Lindeman indicated its importance when he stated, "In a democracy, it is not essential or even desirable that citizens should agree,

---

[1]Volunteer: National Center for Citizen Involvement developed a statement regarding volunteers and social workers. This statement was prepared by Beth Gill, a social work student.

[2]Violet M. Sieder and Doris C. Kirschbaum, "Volunteers," Encyclopedia of Social Work, 17th ed. (Washington, D.C.: National Association of Social Workers, 1977), p. 1582.

but it is imperative they should participate. The health of a democratic society may be measured by the quality of services performed by citizen volunteers." Citizen participation represents a dynamic, diverse and pervasive force in our society. In the field of social service, early volunteers expressed their sense of social responsibility and their religious convictions by direct help to the less fortunate. Citizen participation has more recently included active roles in the formulation of policy, in community education, in fund raising, in advocacy, in administrative decision making, as well as in direct service of many kinds. Voluntarism and citizen participation have become even more important because of the requirement by the Federal Government that there be maximum feasible community participation in various government programs. It is recognized that voluntarism can be an avenue for self-realization and personal growth for many volunteers. The growing needs of social service organizations for human service personnel, in addition to professional staff, have caused many to turn increasingly to volunteers.

In the field of social work, we are particularly sensitive to the fact that voluntarism simultaneously performs two significant functions; volunteers both serve and are served. The act of volunteering yields many benefits to the volunteers while enhancing the effectiveness of the institutions in which the volunteer functions.

The successful integration of volunteers involves a cooperative relationship among several elements in the social work system, based on common undertakings and objectives. Among the elements are social workers, schools of social work, community agencies, national organizations concerned with voluntarism and volunteers themselves.

In the current scene, there is a need to provide a firmer basis for the systematic deployment of volunteers based on data regarding knowledge of voluntarism, its nature and objectives, and also on the perceptions of all participants in the system of their relationships with one another.

Providing such a basis must involve input from agency boards, agency staff, social work faculty and volunteers in the significant areas of volunteer activity: policy making, direct service and advocacy, as well as citizen and consumer participation in service delivery. Volunteer participation serves as a check and a balance, and it identifies and demonstrates new services.

ORGANIZATION

The project was based on a model of collaborative relationships among the elements of a social work system emphasizing the use of volunteers. Participants were to include representatives of agencies, volunteers, professional social workers and faculty of schools of social work. The Inter-Agency Task Force, which provided general guidance and direction to the project, selected six study sites.

As the Task Force investigated which schools of social work to approach, consideration was given to geographical location, public or private schools, size of schools, and schools serving a wide spectrum of racial and ethnic groups.

A major factor in the determination of the sites was the support by the Dean of the school of social work for the aims of the project. Each network unit included local members of the Inter-Agency Task Force, staff members of social agencies and volunteers (Board/advocate/direct service) in addition to a faculty member from the participating school of social work. The participating schools of social work and sites were:

> University of Atlanta - Atlanta
> University of Texas - Austin
> University of Maryland - Baltimore
> University of California - Berkeley
> Case Western Reserve University - Cleveland
> University of Toronto - Toronto

The Deans of all of the schools indicated their interest by assignment of a senior faculty member to serve in the Network. The six units all reflected the basic model, but each organized itself individually based on the differences among communities throughout the nation, differing experiences of the participants and varying philosophies among the agencies and schools of social work.

The Convenors

It was planned that a representative of the participating organizations would serve as convenor and take on the task of planning, arranging, chairing and organizing all the meetings for each of the six units. Three of the units (Atlanta, Baltimore, and Toronto) were convened by the Association of Junior Leagues; one (Cleveland) by the National Council of Jewish Women; one (Berkeley) by Family Service Association of America; and one (Austin) by the Governor's Office on Volunteers.

A small budget was made available for mailings, meetings, etc. The convenors, together with the faculty member and in some instances an executive group, called the meetings, prepared the agendas, prepared and distributed the minutes and frequently chaired the meetings.

Procedure

As the groups were formed, informational and educational materials were sent to each participant, including a suggested guide for procedure. The guide suggested a framework that developed in different ways in different communities.

Each network unit of 10-30 participants started to meet in December, 1980 and continued through June, 1981. Each did continue in the Fall of 1981. Several of the network units formed task groups to explore different issues from the perspective of: agency executives and staff, volunteer administration, volunteers and academia. Most of the groups gathered information about the attitudes and practices concerning volunteers in the social agencies in their communities. Several of the units also circulated a questionnaire to students to assess their experience in the school of social work and their field placements as related to the area of volunteers, board or direct service.

A questionnaire regarding Voluntarism and Social Work Practice went to all the graduate schools of social work accredited by the Council on Social Work

Education. Seventy-five (85.2%) of the schools responded to the questionnaire.

One meeting with representatives of all of the units in the network was held in Louisville, Kentucky in March, 1981 in connection with the Annual Program Meeting of the Council on Social Work Education and the Project Director also met with four of the units from March to June.

ACHIEVEMENTS

The project has already made some significant contributions by the very fact of its existence, and by the work of the various network units. These achievements were outlined in a summary report submitted by the Cleveland Unit (July 6, 1981).

> The Network activity has introduced an important dimension to the relationship of social agencies, the volunteer organizations, and the School.
>
> A new configuration of voluntary agencies and voluntary organizations has addressed important common concerns.
>
> The Network has engaged the interest of a significant sector of the School faculty.
>
> The energy and work of the Network has resulted in an ongoing set of objectives and plans for Network/School communication and involvement in the immediate future.

Specifically, the Deans and senior faculty at six schools of social work have already begun to move toward making the subject of voluntarism part of the education of social workers. Their resolve in every case has been clearly communicated to their respective network units and to the Inter-Agency Task Force.

At the same time a large number of agencies, organizations and people representing a national constituency have indicated to schools of social work and to the social work communities their interest in making the subject of voluntarism a part of the formal training of social workers. They have already offered some specific models through which this can be accomplished; they have made available their knowledge and experience for the purpose of developing appropriate material, and they have offered to make themselves available to deal with specific tasks.

The project has provided an effective way for agencies' operational personnel, professional and volunteer, to share ideas and experiences with each other and with academics. Many have suggested and will continue to suggest ways to enhance the use of volunteers in agencies. A model has been created for a continuing process of narrowing the distance between field and classroom, a process which can only bring benefit to both. The energy and work of the network units has generally resulted in an ongoing set of objectives and plans not only for themselves, but for additional similar groups in the future.

The following was expressed in a letter from a member of the Berkeley unit:

"The final spring meeting of the Berkeley Voluntarism and Social Work Practice Project has just concluded. We have set a date for reconvening in September and have all taken assignments for the summer so that we will be ready to continue our exciting and fruitful work together in the fall. We hope you share our tremendous enthusiasm for this project.

We are very excited about the progress our Task Force has made in the few short months we have been meeting. Plans are currently being made for -

Teaching a 30-hour course on Voluntarism and Social Work Practice at San Francisco State University School of Social Work in spring 1982; Morris Levin of the Network Unit will serve as coordinator, with heavy involvement of agencies, directors, volunteers, etc.

Developing case work studies on the use of volunteers in specific disciplines at local agencies for fall 1981 presentation at Brown Bag Seminars at University of California, School of Social Welfare at Berkeley, and

Developing a satellite task force in Sacramento to continue initial contacts with California State University at Sacramento School of Social Work.

These are only the high points. We have many more strategies we are eager to continue in the fall." (June 19, 1981)

The Austin unit was approached, and its members very likely will take responsibility for developing a course at the University of Texas. Plans are being developed for continuing education courses. (July 28, 1981)

MAIN THEMES

Certain themes emerged out of the investigations and deliberations of the various network units. Repeatedly expressed in many ways was the importance of an atmosphere and attitude of collaborative effort between professional staff and volunteers.

The following concepts took focus:

1. Voluntarism must be integrated into schools and agencies at various levels and functions. It is necessary for boards to state policies regarding the importance of voluntarism, for staff to realize that it is an integral part of their responsibilities, for budget directors to fund, for volunteers to commit, for students to study and for the community to respect.

2. Material needs to be provided to schools of social work to educate and train people in the understanding of voluntarism and the use of volunteers. Cases must be written up, teaching modules created, handbooks written, research conducted, bibliographies compiled and illustrative material prepared. The project itself made some progress in this direction.

3. Having provided forceful leadership and creativity for the entire project, the Inter-Agency Task Force can become a continuing force in guiding schools of social work, national and local agencies and governmental bodies regarding the importance of further developing voluntarism. The Council on Social Work Education, whose 1980 resolution provided the immediate motivation for the launching of the project, is interested in pursuing the objectives of the project.

4. The model developed in this project involving the various network units is readily applicable to other social work communities; the point of entry in each situation can be different as demonstrated by the model. In all cases the existing network units have arranged to continue their work and expect to involve additional participants.

5. The positive responses of the Deans of the respective schools provided encouragement to academic, agency and volunteer participants and indicated the current importance of voluntarism.

6. Though the historical significance of voluntarism and social services is considered by most schools of social work, the key finding of the questionnaire showed that schools provide students with few opportunities to work with volunteers, and little examination of the current roles volunteers play in the various fields of social service. Some attention is given through field work agencies, but there is rarely any reinforcement in the classroom.

7. A major need exists for Continuing Education programs for practicing social workers in order to reorient and reeducate those whose basic professional education might have been deficient in anything related to voluntarism. Schools of social work as well as agencies should sponsor such programs.

8. Continuing Education programs for volunteers (Board members and direct service) are needed for increased knowledge and understanding of the social welfare system. School of social work faculty members teaching these courses can enhance the perception and appreciation of each group's contributions.

RECOMMENDATIONS

As the project concluded, a number of recommendations were developed by examining the minutes of unit meetings, responses to questions, interviews, conferences with the project director, summaries and reports. They take into consideration both attitudinal as well as structural factors in social work practice.

The network units expressed belief that a national meeting would bring together the various ideas and findings of each of the networks as well as introduce new material.

Goals regarding voluntarism in the social work curriculum are to provide cognitive material regarding the voluntary sector of our society, particularly as related to the profession; to provide skills-training for working with volunteers; to influence the attitudes of social work students toward a respectful constructive collaboration with volunteers as members of cooperative teams, with a sense of shared responsibility and common concern for the purposes of the organization. Schools of social work must examine their curricula and include materials related to voluntarism across the board starting with a statement of commitment regarding the importance of voluntarism, the development of special courses in certain aspects of voluntarism and the integration of a component on voluntarism into appropriate courses.

Aside from including material on voluntarism as part of the social work curriculum, a number of other actions can be taken by schools to recognize the importance of voluntarism:

- Familiarize faculty and students with statements of policy reflected in the 1977 resolution of N.A.S.W. and the 1980 resolution of C.S.W.E.

- Recognize the fact that many members of the faculty volunteer in a variety of community activities, serving as role models to students and underscoring voluntarism's importance.

- Involve Board members and advisory committees of the school itself in a program to bring voluntarism to the attention of faculty and of students.

- Designate a faculty member to take responsibility for investigating the school's involvement in voluntarism in all ways, reporting the results back to the faculty and making appropriate recommendations.

- Provide formal and informal events at which professionals, volunteers and administrators of volunteer programs can meet with faculty and students and with each other.

- Include presentations by volunteers as part of appropriate courses.

- Sponsor continuing education for practicing social workers to update their knowledge and skill in understanding and working with volunteers.

- Include subjects related to voluntarism as suggested material for masters' theses.

- Provide extra recognition for students who engage in relevant volunteer activity.

- Require some form of proof of mastery in the area of voluntarism as part of degree requirements.

- Set up a specific advisory committee on voluntarism to assist the school in dealing with the subject.

- Recommend inclusion of content on voluntarism in the Curriculum Policy Statement of the Council on Social Work Education.

The important guideline for agency practice and successful volunteer activity is the need to involve the entire agency, at all levels and in all functions, in the volunteer program.

References to voluntarism should be in statements of purpose and policy, indicating that volunteers are an integral part of the service delivery system to clients and that staff will involve volunteers whenever possible.

Voluntarism should be integrated into budget discussions and allocations; planning for all departments; annual statement of agency goals; discussion at staff meetings; and staff evaluation.

Among the problems which can be solved by using the ideas and principles expressed in this project are:

> underutilization and inappropriate involvement of volunteers; attitudinal barriers that prevent agency staff from accepting the placement of volunteers;

> lack of clarity in responsibility for administration and supervision of volunteer programs;

> lack of understanding of the role of board member as volunteer;

> correcting various myths and stereotypes regarding volunteers, i.e., volunteers are cheap labor, volunteers are generous "Lady Bountiful" altruists, volunteers have unlimited free time, volunteers do not want supervision, volunteers cannot be fired, volunteers do not have skills.

Though many of the recommendations of this study relate to the volunteer as direct service provider, the network units were aware that other roles of the volunteer-policy making, citizen participation advocacy, self-help, etc.- need to be expressed in greater depth.

Consideration might be given to the establishment of a task force on volunteers by the National Association of Social Workers and the Council on Social Work Education, which would continue to examine the relationship between volunteers and practitioners and develop curriculum materials for schools of social work.

The collaborative effort has begun. Its benefit has been proven. Its momentum should be maintained.

SOCIAL WORK EDUCATION AND VOLUNTARISM

Winnifred Herington
University of Toronto, Toronto

For many social workers and social work educators, it may seem a truism to state that every social work curriculum should include content on voluntarism and its relationship to social work practice. It cannot be denied that the historical roots of the social work profession are strongly grounded located in voluntarism.

One of social work's basic value principles of people helping people to help themselves can be traced to our religious institutions which were the original groups providing what is presently referred to as social services. An historical examination of the Judeo-Christian religions show that these sects were committed to performing charitable acts. In fact, the Talmud, an ancient collection of Jewish law and traditions and the Decretun, a collection of papal and church decrees, which dates back to the 12th century, both discuss the subject of charitable giving. Later, as society became more industrialized and the cities became overcrowded, our religious institutions found themselves unable to continue along in this role. Subsequently, these responsibilities were shared by non-sectarian voluntary and private groups, government agencies and eventually by professional social work organizations.

With thanks to Susan McGrath, M.S.W., of The Association of Junior Leagues, for her contribution to this article.

The stereotype of one helping another in distress may carry the "Good Samaritan" or "Lady Bountiful" label but in fact most volunteer helping activities from earliest times was developed and offered within the context of some sort of institution such as churches and voluntary service associations.

It is both these historical roots: the Judeo-Christian concept of helping and the context of help being offered through a voluntary or community institution, that a social work student needs to understand in order to develop a firm professional value base and an identification with the context in which he/she will practice.

While most social work education programs do include this early history of social work and social welfare, there is considerable evidence that many social workers have not incorporated the relevance of our history into their practice. Rather they have relegated history to the past and practice as if professionals and their professional services are full substitutes for the volunteer efforts of former days. The consequences of this attitude are that volunteers become either an "irritating intruder" or a "nice extra" rather than a necessary partner in the delivery of social services.

Clearly the status of volunteers needs to be amplified. With this in mind, an inter-agency Task Force conducted a two-year national demonstration project called Voluntarism and Social Work Practice. The goal of the project was to promote a better working relation-ship between social workers and volunteers.

To accomplish this goal, the Task Force set up a pilot program (or network) in six different cities. Each network explored the status of voluntarism in their communities, the role of volunteers in their social agencies and the curricula in local social work schools that prepare students to work with volunteers.

The networks, located in Atlanta, Austin, Baltimore, Berkeley, Cleveland and Toronto included representatives of social work agencies, volunteer organizations and faculty members of schools of social work. In less than a year's time, each of the parti-cipants reported that they had gained a broader insight into the issues and also the workings of the other groups in the collabora-tion.

Social workers have learned that there is a new breed of volunteer: one who wants structure, training, and the assurance that his/her service is appreciated and effective. Agencies must provide a professional environment if they are to attract today's volunteer.

Volunteers in turn have learned that they need training, supervision and defined responsibilities and, like other agency staff, need to be accountable. Educators and agency administrators recognizing that they provide few opportunities for students to work with volunteers, are examining new ways to incorporate voluntarism in agency practice and school curricula.

Before establishing educational objectives for a curricula, a deeper understanding of the factors determining the current uneasy volunteer/professional relationship is required. These factors can be classified into at least two groups, those which result from changes in social workers and volunteers as collectives and as individuals and those factors of a socio-economic-political nature which have resulted in major changes in the social welfare system.

A number of sociologists (Etzioni, Friedson, Greenwood, Toren and others)[1] have studied the development of helping professions, including social work. Social work has been described as a "semi-profession" in relation to the older professions of medicine and law because it possesses less professional autonomy and has a weaker knowledge base than the "true" professions. These writers also describe the "semi-professions" like social work as striving to become more professional; i.e., to be accorded higher status, to achieve greater autonomy; to establish a more scientific base for practice.

"Social work is also differentiated from other professions concerned with meeting human needs in the fact that it is a relatively late outgrowth of a mature and highly specialized form of society. Even before we reached the complex conditions of modern industrial and urbanized society, law, education and medical service had become separate aspects of community life, largely unrelated to each other and to the depersonalized character of the production and distribution of goods and services." (Lurrie)[2]

Social work has, over the past fifty years, greatly increased its stature as a profession through building and testing its practice knowledge and technology. Social work must continue this important development of its professional knowledge and skills if it is to make its contribution to the alleviation of increasingly complex social problems.

This positive development has its negative aspects. First, by focusing on achieving a higher professional status some social workers tend to be or appear to be overly emphasizing their "domain" or functions rather than accentuating their contributions. Second, as they have received more recognition from other professional colleagues, social workers in their search for professional status has often felt a closer sense of identification with other professions than with their own unrecognized peers. These occurrences have contributed to the "psychological rift" in the professional/volunteer relationship. The individual social worker, especially the new social worker, is under pressure to demonstrate how professional he/she is in the conduct of practice, i.e., that his/her practice reflects an integration of knowledge and a critical stance in the use of that knowledge. Therefore, the "caring help" of the professional must be clearly differentiated from the "caring help" of the volunteer. One could hypothesize that the social worker who is more secure in his/her professional identification and practice competence will be more accepting of and more comfortable in his/her relationship with volunteers.

While social work has become more professional, so volunteerism has in its way become "professionalized." A large proportion of "volunteers" as now recruited, selected and trained by professionals are using professional methods. The competence of and time commitment by volunteers has led many of them to be labelled "professional volunteers." Indeed, apart from the fact that they are unpaid, the performance of many volunteers is indistinguishable from professionals performing similar functions. Having institutionalized roles for volunteers and standards for performance, volunteers have every right to expect recognition for their service contribution in the form of a partnership relationship. This positive development in the competence of volunteers in the social service sector also has its negative impact on relationships with social workers. Training volunteers helps them not only to know what their special skills are but also leads to inevitable comparisons of these skills with social work skills and some negative competing for who is the "best helper."

These are only some of the consequences of the developments in the competence of both social workers and volunteers over the past fifty years. These developments have the potential for much stronger and more effective social services if the negative aspects of the collaborative partnership can be eradicated.

A second group of factors, those of a broader socio-economic-political nature, have also influenced the professional/volunteer relationship.

The Depression during the 1930's and World War II in the 1940's were major economic and political upheavals which caused serious social disruption for families and individuals. Social Services were faced with new social problems as well as with the task of redefining the nature and origins of "old" social problems.

The emergence and continuation of the Depression jolted the country. Workers lost their jobs, banks closed, businesses shut down and farmers lost their land. No longer were voluntary agencies working exclusively with individuals and families that had history of being poor. The chaos of the 1930's created a middle class clientele with problems that had previously been identified as only belonging to members of the lower class. The Great Depression demonstrated that all people living in an industrial society were vulnerable to economic hardships and that new methods for providing relief were needed.

Even with increased understanding, knowledge and technology of practice, the voluntary agencies like the religious institutions which preceded them in providing help for the needy could not meet the overwhelming demand for services.

The resultant growth of government responsibility for many social welfare needs created a sudden expansion of public social services including the employment of professionally educated social workers. This was particularly true in child welfare, veterans services, vocational rehabilitation and mental health. Social workers became part of the growing public bureaucracy and potentially subject to greater regulation of their practice and reduced autonomy. Friedson[3] describes this change for professions the "industrialization" of service delivery in which professional functions and tasks are specified and distributed by the administration of the organization, somewhat analogous to the assembly line industrial plant. In such a setting where only the role of the professional is delineated, the role of the volunteer, if it exists at all, is very much an auxiliary one and not linked to any professional service. Examples of this are, the hospital friendly visitor or library volunteer. Only more recently have some of the public services given serious attention to the volunteer as a partner in service delivery. A notable example of this is the use of volunteers in the probation service in Toronto in which trained volunteers are assigned to juveniles on probation to act as a special friend to the young person and his/her family. Their caring support compliments and supplements the professional help of the probation officer who also must fulfill the legal requirements of the court.

The middle class continued to utilize the services of social workers after the Depression ended. By the time World War II began many social workers had established private practices to accommodate this new clientele. Although private practice proved to be both financially and professionally rewarding to social workers it did nothing to preserve the role of the volunteer.

Developments in social work education over this period of time clearly reflected the interdependence among the schools, the profession and the employing agencies. Social work educators are often professional social workers who have moved from practice roles to academic. Subsequently, they educate students to a particular view of themselves as a professional. The emphasis on research and scholarship in the academic environment combined with the employing organizations' expectations of accountability and effectiveness, require students to concentrate their studies on the knowledge component of practice and the importance of professional judgment. The profession wants graduates with a strong sense of professional identification and a high level of professional competence, to insure the profession's reputation and status among professionals. The government and other large employing agencies have a primary concern for graduates with the particular knowledge and technical skills required to perform the specific functions and tasks related to their services including the skill of being able to function well within a large organization. Until this recent time of financial constraint, public service agencies and government have offered monetary grants along with work commitment programs to insure the flow of social workers trained to meet their requirements. Neither of these two somewhat contradictory goals for social work education is particularly compatible with any educational objective related to improving the relationship between social workers and volunteers. However, there is some evidence that some social work educators are ready to review and alter curricula to include such an objective.

The resolutions of the Council on Social Work Education (CSWE) and the National Association of Social Workers (NASW) which created the earlier mentioned Voluntarism and Social Work Practice project, confirmed that educators and practitioners agree that changes in social work education programs are required. An exploratory survey carried out through the Voluntarism and Social Work Practice project indicated from those who responded, that very few Schools of Social Work included specific content on voluntarism in their curricula. Some of those who did, offered special courses for social work students, some offered only modules as part of a course, while fewer offered practicum opportunities to work (train and/or supervise) with volunteers.

Social work is making important gains in developing and testing its own knowledge and technology. With more security about their professional functions and identity, social workers should be ready to devote more professional energy to developing effective collaborative relationships with other helping colleagues including volunteers. Additionally, with less public support for social work education, school curriculum planners are freer to be more flexible and creative in developing programs which will prepare and encourage graduates to value volunteer citizen participation in all aspects of the social services. Finally, it is more important than ever in these difficult economic and political times, that social workers seek the support of the voluntary sector if they are to meet social service needs as well as fulfill those traditional social work functions of advocacy and brokerage. These problems cannot be tackled in the practice arena alone.

There are several possible locales for social workers to acquire the knowledge about voluntarism and the skills for working with volunteers. These include: university degree programs in social work; community college certificate programs for social service workers; and in-service and/or continuing education programs offered by employers or professional associations. In recognition of the importance of beginning with the basic level of professional training, the following discussion of curriculum planning is focused primarily on university level programs.

Introducing new content or restructuring old content in a curriculum begins with good educational planning, i.e., development of educational goals followed by the identification of knowledge and skills to be taught. The following is a summary outline of goals, knowledge--content on voluntarism and skills for inclusion in social work curricula.

Goals

    (1)   To provide knowledge of the role of the voluntary sector in social welfare services.

    (2)   To provide knowledge about roles of volunteers in social services and the relationship between volunteers and professionals.

    (3)   To develop skills in collaborating with volunteers in a range of role relationships.

Knowledge-Content

    I   History of Social Welfare in Voluntary Sector
           How social services developed historically through voluntary community effort

    II   Present role and status of Voluntary Social Welfare Organizations
           How voluntary social service organizations fit into our present complex system of public and private social services and how influential voluntary organizations are in our community today.

III   Comparative study of organizational structure of public and private voluntary social welfare organizations

         What are the similarities and differences between government and voluntary organizations and their ways of providing services?

IV   Voluntarism in our Society - value, motivations

         Is volunteerism still valued in our society and how do persons decide to become a volunteer?

V   Roles of volunteers in direct service activities e.g. the friendly visitor in the hospital, the big sister to a troubled teenager

VI   Roles of volunteers in indirect service activities e.g. board or committee member, receptionist

VII   Professional - Volunteer Relationships

    (a)   in indirect service - e.g. Does the social worker feel intimidated by the important business executive member of the board?

    (b)   in direct service - e.g. Does the social worker show respect for the volunteer and value his/her contribution to the service?

    (c)   Supervision, facilitator, trainer, collaborator

Skills

The skills required by social workers in working with volunteers should be similar to those used for interacting with colleagues and other professionals.   Therefore, the major focus for learning to work with volunteers needs to be on developing positive and constructive attitudes.   Social work students need to learn to perceive volunteers, both direct service and board volunteers, as colleagues in service to people in need.   One location where this learning can occur is in a practicum setting provided the professional staff is experienced in working with volunteers. The other site for learning these skills is in the classroom setting.

There are a number of approaches to incorporating the content into a curriculum.   The following are suggested ways in which traditional content areas can be strengthened and/or fovused to enhance social work students' competence in working with volunteers and with the voluntary sector of social welfare. Presentation of these ideas in the context of the traditional curriculum areas is for convenience only and is only one way of many to organize content.

1. History of Social Welfare and Social Work: Professional Values

This component is and should remain core to any professional social work degree and should include an historical overview outlining the emergence of social work as a profession as well as its origins in voluntarism. Understanding of the linkages between social work and voluntarism today can be greatly enhanced by introducing curricula which has an historical parallel between these two activities and the important contributions both have made to the profession.

2. Human Behavior and Social Environment

This course should be designed to promote students' understanding of the relationship between human behavior and social environment by familiarizing them with the basic concepts of subject areas other than social work. These include, but are not limited to, psychology, social sciences, history, economics and philosophy. A well balanced educational background is essential as a foundation for social work practice.

> For example, it is important that individuals experience intimate human relationships and social contacts in order to achieve maturity and self actualization. Social workers understand this and apply this knowledge in professional relationships with clients as part of their helping intervention. Many clients need additional help to incorporate the intervention process with the process of initiating and sustaining personal relationships and to developing or improving social skills. The use of a volunteer trained to offer such assistance to clients, can become another form of intervention which can be used following or concurrent with professional help.

3. Social Welfare Policy

A social work education should help students master the analytic skills required to understand the complex social policies which are the basis of the social welfare legislation and regulations for our large public social service programs. Social welfare policy courses should be designed to acquaint the student with volunteer citizen participation in the political process which begins with an identification of need and ends with a service delivered. Indeed, as Kramer[5] suggests, the role of the voluntary sector in the social services is being challenged by some as no longer being distinctive from government services while

59

others perceive the need for a redefinition and strengthening of the voluntary sector. This latter view appears to be the one most strongly supported in the North American communities. Finally, social work students must be taught the role volunteers have played in identifying and interpreting community needs and in lobbying to gain public political support for services to meet these needs.

4. Social Work Practice Methods

As presently taught, most methods of social work practice tend to focus primarily on the skills (interviewing, communication and problem solving techniques) social workers need to work with clients (individuals, families, groups and communities).

This course should include content that teaches students how these skills can be transferred to non-clinical settings. Particularly when establishing professional relationships with community leaders, citizen committees, boards and volunteer members of social welfare organizations,

5. Social Work Research

The research component of the curriculum could include researching the current use and effectiveness of volunteers and voluntary organizations. This content would allow students to acquire and utilize research skills in addition to gaining insight into the different roles played by volunteers as helping individuals and voluntary organizations and social service providers.

The five social work education components listed above suggest one curriculum model for incorporating and teaching this content. This is an integrated model with content on voluntarism planned to permeate all courses. Since any curriculum should contain clear and specific objectives, this model could be defined as having an educational objective related to voluntarism. It has a number of advantages and some disadvantages.

Any model in which certain content has linkages across curriculum areas, assists the student in his/her integration tasks and that content is more likely to be internalized and incorporated into practice.

A second advantage of an integrated model is that it specifically focuses in on voluntarism without overloading the curriculum. This model could also include field assignments as a practicum objective requiring each student to serve an internship working with volunteers.

There are four disadvantages of this model. First, not all

faculty will be equally committed to the objective and therefore, it will be difficult to ensure or determine to what extent the desired content is taught. However, this problem could be overcome if social work schools introduced the voluntarism curriculum as required components to social work courses complete with a mechanism for evaluating its viability.

Some schools might also object to the inflexibility that prescribed or required content sometimes imposes. If some content on the subject is taught throughout the curriculum, specialized courses will not likely be considered. Lastly, content that is integrated across a curriculum tends not to be visible and at this point in time it may be necessary to highlight this content in a different way.

One way to highlight content on voluntarism is by introducing an "independent" curriculum model in which content on voluntarism would be taught in separate courses or in identified modules within courses. Within this model, there might or might not be an educational objective related to voluntarism. If there was such an objective, the curriculum could include one or more required course(s) on voluntarism and one or more electives to allow for in-depth study on special aspects of voluntarism. If there was not such an objective, the availability of courses on voluntarism could be made known to interested students. Although the "independent" curriculum model would result in fewer students studying voluntarism those that did would have a stronger commitment to and more enthusiasm for working with volunteers and the voluntary sector than students who did not participate in such courses.

Fewer students studying voluntarism is one disadvantage of this model. Another is that instfead of providing field experience with volunteers for all social work students it can only promote that type of internship program for students participating in voluntarism courses.

A final issue for social work schools is whether to develop specialist education programs to professionalize the volunteer coordinator role. Undergraduate schools have been offering similar courses for at least the past decade. In 1974 the University of Califorai at Riverside offered, under a federally funded program, a two-semester course in volunteer administration. During the fall of 1975, the University of Denver introduced a four-year course leading to a bachelor's degree in volunteer administration. By 1976 six community colleges in California had established A.A. degrees in the field.(Lobb)[6] Perhaps it is time for graduate schools of social work to explore the possibility of offering curriculum that focuses on educating future volunteer coordinators. Precedents have been set. In fact, the majority of social work graduate schools presently offer some form of specialized curriculum. Also, the proposed new educational policies in the United States and Canada recommend some concentration/specialization study at the Master's level. If these developments and policies prevail future curriculum may well include a specialized volunteer coordinator program.

The knowledge and skills (i.e. communication, interviewing techniques, organizational abilities, etc.) required for this role conform with those of the social work profession. Therefore, education for volunteer coordinators could be readily accommodated within a Master's level social work education program. However, before any school moves to offer such a program, several questions need to be answered.

One is whether the role of volunteer coordinator lies primarily in the domain of the profession of social work by reason of its particular values, knowledge and skills or whether education in social work is only one of several appropriate forms of preparation for this relatively new occupational role. Another is what would the career prospects be for graduates with this specialization?

CONCLUDING SUMMARY

This article has addressed how social work education can participate in the objective it shares with the profession to strengthen the relationship between social workers and volunteers and between the profession and the voluntary sector of social welfare. The historical context of the relationship was briefly explored and some factors contributing to some of the present concerns were identified. Curriculum goals are suggested as well as specific knowledge content and resultant skills. Two possible curriculum models are presented: an integrated model with content on voluntarism included in all areas of the curriculum and an independent model with most content on voluntarism being offered in special courses or modules within courses. The advantages and disadvantages of both models are discussed as well as the proposal of a specialist program for the volunteer coordinator role.

Curriculum designed to familiarize social work students with the past and present roles and contributions of volunteers would be incomplete without a mechanism for feedback and evaluation. Without this last component, social work education would be unable to measure the effectiveness of the curriculum. Pre- and post-testing of participating students is but one method that could be employed. For instance, prior to taking a course on voluntarism students could be polled to determine their attitudes and test their knowledge about volunteers and voluntarism. Upon completion of the course the same set of questions could again be administered.

FOOTNOTES

1. See Etzioni, A. "The Semi-Professions and Their Organization,"
   New York: Free Press, 1969: Friedson, Eliot, ed.
   "The Professions and Their Prospects," London: Sage
   Publications, 1973; Greenwood, Ernest, "Attributes
   of a Profession," Social Work, II (July 1957);
   Toren, Nina, Social Work: The Case of A Semi-
   Profession, London: Sage Publications, 1972.

2. Lurrie, Harry L. "The Responsibilities of a Socially
   Oriented Profession," New Directions in Social Work.
   Cora Kasus, ed., New York: Arno, 1954.

3. Friedson, Eliot, ed. op cit.

4. See Brewer, Lyla. "A Master's Emphasis Vol. Administration."
   Vol. Administration, IV, No. 4, Haeuser, Adrienne and
   Florence S. Schwartz. "Developing Social Work Skills
   for Work with Volunteers." Social Casework, December,
   1980; Richards, L. "Education for Voluntary Program
   Management: One Model in Canada." Vol. Administration,
   Vol. IV, No. 4, 1981; Schwartz, Florence S. "Training
   the Professional Staff to Work with the Program Volunteer."
   Vol. Administration, Spring, 1977.

5. Kramer, Ralph. Voluntary Agencies in the Welfare State.
   University of California Press, Berkeley, 1981.

6. Lobb, Charlotte. Exploring Careers Through Volunteerism.
   New York: Richards Rosen Press, Inc., 1976.

REFERENCES

Allen, Kerry K.
   1980   "A Volunteer Agenda for the 1980's," Voluntary Action
           Leadership (Summer)

Brewer, Lyla
           "A Master's Degree Emphasis Vol. Administration,"
           Vol. Administration, Vol. XIV, no. 4.

Chapin, Henry
   1977   "Tapping the Untapped Potential: Toward a National Policy
           on Volunteerism," Canadian Council on Social Development
           (October).

Davies, Bleddyn
           "The Cost-Effectiveness Imperative to the Social Services
           & Volunteers," Occasional Paper, The Volunteer Centre.

Education for Giving
   1980   Vol. Action Leadership (Spring)

Haeuser, Adrienne A. and Florence S. Schwartz
   1980   Developing Social Work Skills for Work with Volunteers,
          Social Case Work (December).

Holmes, A. and J. Maizels
   1978   Social Workers & Volunteers, B.A.S.W. Allen and Urwin,
          London.

Kramer, Ralph
   1981   Voluntary Agencies in the Welfare State, University of
          California Press, Berkeley.

Kreps, G. M.
          "Volunteerism, Vol. Coordinators & Continuing Education,"
          Vol. Administration, Vol. XIII, no. 4.

Richards, L.
   1981   Education for Voluntary Program Management, One
          Model in Canada, Vol. Administration, Vol. IV, no. 4.

Schwartz, Florence S.
   1977   "Training the Professional Staff to Work with the
          Program Volunteer," Vol. Administration (Spring).

Scheier, Ivan
   1977   "Staff Non Support of Volunteers," Vol. Action Leadership
          (Fall).

Sieder, Violet M. and Doris C. Kirschbaum
          "Volunteers," Encyclopedia of Social Work, 17th Edition.

Trost, L. S.
   1977   "M.S.W. Attitudes toward Direct Service Volunteers,"
          Vol. Administration, Vol. X, no. 3 (Fall).

SOCIAL WORK PRACTICE WITH SENIOR ADULT VOLUNTEERS IN ORGANIZATIONS RUN BY PAID PERSONNEL

Mary M. Seguin
University of California, Los Angeles

Social Workers have only begun to realize the implications that an aging population has for their practice. Of about 24.7 million men and women age 65 or
older in the United States as of July, 1979, only about 3 million or 13% were
working or actively seeking work; 1 man in 5, and 2 women in 25. Men at age
65 can expect to live 14 more years, and women 18 (Weg, 1981). This means that
most men and women today can expect to be retired for a number of years.
Through retirement they have lost both a principal source of income from wages
and a principal means through occupation for establishing personal identity
and socially valued productivity. Older persons and others -- youth, women,
and racial minorities -- who tend to be excluded from full participation in
the labor-force attest to the urgency of modifying current ways of making income and meaningful tasks available to all persons through the life-cycle.
Each cohort that retires is expected to be healthier, better educated and live
longer than the previous one. Older persons have coped with rapid change
throughout their lives. They can help to create the social inventions needed
to make the institutions of society responsive to the changing requirements
of its people.

Older men and women for whom paid work has long been an important means for
productive involvement, often no longer have that option available due to retirement practices. Volunteer or unpaid work affords them a means similar to
paid employment for identity and participation in community life through work
in organizations. Older volunteers, i.e., workers who are both retired and
unpaid, afford organizations a largely untapped personnel resource. If
established organizations operated by paid personnel are to utilize this
resource they must modify their operations to accommodate the new older
volunteers. The paid staff often recruit and deploy volunteers just as they
do paid personnel in those organizations which utilize service volunteers.
Volunteers may, therefore, perform tasks which are limited in variety or
challenge due to paid workers retaining administrative, professional and

supervisory roles.

The guidelines for practice presented here are for a different model of volunteer involvement in which the volunteers have access to the full range of roles and have opportunities for innovation as they discover ways to complement the work of paid personnel. These guidelines are derived from the experience of about a hundred senior adult volunteers and two paid workers, a social worker/gerontologist and a coordinator of volunteers, as together they developed a cadre of older volunteer personnel in an institution of higher education (The Andrus Volunteers, Andrus Gerontology Center, University of Southern California). From their evolving position in the center, these retired men and women have been able both to help accomplish the mission of the organization and to engage in growing numbers and kinds of self-enhancing, satisfying personal experiences. Although based upon a single case study, the principles presented seem to be applicable to other similar settings. This example is intended to highlight the challenge and excitement of helping today's senior adult pioneers generate the social inventions that can improve the quality of life for the growing older population -- of which we all are members now or in the foreseeable future.

Social workers who serve this well elderly population function primarily as catalysts, enabling older individuals and groups to meet both their own needs and those of others for whom they act as advocates, and as colleagues with professionals from various disciplines, developing and adapting ways to meet changing needs of all persons in an aging society. The social worker's objective in this instance was to help retired persons create one kind of "social invention" that enabled them to participate in the mainstream of community life through meaningful work in an established organization which they and their paid associates could then operate without further intervention of the social worker. The guidelines that follow are written from this perspective.

Presented first is a profile of the Andrus Volunteers (AVs) and their current (1980-81) program in order to illustrate the mutual benefit to retired persons and to the organization that can come from having older volunteer personnel functioning in a range of roles in an organization. Next are stated the principles for practice which emerged and guided volunteers and paid staff during the evolution of the AVs from the initial literature search on older volunteers (Seguin, 1972), through the research and demonstration period (Seguin, 1973-75), and the transition to an on-going status in the Gerontology Center, 1976 to the present time. The paper concludes with observations about application of the guidelines in other settings.

THE ANDRUS VOLUNTEERS

Profile: There were 64 active and 45 sustaining members in 1980-81 (Birren, 1981). One hundred active individuals (By-laws, 1981) are as many as can be physically accommodated in the Andrus Center and absorbed into the volunteer's supportive structure of interpersonal relationship and work. There were 20 men and 44 women; 49 were White, 14 Black, 1 Hispanic. Their demographic profile showed AVs to be similar to other volunteers (Payne, et al., 1972) with respect to socio-economic-status, educational level attained and different from other volunteers with respect to age, AVs being older (median age, 70; range, 48 to 85). The AVs were different from their age peers in that they had more schooling and higher socio-economic-status. Although the majority of AVs were

66

in professional/managerial positions prior to retirement, approximately one-fifth were not. While some members in retirement had sharply limited incomes, they continued a life-style compatible with that of their more affluent peers. It is not surprising that the university setting attracted many volunteers who had gone to college and enjoyed campus life.

An active Andrus Volunteer, in addition to giving regular volunteer service in projects sponsored by the AVs, is expected to participate in a weekly membership meeting, either general or committee, and pay $3.00 per year to defray the cost of mailings and publishing their monthly newsletter, the Volunteer News. Members are inducted into the AVs through an initial interview with a member of their Membership Committee, through participation as a docent (described below) and through the weekly meetings.

The weekly meetings serve a triple purpose, they: 1) provide a forum for the exchange of information about gerontology, including the research findings of the Andrus Center staff, the various activities of the AVs, the requests for volunteer service made by staff and students from the university and by groups from the wider community; 2) afford members an affective support group; and 3) structure the volunteer program by receiving and evaluating requests for service.

Sustaining members are AVs who were once active but can no longer meet all of the requirements of active membership due to such circumstances as moving away, taking paid employment, extended travel, illness, or family responsibility. They attend when they can and pay their membership fee to keep in touch via the newsletter.

Of the 30 volunteers who were active in September, 1974, the beginning of the first full year of operation, six were active in 1980-81, and eight were sustaining members. After six years, almost half of the initial elderly group were still affiliated.

Structure: Activities of the AVs are designed to help accomplish the mission of the university, namely research, education, and public service. The structure (Seguin and O'Brien, 1976) which the AVs have evolved for themselves shows this articulation. Their volunteer services are administered by the Vice-Chairperson for Program through their committees for Research, Education, and Community Programs (public service). In addition, the AVs engage in activities required to maintain themselves as a viable group. Their Vice-Chairperson for Personnel, Development and Communications administers the work of their Membership Committee which is in charge of recruitment and placement, orientation and reimbursement of volunteers; and of their Communications Committee which is in charge of publications, tours, and the speaker's corps. A Nominating Committee presents a slate of officers to be elected by the membership; and Ad-hoc Committees are formed as needed to deal with projects, e.g., Peer Leadership Project, Peer Counseling, structure and by-laws, fund-raising, and office management. The Executive Committee coordinates the work of all AVs.

The AVs, like other components of the Andrus Gerontology Center, are expected to find their own fiscal support. The salary of the paid coordinator is their major expense. Other items include reimbursement for out-of-pocket expenses (mileage), office supplies and telephone. Source of income are from: 1) grants for projects, e.g., research and demonstration on older volunteers, volunteer leadership development; 2) publications, e.g., <u>Releasing the Potential of the Older Volunteer</u>, <u>Aging; Today's Research and You</u>, <u>How to Set Up a Volunteer Blood Pressure Screening Program</u>, 3) operating the food concession during summer institute class breaks; 4) fund-raising events, e.g., bazaars, and plant sales, and 5) inclusion in grants of other departments for specific services rendered by the volunteers to those projects, e.g., an item for interviewers, or research subject recruitment.

<u>Program</u>: Andrus Volunteers engage in <u>research</u> on aging in several ways: 1) They regularly supply faculty and graduate students with a pool of research subjects over age 65 for various studies of the aging processes; 2) They sometimes serve on panels to test research instruments and to plan and evaluate research projects; 3) Some are trained as research interviewers on projects initiated by Center researchers; 4) The volunteers also initiate their own research projects, e.g., "Organizational Response to Older Volunteers," "Life Enrichment through Humor in Long Term Care Facilities," and evaluate the educational series, "Aging: Today's Research and You," which they sponsor.

<u>Educational Programs</u> have been developed by AVs principally for older persons. Their first major educational effort was an intellectually stimulating oppor- tunity for retired professionals. They organized an advisory consortium of paid and volunteer educators from three universities, the Los Angeles Unified School District, and the Los Angeles County Area Agency on Aging, and began an experi- mental "class," entitled "New Perspectives for Adult Learners," funded through the public school district. The class was composed of twenty-five men and women from different backgrounds who became the recruiters, organizers, curricu- lum developers, students and teachers. The "class" was repeated for two semesters and held in different parts of the city.

Subsequently, they have designed educational events that translate aging re- search findings into lay language. Upcoming is their sixth annual series of lectures and discussions entitled, "Aging: Today's Research and You," covering such topics as drugs and the elderly, memory, adult learning, coping with widow- hood, planning to make the rest of your life the best. Each series is planned in cooperation with the continuing education component of the Andrus Center. Each monthly event features a lecture by a faculty member or researcher of the Center. Following the lecture is an opportunity for small group or panel dis- cussion of the content facilitated by AVs who have studied the subject and have prepared to be discussion leaders. Each year the series has sold out in advance, attendance averaging 175/event in 1980-81. Participants include re- tired persons, professionals serving older adults, Andrus Volunteers, and graduate students. Andrus Volunteers also serve as teaching assistants and librarians for some Leonard David School of Gerontology regular courses; take courses in the school; serve as guest lecturers. These classroom experiences provide intergenerational opportunities of mutual benefit to young and old and give AVs a chance to help disspell negative stereotypes of aging.

"Who me--A Leader?", an audio slide presentation and a leader's manual are products of the AVs' Leadership Development Project, PEERS. Twenty AVs designed the project and secured federal funding (Title IA, Higher Education Act, administered by California Post-Secondary Education Commission) to implement it. They prepared the curriculum and taught themselves to teach others how to develop volunteer leadership for programs serving seniors, e.g., an information service in a Savings & Loan Association; program development in two multi- service senior centers; two workshops on Retirement/Aging with church groups;

volunteer services in a convalescent hospital. In the two year development of the PEERS Project, AVs have discovered how to work with their volunteer leader counterparts and paid staff in different kinds of organizations in the community, thus expanding opportunities for older volunteers in serving senior adults.

In May, 1980, the AVs staged a gala educational/fund-raising event, "Ethel Percy Andrus Day," to honor the memory of Dr. Andrus, founder of the National Retired Teacher's Association -- American Association of Retired Persons, and for whom the Gerontology Center is named. The day featured well known speakers, colleagues of Dr. Andrus, lunch and a bake sale. This effort took months of planning and work by many volunteers. The money raised was used for scholarships for members to take courses in the School of Gerontology. The recipients not only benefitted personally from this educational opportunity but became better prepared to perform their volunteer work.

The Community Programs division of the Center (now called the Institute of Policy and Program Development) sponsors projects which link the Center with the wider community. The volunteers have been administered through this division from the beginning (1973). As their talents became known, the AVs affiliated in some way with almost all of the Community Programs. They have served as members of advisory committees, technical assistants, panelists and in other roles with such projects as Pre-Retirement Planning, Multi-Service Senior Center Development, Health Screening, and Nutrition.

Guiding visitors on tours of the Center was an early service provided by the AVs that has continued. The AVs docent program, mentioned earlier, places friendly, knowledgeable, older persons at the entrance to the Center to greet and guide newcomers and to perform whatever incidental tasks that need to be done. New volunteers serve as docents for a few months as part of their orientation. By being in the lobby they get acquainted with faculty, staff and students, and become familiar with what is going on in the Center. The AVs Speakers' Corps responded to 73 requests in 1980-81 from groups throughout Southern California to speak on such topics as successful aging, sexuality and aging, exercise physiology and facts about aging.

Some AVs received training and became peer counselors as one part of the Adult Counseling service developed primarily to train younger professional counselors. As colleagues of the student counselors, the AVs afforded the students the opportunity of knowing well elderly persons to balance their experience with frail and disordered older adults, and also provided practical knowledge about how to deliver services responsive to the needs of people of similar age to themselves.

Individual AVs participated on Boards and in other leadership positions in community groups that advise and support the Center, e.g., Goldenera, a financial support group which some AVs helped to create; and the Board of Councillors which is advisory to the Center. AVs not only attend conferences of professional groups such as the Western Gerontological Society (WGS), but also make presentations based upon their own projects and in conjunction with Center faculty and graduate students. Of the ten AVs who attended the 1981 WGS Annual Meeting in Seattle, seven were presentors. One AV has been appointed by the Governor to the newly formed California Life Care Contract Advisory Board. Another has been named a Center Fellow of the UCLA/USC Long Term Care Gerontology Center. Another was co-chairman of the Los Angeles Regional Mini-White House Conference on Aging, and was elected as a delegate both to the State House and to the White House Conference on Aging. Nine other AVs were elected as delegates to the State House Conference on Aging.

The above description only highlights some of the AVs involvement. It is apparent from their productivity that the AVs have generated ways of relating to one another and to their work that releases person power and potential. More exciting even than the ever-evolving things they do is the feeling of mutual support and encouragement they give to one another. The norms and expectations which they have established for themselves encourage cooperation, innovation and some risk-taking. They celebrate special events, recognize special contributions and serve to support members through crises.

Stated in the next section are some of the conditions required to permit older volunteers to flourish in an organization operated by paid personnel.

GUIDELINES FOR OLDER VOLUNTEER PERSONNEL DEVELOPMENT

Testing the Organizational Climate:

The social worker who is about to help develop a cadre of older volunteers in an established organization run by paid personnel must test the readiness of that organization to utilize fully the volunteers' potential. Answers to the following questions must either be positive at the outset or are likely to become positive through demonstration.

1. Is there a viable relationship between the mission of the Organization and the contribution Older Volunteers can make to it?

The presence of senior adults in a gerontology center, for example, "made sense." Older adults could not readily be denied access to an organization whose mission was to study aging processes and prepare professionals to work with older people and on their behalf. This natural connection may not be as easy to perceive in some settings, and would require exploration to understand how the older volunteers can "visibly" contribute to the productivity of the organization.

2. Is the Organization attractive to Potential Older Volunteers?

Does the setting afford opportunity for at least the following three things:

a) stimulating relationships with the "regulars" in the organization, e.g., paid personnel and "consumers;" with others in the community, through this organization; and with other volunteers in the organization;

b) "real work" that is important, needed and recognized? that can be done within the time, talent, and energy constraints of the older volunteer?

c) positive identification for the individual through affiliation with the organization? This is an important consideration for retirees who can no longer identify themselves by stating their place of work.

3. How open is the psychological climate in the organization to accepting older volunteers?

a) <u>Is the organization ready for older persons?</u> The retirement process by which older workers were separated from the workplace may have overtones of prejudice against older adults that could re-activate feelings of being rejected in retirees who seek to enter this organization, and reinforce ageist stereotypes of young workers should they feel threatened by more experienced workers in their midst. On the other hand, retirees who volunteer may be welcomed because they are too old to pose a job threat to younger employees.

b) <u>Is the organization ready for Volunteers?</u> This may be a more salient attitudinal problem than age (Seguin, <u>et al.</u>, 1977). Money symbolizes the contract between the individual worker and the organization. Without the exchange of money, paid workers and volunteers alike may have difficulty conceptualizing that relationship. Money also is used to symbolize the worth attached to the work or to the worker or to both. Feelings about "free" work may range from "Whatever is worth doing, is worth being paid for" to "Tender loving care cannot be bought, but only freely given." Most people have definite, often unspoken feelings about unpaid (volunteer) work that are likely to surface when the idea of bringing volunteers aboard as full partners with paid personnel is introduced. The climate should be tested at all levels -- with decision makers, Board and staff; with line workers and support staff and with "consumers" -- to determine whether or not volunteers have at least a fifty-fifty chance of ultimate acceptance in the organization.

4. <u>Does the organizational structure permit development, innovation and tolerance for difference?</u>

The introduction of volunteer personnel will require such innovations as: a) a set of policies for volunteer personnel different from those that govern paid personnel; b) work that complements or supplements and does not compete with or duplicate tasks performed by paid employees; and c) cooperation between paid staff and volunteers in getting and deploying resources required to reach their common goals.

5. <u>Is the organization willing to allocate resources enough for older volunteers to demonstrate their value to the Organization?</u>

A minimal committment of resources is required to start up and to continue the support of volunteer personnel. Answers to the following questions should be positive:

a) Will the organization hire a competent, full-time Coordinator of Volunteers? This should be a paid position, at least initially, so that it is similar to positions of other paid staff in having a credible place in the organization, sanctioned by other paid employees, and governed by the same rules that apply to the core personnel responsible for the productivity of the organization. To perform a bridging function the Coordinator of Volunteers must have access to paid personnel as well as volunteers. To provide continuity for the volunteers who usually work part-time, the Coordinator of Volunteers should be full-time.

b) Are physical space and appointments not only available for the volunteers to do their work efficiently but also for them to interact with one another as a group? Suitable facilities for social interaction in the work place is vital both for the morale of the volunteers and for the exchange of work related information to stimulate their effective growth and innovation.

c) Is there fiscal support for: 1) the salary of the Coordinator of Volunteers, the most costly item; 2) reimbursement of volunteers' out-or-pocket expenses, an important consideration for retired persons on limited incomes who cannot afford to give both time and money; and 3) equipment, supplies, material and other items that support productive work?

6. <u>Where will the administration of the volunteer personnel be located in the Organizational structure?</u>

The volunteer personnel should be located as close as feasible to the center of the administrative structure in order for the volunteers to gain access to a range of paid personnel, tasks, recognition and resources not possible when confined to one part of the organization especially if that part has low priority; and to understand the organization of which they are a part.

<u>Developing Older Volunteer Personnel in an Established Organization</u>

Having located an organization in which senior adult volunteers might establish themselves and flourish, the social worker now thinks about the potential volunteers, the work they may undertake, and the organizational setting in which they will work -- both the existing arrangements and the structure the volunteers will create in order to govern themselves and their work. The worker operates from the belief that the older volunteers will generate meaningful work which is: a) responsive to their own needs and interests if they take charge of the development of the older volunteer personnel, and b) responsive to the needs and interests of the organization if they work closely with the paid personnel and "consumers."

The <u>volunteers</u> must share the challenge of opening opportunities for "non-traditional" workers in this setting and take the responsibility for inducting older adults into the organization from the outset if they are to be in charge of what they do. The Coordinator of Volunteers' first task is to locate a few individuals who respond favorably to the challenge of finding out whether or not there is a contribution that older volunteers can make to the work of this organization. The Andrus experience suggests that men and women who take up this challenge are likely to be experienced problem solvers such as administrators, other professionals, and homemakers who enjoy helping people organize and get things done. The next task for the Coordinator is to help these potential volunteers get acquainted with one another, the work and workers in the organization and assess where their own talents can be put to use. Once they decide where and how to get started and begin to interact with one another enough to offer some support for their efforts and a way to evaluate the results of their work, they have become volunteers. The Coordinator brings to their attention volunteer opportunities suggested by staff and also encourages the volunteers to explore their own ideas about creating programs that meet the objectives of the organization. Together, Coordinator and volunteers address obstacles they face in gaining acceptance in the organization and in developing the cadre of volunteers to perform the tasks that become more numerous as the volunteers establish a track record of service. The Coordinator provides: a) Continuity for the volunteers, giving them information about events that take place between the times that they are present, and b) a locus for the staff to request volunteer services and provide feedback as to results. As the numbers of volunteers and the kinds of work increase, the Coordinator performs more complex tasks: of providing administrative support to the volunteer leadership and accountability for the volunteers' work to the organization's Director and Policy Board; of exercising interpersonal and managerial skills in expediting the timely flow of information and other resources between and among volunteers and staff; of serving as consultant to volunteers and to staff about their work and relationships together. The Coordinator serves as bridge, advocate, interpreter, trouble shooter, colleague, leader, expeditor, mediator and lender of vision.

The work itself brings together the interests of the volunteer and the organization. To be meaningful, the work must do two things: induce the volunteers' psychological development and help to accomplish the central goals of the organization. The Coordinator and volunteers look for individual and organizational indicators of "good" work when assessing requests for volunteer services. Meaningful tasks provide for the volunteer a means for accomplishment, recognition, interest, challenge and growth (Herzberg, 1966; Pitterman, 1973; Seguin and O'Brien, 1976). The volunteer must also do "real," not "made" work, as noted earlier. If the work is to have clear and important meaning, both volunteers and paid personnel must be able to see the connection between the work the volunteers do and the outcomes for the organization. In addition, as also stated earlier, the work of the volunteers must complement, not compete with the work of paid staff. Volunteers will not gain acceptance by paid workers who believe that volunteers are taking over their jobs; even when volunteers extend the service over the lunch hour or release the paid worker for jury duty. Volunteers and paid workers may perform identical tasks, but if done by volunteers the work must be for the volunteers' own projects, e.g., typing the Volunteer News, not for work normally done by a paid worker.

The organizational structure created by the volunteers to govern themselves and their work should be independent of, but closely articulated with, the structure of the parent organization. An independent, volunteer-directed structure is important for several reasons. First, the volunteers need to take charge of volunteer personnel and its deployment to work under supervision of: a) paid personnel in the organization, in response to requests for volunteers to help with work for which the paid staff is responsible, b) volunteer personnel in the organization for volunteer initiated work, and c) either paid or volunteer personnel in other settings which have requested volunteer services from the organization. Second, the older volunteers need to develop their own peer group, one that is responsive to their common circumstance of being retired and unpaid workers in the midst of non-retired employees, and designed for their personal growth and support as well as for meeting the needs of the workplace. Third, the volunteers need to generate a range of tasks to accommodate volunteers with different talents, especially administrative, managerial and professional work, which may not be as available when volunteers are organized by paid personnel who retain the management roles. Close articulation is essential between the structure generated by the volunteers which should reflect the central functions of the organization, as should the structure of work of paid personnel. Both formal and informal contact and communication should be established between volunteers and their paid counterparts who perform similar functions in order to exchange information, develop complementary tasks and evaluate outcomes in relation to organizational goals. The volunteers' existence is almost totally dependent upon their capacity to operate within the constraints of the organization and gain access to and expand its resources. They must, therefore, establish structure and relationships that are compatible.

APPLICATION TO OTHER SETTINGS

Helping older volunteers open work opportunities in organizations as a means for well elderly persons to stay in the mainstream of community life can, presumably, be carried out in any socially sanctioned institution. Social workers and other coordinators of volunteers may be unfamiliar with some desirable workplaces that are familiar to senior adults and accepting of older workers. The McKinsey report (1974) entitled, "Developing New Roles for Older People: A Strategy for the New Careers Program," indicated four fields likely to provide expanding opportunity for older paid workers; namely, health, education, justice and commerce. These four fields were sampled in the study of organizational response to older volunteers in Los Angeles (Seguin and Andrus Volunteers, 1977). Data were gathered from 98 organizations, half that had older volunteers and half that did not. The findings indicated that many organizations with no older volunteers would consider the possibility of utilizing them, even commercial and justice enterprises which tended not to engage volunteers. As indicated earlier, to introduce volunteers may prove more difficult than to introduce older persons due to negative attitudes held by some paid personnel about unpaid work and people who perform it.

The potential supply of older volunteers is large and growing each day as more people retire at age 65 or earlier, in good health and with enough income to exercise options about how to spend their free time. Some will choose to work in organizations, either as paid workers or as volunteers, if they feel that the work is worthwhile and satisfying.

The model for older volunteer involvement presented here may be developed more readily in organizations that have not previously had volunteers or where they have been marginal. If staff have established different workable arrangements for utilizing volunteers, they are not likely to change. Nor do all organizations lend themselves to a cadre of volunteer personnel engaged in a wide range of roles. When free to discover new ways to help accomplish the organization's goals, however, volunteers can benefit the organization in initially unforeseen ways.

Benefits to the organization and to the senior adults that result from following the model of older volunteer development described here do not insure continuity for the program. There are several reasons for this: volunteers are perceived as marginal workers in organizations run by paid personnel; the Coordinator of Volunteers is a highly skilled professional occupying a marginal position both within the organization where this worker is usually one of a kind and in the classification of occupations where this position is recently listed and the kind of preparation needed for it has not yet been clearly developed; fiscal resources required for the program, though small in relation to results, are not likely to be incorporated into the regular, on-going budget of the organization in periods of recession.

The rewards in generating and maintaining this kind of older volunteer program are long range, in helping organizations adapt to the requirements of our new aging society; and short range, in helping today's elders find new

74

ways to express their considerable potential.

REFERENCES

Andrus Volunteers
   1980   <u>By-Laws</u>.

Birren, J. E.
   1981   "Andrus Volunteers Recognition Day." Focus No. XIII. A bulletin to
          all personnel, Andrus Gerontology Center, University of Southern
          California, March 27.

Herzberg, Frederic
   1966   <u>Work and the Nature of Man</u>, Cleveland, Ohio: World Publishing Company.

Little, M.
   1981   <u>How to Set Up a Volunteer Blood Pressure Screening Program</u>, Los
          Angeles, Calif.: Andrus Gerontology Center, University of Southern
          California.

McKinsey and Company
   1974   <u>Developing New Roles for Older People: A Strategy for the New Careers</u>
          <u>Program</u>. (A report to the Edna McConnell Clark Foundation.)

O'Brien, B. (ed.)
   1978   <u>Aging: Today's Research and You, Lecture Series I, 1976-77</u>, Los
          Angeles, Calif.: University of Southern California Press.

O'Brien, B. (ed.)
   1979   <u>Aging: Today's Research and You, Lecture Series II, 1977-78</u>,
          Los Angeles, Calif.: University of Southern California Press.

Payne, R., B.R. Payne and R.D. Reddy
   1972   In D. H. Smith, R. D. Reddy and B. R. Baldwin, (eds.) <u>Voluntary Action</u>
          <u>Research</u>, Lexington, Mass.: D. C. Heath and Company.

Pitterman, Lawrence
   1973   <u>The Older Volunteer: Motivation to Work</u>. Prepared for Older
          Americans Volunteer Program Action, Washington, D.C.

Seguin, M. M.
   1972   <u>Older Volunteer Training Program: A Position Paper</u>, Los Angeles,
          Calif.: Andrus Gerontology Center, University of Southern California.

Seguin, M. M.
   1975   <u>New Roles for Older Adult Volunteers</u>. (Paper presented at 102nd
          Annual Forum, National Conference on Social Welfare, San Francisco,
          May.)

Seguin, M. M.
   1975   <u>Older Volunteer Project: A Study of Senior Volunteer Personnel</u>
          <u>Development</u> (1973-75). (A report submitted to the Andrus Foundation,
          NRTA-AARP.) Los Angeles, Calif.: Andrus Gerontology Center,
          University of Southern California.

Seguin, M. M. and O'Brien, B. (eds.)
1976   Releasing the Potential of the Older Volunteer. Los Angeles, Calif.:
        University of Southern California Press.

Seguin, M. M. and Andrus Volunteers
1977   Organizational Response to Older Volunteers in Los Angeles. (A
        report to the Andrus Foundation, National Retired Teacher's
        Association - American Association of Retired Persons.) Los
        Angeles, Calif.: Andrus Gerontology Center, University of Southern
        California.

Volunteer News
1973-81 Vols. I-VIII, published 10 times per year by Andrus Volunteers,
         Andrus Gerontology Center, University of Southern California.

Weg, R. B.
1981   "Selected Characteristics of the Aging in the United States."
        In Helen Dennis (ed.), Retirement Preparation: An Update. Los
        Angeles, Calif.: Leonard Davis School, Ethel Percy Andrus Gerontology
        Center, University of Southern California.

INVOLVEMENT OF SENIOR CITIZENS IN NEEDS ASSESSMENT AND SERVICE PLANNING

Marie Weil
University of Southern California

The involvement of senior volunteers in needs assessment research and service planning empowers seniors and strengthens voluntary action. Volunteer senior leadership can be strengthened through direct and active participation in assessment of senior population needs and program planning. Such participation in service planning is mandated in federal regulations, yet the effective involvement of citizens and consumers in planning is frequently problematic. This paper presents the results of the successful experience in needs assessment and development of a service model by the Orange County (California) Senior Citizens Council and program staff from various senior programs. The project was sponsored by the Extension Division of the University of California at Irvine (UCI) and the Council.[1] Volunteers were involved in all phases of the project which focused on developing and analyzing needs assessment information and developing a service model for seniors.

BACKGROUND

The needs assessment and service planning processes were carried out through a Study Team, a group of 22 individuals who met biweekly for a six-month period to examine senior concerns and develop a plan for a comprehensive service delivery system for seniors in Orange County. The Study Team was convened and administered by a staff member of UCI's Extension Division and was led by the author.[2] One-half of the Study Team was made up of volunteers who were members of the Orange County Senior Citizen's Council or other senior groups; the other half was staff members of agencies providing or planning services for seniors.

The idea for the Study Team project originated with the Title I Program's local advisory committee composed of representatives of the Senior Citizens Council and staff. The Council members and Extension staff held the belief that seniors in volunteer and staff positions should be involved in research and program model development to assure a service system responsive to the

needs of the senior population of the county. Coinciding with the documenta-
tion by the Senior Citizens Program Office that Orange County lacked a coordinated system of senior centers and services was the recommendation in the
Comprehensive Older American Act Amendments of 1978 (Public Law 95-478) that
focal points for comprehensive service delivery for seniors be designated.[3]

Hence, the Study Team was convened (1) to examine the current status of the
delivery system for social services to the elderly in Orange County; (2) to
consider the potential of senior centers in fulfilling the role of delivery
"focal point"; and (3) to develop a desirable service delivery system for Orange
County, with guidelines and criteria for facilities, program and staffing of
senior centers.[4]

A diverse membership of staff and volunteers from public and private agencies
and organizations in Orange County's aging network was invited to participate
on the Study Team.[5] The Study Team reviewed current literature and legislation
relating to senior services and designed and implemented a survey of senior
centers and nutrition sites throughout the county.

After completion of the study, the group sponsored a conference which presented
their findings and model and elicited community feedback. The Study Team's
recommendations received the overwhelming support of the nearly 100 senior
citizens and senior service agency staff in attendance. The conference extended
volunteer and staff knowledge about senior program issues and broadened the
base of support for the Study Team's Comprehensive Service Plan, which was
ultimately adopted by the county.

The success of the program, then, was threefold: 1) it demonstrated the
effectiveness of senior volunteers in needs assessment research and service
planning; 2) it demonstrated a positive model for joint planning and action
among volunteers and program staff; and 3) it produced a needs assessment research report and a monograph describing and recommending a service model for
senior programs for Orange County.[6]

Basic Premises of the Study Team

Study Team members believed that implementation of the "focal point" concept
could improve the quality of services to seniors. They sought to increase outreach to vulnerable populations and increase programs for under-served geographic areas. Members also desired a more formal system of case management
and accountability. The Study Team was concerned that service focal points be
developed in a manner that would 1) meet the legislative intent, 2) implement
coordinated and comprehensive services for seniors, and 3) provide for productive citizen and consumer input for planning and feedback regarding program
development.

Process of the Study Team Project

Adopting the "Senior Center Philosophy," the Study Team held that senior
service center programs should be planned with not for older people.[7] The
importance of seniors as service planners and monitors as well as consumers was
stressed throughout the Study Team's work. Volunteer involvement was viewed as
essential for sound program development and accountability to the community.

The senior volunteer members of the Study Team brought considerable knowledge, experience and expertise to the endeavor. Several had been members of the Senior Citizen's Council and its working committees for quite a period of time, and some had professional experience in business, social work and law. This group of senior volunteers was thus sophisticated in program areas and was generally skilled in working with program staff and the Study Team leader and administrator. The program staff members tended to be younger, but their knowledge of program issues and senior needs enabled strong collaboration and positive relationships among the very diverse members of the Study Team.

Roles of volunteers and staff were complementary. Volunteers headed sub-committees and engaged in special literature, facility and program research and provided reports to the Team. Program staff members served on sub-committees and aided in instrument design, data coding and analysis. When there were differences of opinion and approach within the Study Team, senior volunteers often mediated. Toward the end of the project, senior volunteers and the Study Team leader presented project findings and recommendations and conducted workshops at the conference which planned for implementation of the model.

A lasting benefit of the Study Team effort was the opportunity for the group to work together for sufficient time to develop understanding of various view-points and to move to consensus. The work of the team was an on-going experience in program study, negotiation and collaboration.

Study Team Research

The research and development aspects of the Study Team project centered on the planning and implementation of a needs assessment and survey of programs to determine current levels and types of service and service needs of seniors.[8] Toward this end, a sub-committee drafted a survey instrument for review, critique and modification by the entire Team.

Data for the needs assessment and program survey was collected from 38 programs from a sample of 43 senior programs which offered some social service. The types of programs participating included: senior centers, nutrition programs, drop-in centers, city-sponsored and recreation department-sponsored senior programs and multi-purpose/multi-age program centers. Program directors and coordinators were interviewed. To assist in planning for local areas, data were analyzed by four geographical sub-areas as well as county-wide.

Responses relating to the following categories were compiled and analyzed: core services and desirable services; planned services; unmet service needs; staff-ing patterns; and categorical comparisons of seniors who utilize service pro-grams. Findings of the needs assessment research and information from other relevant data sources guided the model development phase of the project.

Recommended Core and Ancillary Services

The Study Team determined through a modified Delphi technique, examination of previous research (notably an earlier study conducted by the United Way of Orange County) and their own research, a set of 26 recommended core services to which all seniors should have access through a senior service center focal point. These services might be provided directly by the center, or the center might serve as a broker to arrange services for center clients through agree-ment or contract with other service provider agencies. Core services range from daily telephone reassurance, nutrition programs and counseling to individual needs assessment and case management. The core services and recommended providers are presented in Chart I.

In addition to core services deemed to be essential, the Study Team further defined twelve ancillary service components listed in Chart II that should be offered through senior service focal points.

Survey Findings

The needs assessment program survey documented the frequency and types of social services offered by senior programs in Orange County. Frequencies were tabulated to determine the availability of all core and ancillary services. Planned services were tabulated and compared with identified unmet needs for service. Staffing patterns and service utilization by special population groups were also analyzed.

Social services such as medical screening or legal counseling tended to be provided on a contract basis through specialized public or voluntary programs. Information and referral services, reassurance calls and home-delivered meals tended to be offered directly by senior programs. Among the ancillary services, crafts, hobbies, recreation and educational programs were most frequently offered.

The Study Team was concerned that no programs reported offering individual needs assessment, case management or 24-hour emergency telephone contact or relay. Only two agencies stated that they offered outreach services.

The programs surveyed offered proportionately more of the desired services than the needed core servies. This pattern indicates the primarily recreational function which a number of senior programs have served. It may also reflect lack of funding, facilities or staff capable of providing more complex services such as senior day care or assistance with out-of-home placement.

Most of the agencies surveyed reported that they planned only one new service for the following program year. Health related programs predominated, followed by expanded or new nutrition or recreation/crafts programs. Agencies reported the greatest unmet service needs as transportation, housing or housing assistance, in-home care, expanded health services and senior day care.

Only 44 planned services were reported versus 110 unmet needs. No programs expected to initiate in-home care services although this was identified as a major unmet need. Two programs planned day care and five planned transportation services. Outreach was planned by three and noted as an unmet need by seven other programs. No programs were planned for frail elderly or handicapped/disabled seniors. No housing programs were planned. The Study Team was also concerned that no programs for case management, emergency telephone relay or individual needs assessment were planned.

Reports of staffing patterns revealed a shortage of full-time staff and great unevenness in staffing patterns. The Study Team concluded that adequate staff and increased volunteer recruitment were major needs to strengthen senior programs.

Analysis of service utilization data revealed that frail elderly were greatly under-represented. This finding reflects the absence of specialized programs

Chart I

Core Services Recommended for All Focal
Points in Orange County

<u>Services</u>	<u>Provided by</u>
Daily Service Telephone Calls (Reassurance)	Center
Personal Physical In-Home Care	Center or Brokered
Home Counseling Service	Center or Brokered
In-Home Care; Chores, Cooking, Shopping	Center or Brokered
Home Delivered Meals	Center or Brokered
On-Site Nutrition Program	Center or Brokered
General Information, Referral, and Follow-Through	Center
Assistance with Loans & Emergency Financial Service	Center or Brokered
Legal Services	Center or Brokered
Tax Services	Center or Brokered
Housing Assistance	Center or Brokered
Home Repair	Center or Brokered
Advocacy	Center or Brokered
Senior Day Care	Center or Brokered
Medical/Health Services/Exercise Programs	Center or Brokered
Counseling/Consultation/Mental Health Services	Center or Brokered
Services for the Handicapped	Center or Brokered
Alcohol and Drug Abuse Services	Center or Brokered
Transportation Services	Center or Brokered
Escort Services	Center or Brokered
Bilingual Services (As Needed by Area Population)	Center
Informational Services on Income Support Programs (SSI and Social Security)	Brokered
Outreach	Center
Case Management	Center
24-Hour Emergency Telephone Contact or Relay	Center
Individual Needs Assessment	Center

Chart II

Ancillary Services Recommended for Focal
Points in Orange County

Crafts and Hobbies
Recreation
Educational Programs
Trips and Travel
Discount Rates on Meals and Merchandise
Cut Rate RX
Employment Services (Job Finding)
Volunteer Opportunities
Home Security/Crime Prevention/Victim Assistance
Protective Services (Abuse/Neglect/Family Violence)
Services for Out-of-Home Placement
Night Care and Respite Care

for seniors with health problems. Services for other senior special needs groups including poverty-level-income seniors and seniors who are members of ethnic minority groups (Hispanic, Black, Native American and Asian/Pacific-- including Southeast Asian refugees) were also greatly under-represented in service utilization counts. The unmet needs identified by program staff and the Study Team were major considerations in development of the Study Team's service model.

A CONTINUUM MODEL FOR COMPREHENSIVE SERVICES

The model developed by the Study Team focused on development of services fitting the continuum of needs experienced by seniors. "Continuum," as defined in the dictionary, is "an uninterrupted ordered sequence." The Study Team was impressed by the applicability of this concept both to the types of services needed by senior citizens and to the organization of physical locations where these services are provided.

Types of services for senior citizens can be categorized in an ordered sequence from those which enhance the quality of life to services which are necessary to support life. The Study Team identified four basic service categories that comprise the continuum of need:[9]

1. <u>Enhancement Services</u>: those services which, although not necessary for physical survival, are desirable and needed to maintain a good quality of life--such as recreational programs, socialization activities, educational and travel opportunities.

2. <u>Sustainment Services</u>: those services which are needed for sound social, emotional and physical well-being--such as nutrition programs, crisis counseling, legal counseling, employment or volunteer opportunities, and mental health maintenance services.

3. <u>Life Support Services</u>: those services which are necessary to maintain life--such as acute or chronic medical care, mental health treatment, day care, night care, and out-of-home care.

A fourth category of services is an essential corollary to these basic service levels, that is:

4. <u>Access Services</u>: services provided to assist seniors in learning about, connecting to and utilizing other services--such as information, referral and follow-through, outreach and transportation services.

The physical locations where the senior makes the contact to receive these services can also be viewed as a continuum ranging from neighborhood drop-in centers, which may be limited in programs but strong in emotional and social support, to a comprehensive service delivery center which provides, brokers for, and coordinates a full range of services to the senior population in a wider geographic area.

Model for Orange County

In Orange County, the geographic and population variation is considerable, ranging from densely populated urban areas with sprawling suburban areas to isolated and generally under-served rural areas. While seniors share some basic service needs (e.g., socialization and access to social and health-related services), the needs of the senior population are as varied as the unique individuals who compose this population. Special population sub-groups, such as the frail elderly, low and marginal-income seniors and minority group seniors, will also have particular needs based on their own situations, interests and characteristics. Therefore, the Study Team developed a flexible model for senior services which was both comprehensive in scope and differentiated in types and levels of service, depending on individual and community need. The Team wanted a service model which would provide for increased and improved coordination of services for seniors in Orange County within a more collaborative and comprehensive service delivery network. The central notion of the Continuum Model is that the senior service center focal points should provide access for seniors to all services which they may need. Such centers can thus function as a community of support, able to respond to changing needs and to offer socialization services, opportunities for friendship and volunteer activities, as well as provide access to sustainment and life support programs and services.

Other practical considerations had to be incorporated into the model to facilitate implementation. For example, the exact mix and balance of services needed in communities will differ. Specialized services will be more costly. Limited county resources will force choices among priorities, with trade-offs between efficiency (the more people served, the lower the unit cost) and effectiveness (the more intense, continuous, and personal the services, the higher the cost). The goal should be to achieve the highest level of both qualities within available resources.

In addition, program costs, political factors and social issues will have to be carefully considered in selecting the level and range of services for each neighborhood and larger service area in the county. The essence of a comprehensive service delivery system for seniors is the communication and coordination among various programs to assure that seniors receive all the services they need and to which they are entitled. The communication network, feedback systems, case management, information, referral and follow-through systems are the muscles that make a network of services effective. The concept of community focal points for service delivery offers a viable focus for maximizing resources, encouraging coordination and promoting communication among agencies and persons who plan and provide services for senior citizens.

FOCAL POINTS FOR SENIOR SERVICES

The Comprehensive Older Americans Act Amendments of 1978 encourages the designation of multipurpose senior centers as focal points. The Study Team believed that "focal point" connotes a concept rather than a structure, and that senior centers can be utilized to develop and strengthen the network of senior services by providing information and referral, brokerage and coordination of services, and direct collateral services. A "focal point" further implies access to services, concerns for equity, locating gaps in services and planning to meet identified needs of senior in its service area. Thus in the Study Team's model, references to senior centers as focal points relate to functions.

After considering survey results and the demographic data for Orange County's older population, the Study Team recommended a Service Model with the three following types of senior center "focal points" which are designed to meet the general needs of the senior population and the more specialized needs of isolated service areas and groups with particular service needs. In combination these three types of focal points form a model for comprehensive service delivery for seniors.

Type I: The Comprehensive Senior Service Center

The Comprehensive Senior Service Center, as a facility-based focal point, will serve a specific geographic area, determined by population and natural service areas, offering direct and brokered center-based services and serve as an entry point for access to specialized community-based services. The Center should be linked to smaller, less comprehensive neighborhood-based senior programs, and should aid them in access, referral and coordination.

The Comprehensive Senior Service Center should have a mandate to serve all seniors within its geographic boundaries who are in need of services, with special emphasis on vulnerable populations, such as low-income, minority and frail elderly. All of the core services, as well as many of the ancillary services, should be provided through direct center-developed and administered services, or through the coordination of brokered services provided through agreement or contract. Case assessment and case management services should be provided. For example, seniors needing services (such as acute care) which are available in the community, could receive information, referral and follow-through services from the center. Access to services, coordination and continued case management for seniors and their families should be major responsibilities of the comprehensive center.

Diagram I represents the Comprehensive Senior Service Center. As is illustrated, a variety of smaller, neighborhood-based senior programs, such as drop-in centers and senior clubs, would feed into this focal point. The comprehensive center would provide access to a variety of center-based and brokered services in the areas of life enhancement, sustainment and life support. Examples of center-based and brokered services are presented in the diagram. This focal point assumes a well-developed physical facility appropriate for offering a variety of programs and services. The center would maintain coordination of its own program and services.

Type II: The Special Population Group Senior Service Center

Some senior population groups have critical and specialized needs which relate to their physical condition and/or their culture. Many of these seniors will need specialized services related to health needs or cultural needs as well as the core senior services.

Some frail elderly and ethnic minority elderly will wish to maintain involvement with their geographic service centers, while others will need or prefer to be related primarily to programs which are designed to meet the particular needs of their cultural group or of frail or disabled persons. Both options should be available to seniors with special problems or situations.

The Special Population Group Centers would draw their service populations from a specific community of interest within a broader geographic area. While

Diagram I
Comprehensive Focal Point

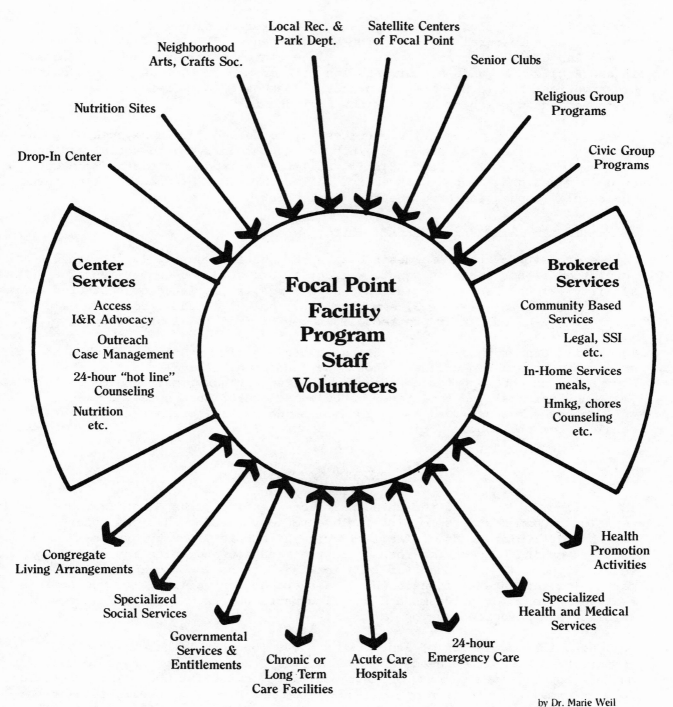

Neighborhood
Arts, Crafts Soc.

Local Rec. &
Park Dept.

Satellite Centers
of Focal Point

Senior Clubs

Religious Group
Programs

Nutrition Sites

Civic Group
Programs

Drop-In Center

**Center
Services**

Access
I&R Advocacy

Outreach
Case Management

24-hour "hot line"
Counseling

Nutrition
etc.

**Focal Point
Facility
Program
Staff
Volunteers**

**Brokered
Services**

Community Based
Services

Legal, SSI
etc.

In-Home Services
meals,

Hmkg, chores
Counseling
etc.

Congregate
Living Arrangements

Specialized
Social Services

Governmental
Services &
Entitlements

Chronic or
Long Term
Care Facilities

Acute Care
Hospitals

24-hour
Emergency Care

Specialized
Health and Medical
Services

Health
Promotion
Activities

by Dr. Marie Weil

85

seniors in a specific ethnic group, for example, might receive some services and participate in some programs through neighborhood-based programs, their primary access to focal point services and access to coordinated larger community-based services can better be managed by the Special Population Group Center staff who will have translation skills, understand the culture and orientation of the group, and will be especially capable of engaging in out-reach to and advocating for the needs of their special clientel.

The Special Population Group Centers should offer culture-specific services that maintain cultural customs, such as observance of Indian festivals and Indian languages and crafts. Assimilation-related services, such as classes in the English language and orientation to American customs as well as cultural preservation, should be offered to assist Southeast Asian refugees in under-standing and functioning in their new environment.

Transportation and translation services may be needed for these special popu-lation groups when they are moved into larger community-based social and health service networks. The staff of this facility can expect to play a much greater role in case management and intensive follow-through. Diagram II illustrates the Special Population Group Center focal point.

Type III: Mobile Senior Service Center

Mobile facility centers are desirable in communities where: 1) the senior population is not large enough to warrant construction or conversion of a facility; 2) the senior population, while large, is isolated or scattered over a wide geographic area; or 3) a mobile focal point, coordinated with various neighborhood-based senior programs, is the preferred model of service.

The Mobile Center should coordinate services closely with local neighborhood programs. Scheduling problems should be handled sensitively to assure equal access to and coverage for core services. Certain services, such as 24-hour emergency referral and assistance, should be located in a specific place, while other services, such as basic health and dental screenings, can be handled from the mobile facility. See Diagram III.

PROJECT COMPLETION

In addition to designing the three part service model, the Study Team developed detailed recommendations for its implementation. Recommendations covered: (1) the particular needs of frail elderly and ethnic minority groups; (2) the decision making process for focal point designation and selection of appropriate service types; (3) the need for technical assistance in program development particularly in areas of outreach, access and accountability; (4) the adminis-trative options for programs and staffing patterns; and (5) concerns regarding facility and resource development.

Following the completion of its work--the development of the service model monograph and report on needs assessment, the Study Team continued to meet for mutual support, idea sharing and strategy development for model implementation. This informal continuation of the Study Team has become a powerful coalition seeking improved services for seniors in Orange County. Senior volunteers led the group in a lobbying effort to disseminate the report and persuade govern-mental officials to consider the Team's recommendations and model for service.

Diagram II
Special Population Group Focal Point for Senior Services

Draws Population from a Community Of Interest — Specific Group Population may come from a wide service area for culture and need specific services.

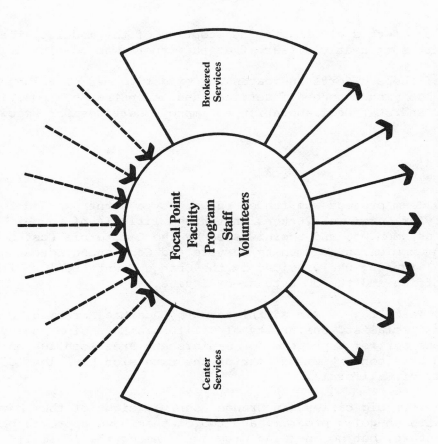

Access to Community Based Social and Health Services

by Dr. Marie Weil

87

Diagram III
Mobile Facility Focal Point

Services a variety of rural communities, or isolated Seniors, or scattered senior population. Delivers services at a variety of neighborhood based points of service.

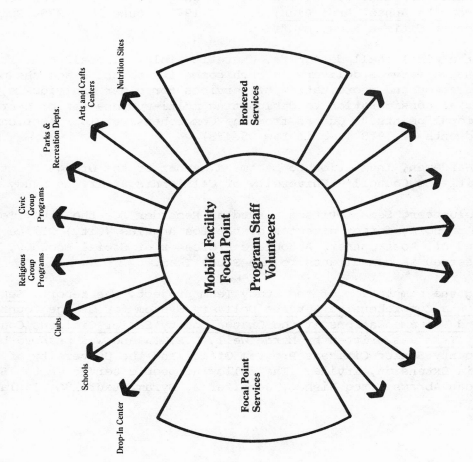

Access to Community Based Social and Health Services

by Dr. Marie Weil

The culmination of this effort was the adoption of the model by the County Board of Supervisors nearly a year after the report was completed.

The success of these efforts indicates the effectiveness of volunteers in planning and lobbying for needed services and demonstrates a positive strategy for volunteer and staff collaboration to improve services for special populations.

Notes

1. The Study Team project was funded in part by a grant awarded to the University of California Extension through Title IA of the Higher Education Act as amended, and administered by the California Post-Secondary Education Commission, Community Service and Continuing Education Program. Additional funding was provided by the Orange County Senior Citizens Program office and the UC Extension, Irvine.

2. The Study Team Project was administered by Ada Mae Hardeman, Continuing Education Specialist, University of California Extension at Irvine. The project was part of a program for Seniors and Area Agencies on Aging, sponsored by a consortium of four of the Extension Divisions of the University of California.

3. "Among the ten big cities (in Orange County), eight of them have senior centers with on-going programs and two of them have approved buildings for senior centers, but no on-going programs. Among the 16 small cities, three have senior centers, six have inadequate centers, three have no buildings, one is under construction; six of them have some on-going programs and the other ten cities have no on-going programs for seniors." Quoted from The Annual Area Plan, July 1, 1978 - June 30, 1979, Orange County Senior Citizen Program Office.

   "Each (area plan) shall designate, where feasible, a focal point for comprehensive service delivery in each community to encourage the maximum collocation and coordination of services for older individuals, and give special consideration to designating multi-purpose senior centers as such focal points." Quoted from the Comprehensive Older Americans Act Amendments of 1978 (Public Law 95-478).

4. Ada Mae Hardeman, Invitation to become a member of the Orange County Senior Citizens Council - University of California at Irvine Study Team.

5. Senior Volunteer, Sema Levinson served as Recorder for the Study Team. Dr. Roy Azarnoff, former director of the Los Angeles (City) Office for the Aging, and Dr. Ross Conner, Associate Professor of Social Economy, UC Irvine, served as consultants to the Study Team.

6. Following the completion of the Study Team project, the report, Senior Centers in a Comprehensive Service Delivery System for Orange County: Report and Recommendations of the Orange County Senior Citizens Council-UCI Study Team was written by Marie Weil, D.S.W., and was printed by the Orange County Senior Citizens Program Office and the University of California Extension, Irvine. The following people served on the Study Team: Joan Abrams, Greg Bishop, Jennifer A. Byram, Laurel G. Caplan,

John L. Clark, Shirley Cohen, Marilyn L. Ditty, Jeanette J. Dutton, Maria Estrada, Mary D. Kerbret, Sema Levinson, Freda Magid, Mark Matthews, Lee McGrew, Muriel Nelson, Aida M. Ramirez, Fred Roth, Gina Ryan, Frances M. Scherman, Isadore Schneider, Patricia Seixas, and Alex Smith. The Report is available through the University Extension Office, University of California at Irvine.

The Report of the Needs Assessment Survey of Orange County Senior Services, sponsored by the Study Team, is on file in the Orange County Senior Citizens Program Office.

7. "The uniqueness of the senior center stems from its total concern for older people and its concern for the total older person. In an atmosphere of wellness, it develops strengths and encourages independence, while building interdependence and supporting unavoidable dependencies. It works with older persons, not for them, enabling and facilitating their decisions and actions, and in so doing creates and supports a sense of community which further enables older persons to continue their involvement with and contribution to the larger community." Quoted from Senior Center Standards: Guidelines for Practice. Developed by the National Institute of Senior Centers, published by the National Council on Aging, Inc., Washington, D.C., 1978, p. 5.

8. The Study Team examined existing senior service data and program information, particularly information on senior club services previously collected by the United Way of Orange County. The Study Team developed the needs assessment instrument. Copies of the Instrument are available from the author.

9. The categories for Enhancement, Life Support and Access services were adapted from a presentation to the Study Team made by Dr. Roy Azarnoff. The Study Team developed the Sustainment category and redefined the categories to fit the continuum model.

INTERFACING MUTUAL-HELP AND MENTAL HEALTH DELIVERY SYSTEMS: IMPLICATIONS FOR POLICY AND ADMINISTRATION CURRICULA*

Norma Radol Raiff
Mon Valley Community Mental Health Center
Monessen, Pennsylvania

and

Barbara K. Shore
University of Pittsburgh

In the past fifteen years, major policy and structural changes have occurred in the nation's mental health service systems. The accelerated movement of patients from mental institutions into the community, coupled with recent legal decisions establishing patients' rights to treatment, has helped to create unprecedented national awareness of the tremendous level of unmet human need (Wittman, 1977).

The President's Commission on Mental Health (1978) addressed this need by issuing a major policy report calling for greater use of local community resources and lay helpers in the service delivery process. Within this report, the Commission's Task Panels recommended that professional schools, as a condition of accreditation, ought to develop curricula:

> ...in all undergraduate and graduate training programs in the social,
> behavioral, educational and medical sciences and professions related
> to mental health services delivery on the nature and function of
> community support systems, natural helping networks and mutual
> help groups (Ibid., Vol. II).

This Federal mandate challenges social work educators to develop innovative curriculum that is sensitive and responsive to the new national policy, both philosophically and in terms of training for emerging patterns of differential skills and staffing.

---

*An earlier version of this paper was presented at the Annual Program Meeting Council on Social Work Education, Boston, Massachusetts, March 5, 1979.

In this paper we provide guidelines for a new curriculum that responds to the Task Panel recommendations that nontraditional help-givers, mutual help groups and community volunteers be re-evaluated and studied as naturally occurring mental health resources. In particular, this paper focuses on the development of a curriculum oriented toward preparing graduate social workers to work with mutual help groups. Although we recognize that some of this information also pertains to interfacing needs associated with other types of health volunteers and natural support systems, we have focused primarily on mutual help groups, first (1) because of a relative absence of scientific information on this subject in traditional social work texts and educational programs; and second (2) because mutual help groups are most likely to be found among those neglected population groups, i.e., the chronically ill, the aged and ethnic minorities, explicitly cited by the President's Commission as most in need. As several curricular models relating to the learning needs of two and four year human service workers involved with mutual help related roles already exist (Vinokur-Kaplan, Bowles, Silverman, 1978), our comments are specifically directed towards the more advanced learning needs of graduate social work students employed in health planning, administration, policy and community organization roles.

RATIONALE AND DEFINITION OF MUTUAL HELP GROUPS

Many students of mutual help groups have adopted the rationale encompassed in Gerald Caplan's approach to community mental health, which has underscored the use of natural supports (including mutual help groups) by lay actors in coping with the requirements of everyday life (1974). According to Caplan's early interpretations, natural supports provide three basic functions: they "(a) help the individual to mobilize his psychological resources and master his emotional burdens; (b) they share his tasks; and (c) they provide him with extra supplies of money, materials, tools, skills and cognitive guidance to improve his handling of his situation." Other rationales have emphasized the importance of mutual help groups as highly technical and expert learning environments (Borkman, 1976), and as useful with nontraditional client populations (Antze, 1976).

In our approach, mutual help groups are differentiated from other forms of natural support systems by (a) their degree of social organization; (b) special constitutency, and (c) philosophical perception of the nature of helping. We have developed the following definition:

> Mutual help groups are units which organize to respond to the specific needs, problems, or conditions which the service constituency believes is being inadequately addressed within professional service delivery frameworks. In mutual help groups, membership is determined by a self-declaration that one possesses a group-salient characteristic or condition, and, furthermore, the possession of this characteristic or condition is defined within the mutual help framework as a "strength" -- that is, a contribution which the person brings to the collectivity and which enables him/her to function as a helping source.

In the arena of mental health, mutual help groups flourish both among those with "diagnosed" mental illnesses, and among those populations who are emotionally stressed by the traumas of life transitions, the need for caring for the aged and retarded, and those who face chronic handicap. These mutual help (mental health) groups provide emotional support and peer-based lay counseling using a variety of agendas, running from highly structured programs, such as that developed by Recovery, Inc., to more spontaneous formats, often patterned after Alcoholics Anonymous.

THE INTERFACE MODEL

The teaching model that we have developed builds upon the Commission's observations that a variety of "natural" lay resources -- family and kin, mutual help groups, churches and schools, and other volunteer resources -- exist as under-developed sources of mental health manpower. In the curriculum we have developed, the basic thrust is to develop the theme that graduate students concentrating in health administration and policy and planning may work within each of these natural lay sectors to promote and enhance the creation, use, and support of mutual help (mental health) groups.

As Figure 1 shows, the various helping sectors mentioned by the President's Commission may be analytically represented as falling into three types of loci. Within each locus, the sectors may be further subdivided, with the least or-ganized or institutionally recognized subsector represented at the perimeter, and the more conventional or organized subsector represented as closer to the center. The three major loci are the following: (I) "natural helping sector"[1], (II) the "non-mental health/non-welfare specialty sector" and (III) the "organized health and welfare sector." The "natural helping sector" (I) in-cludes (A) informal community structures and relationships, (B) "nonregular" health workers--such as herbalists and spiritual readers, and (C) family, kith and friends. Sector II, the "non-mental health/non-welfare specialty sector, includes those institutions and agencies which are found in local communities, but which are not specifically identified as providing mental health or welfare services. These include: (A) traditional civic agencies such as courts and schools; and (B) general health practitioners such as general physicians or paramedics. These structures often are the help-seeker's first source of referral or professional identification. Lastly, (III) the "organized health and welfare sector" consists of social welfare and health systems which specialize in mental health content. The subsectors range on a descending level of tradition and professionalization from: (A) conventional health and welfare agencies; (B) the newer "alternative" agencies[2] (i.e., rape centers, hotlines, women's shelters) and (C) mutual help groups. In talking about the contribution of each sector, we are philosophically committed to the belief that direct social work intervention with specific "clients" ought to be the last resort; that is, after possible services to the client group have been delivered with maximum effectiveness by the other "natural" or less social work identified sectors. Social work curriculum must reflect this emphasis.

The salience of mutual-help groups and other forms of indigenous helping behavior ought to be included as components throughout the entire social work curriculum ladder with special emphasis upon the role of human network supports in mental health and stress reduction. The importance of peer learning environments and non-directive therapies typical of mutual-help groups ought to be included in human behavior and methods courses. In the policy and administration components

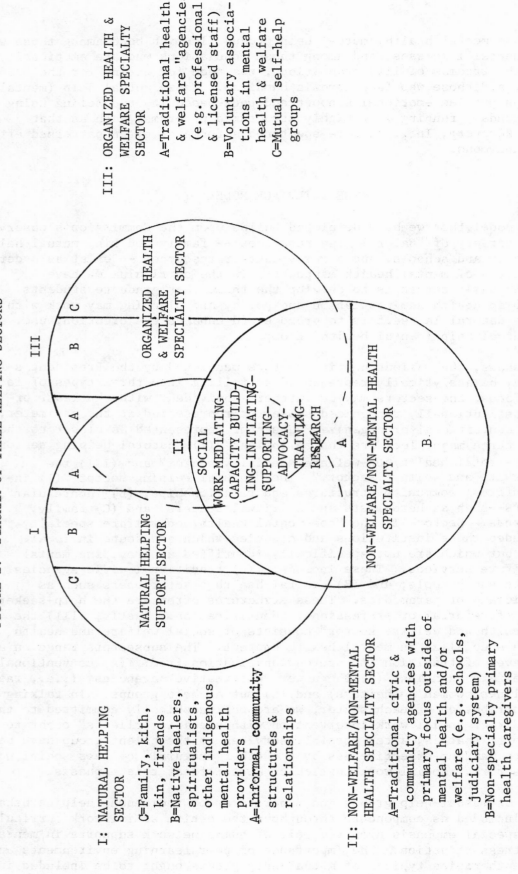

FIGURE 1: DIAGRAM OF THREE HELPING SECTORS

I: NATURAL HELPING
SECTOR

C=Family, kith,
kin, friends
B=Native healers,
spiritualists,
other indigenous
mental health
providers
A=Informal community
structures &
relationships

II: NON-WELFARE/NON-MENTAL
HEALTH SPECIALTY SECTOR

A=Traditional civic &
community agencies with
primary focus outside of
mental health and/or
welfare (e.g. schools,
judiciary system)
B=Non-specialty primary
health caregivers

III: ORGANIZED HEALTH &
WELFARE SPECIALTY
SECTOR

A=Traditional health
& welfare "agencie
(e.g. professional
& licensed staff)
B=Voluntary associa-
tions in mental
health & welfare
C=Mutual self-help
groups

of the social work curricula, we propose that the learning program must focus on the development of knowledge, attitudes and skills which articulate with the "interface" model.

CURRICULUM REQUIREMENTS

The curriculum should attempt to develop knowledge, attitudes, skills and strategies oriented toward the special needs of mutual helpers, including their general lack of public recognition, lay backgrounds and general social invisibility. Generally, the roles and skills which we single out as appropriate to the Interface Model are: (1) mediating; (2) capacity building (including consultation and technical assistance); (3) initiating and supporting; (4) advocacy; (5) training; and (6) research. The curriculum calls for an integrative seminar and a field practicum.

Knowledge Requirements

1. Importance of community supports and social interaction to mental health.

2. Uses of indigenous healing systems and group rituals in non-Western and non-modern societies.

3. Similarity between mutual help dynamics and group dynamics/psychological theories of behavior.

4. Information relating to absence of social network supports among "welfare hotel" residents, the aged, and other mental health vulnerable populations, including knowledge of how background variables such as the rural-urban-suburban continuum are associated with social network deficiencies among these particular subgroups.

5. Models of articulation used by different mutual help groups - i.e., Alcoholics Anonymous, Parents Anonymous, Make Today Count, Recovery, Inc., and Widow to Widow (Silverman, 1978; Gartner and Reissman, 1964; Borman, 1975, 1979).

6. Administrative models common to mutual help groups, with emphasis on their departure from more conventional "bureaucratic" models.

7. Inventory of mutual help (mental health) groups.

Attitude Requirements

Teaching attitudes and consciousness raising are among the most difficult tasks in the social work curriculum. When working with mutual help groups, the learning situation is sometimes aggravated by the anti-professional and aggressive ideological rhetoric occasionally found in these contexts; by mutual help vocabularies, which the learner may react to as "jargon" and "unscientific"; and by the often rapid flow of mutual help personnel throughout their organization, which tries the worker's patience with reoccurring demands for "proving oneself" and establishing trust. Within the educational process, the following attitudes need to be openly inspected and encouraged:

1. Recognition of positive contributions of mutual help groups.

2. Support for a pluralistic approach that grants the right of people in need to have a wide range of options available to them.

3. The value of enabling people to attain independence by being helpers rather than helpees.

4. Support for eclecticism in definitions of problems and solutions.

5. Openness to experimentation.

6. Willingness to confront the limits of professional knowledge and approaches.

    In addition to these general attitudes, students must be helped to recognize some of the ethical dilemmas which the Interface Model raises.

7. The client's right to privacy vs. "testimonial" nature of mutual helping.

8. Dilemmas of sponsoring referral to mutual help structures which may be non-professionally derived and delivered.

9. Whether a mutual help "advocate" role is appropriate to social work as a profession.

10. Dilemmas of policy implementation: i.e., will encouraging formation of mutual help groups enable tax reductionists to claim that costly programs of professional service are necessary?

11. Dilemmas of scarce resources: Will involving mutual helpers on agency and institutional levels of participation encourage them to lose their peer orientation and status? Will this deprive mutual help groups of internal workers needed to the mutual help organization?

Skills Requirements

The skills emphasized in the Interface Model pertain to those roles and functions which enhance the social worker's ability to:

(1) serve as consultant;

(2) referral agent and resource;

(3) initiate new roles into agency contexts;

(4) assess community needs and develop mutual help resources and advocates;

(5) disseminate knowledge;

(6) recruit individuals with strong mediating capacities and ability to articulate with indigenous helpers;

(7) train mutual helpers and professionals in techniques of program development and evaluation;

(8) build linkages.

ACTION STRATEGIES

The Interface Model generates three clusters of strategies to be emphasized in both class and field skills-based courses: (A) strategies oriented toward "traditional" agencies; (B) strategies designed to strengthen and mediate free-standing mutual help groups; (C) strategies oriented toward linking mutual help groups and other helping systems. Within each identified context, explicit strategies and short and long-range goals need to be mutually negotiated among the acting partners on a peeristic basis.

A. Strategies oriented to traditional and agency environments

   1. Develop socialization groups which prepare clients to interact in mutual help contexts by providing specific information; helping to discriminate between varied contributions of "professional" and mutual helper; rehearsing in "going public," etc.

   2. Develop and staff mutual help groups within agency contexts.

   3. Develop transitional service arrangements which facilitate client's participation in mutual help groups.

   4. Develop mutual-help oriented support networks among (a) professionals; (b) mutual help groups of various kinds; (c) mutual help peer therapists and group administrators; or (d) any combination for purposes of information sharing, policy discussion and emotional support.

   5. Recruit and train mutual helpers as part of the agency's service delivery program.

   6. Identification and training of mutual helpers to meet unmet community needs.

   7. Recruit mutual helpers for agency board and committee membership and provide socialization and support services if needed.

   8. Provide in-agency training programs on mutual help.

B. Strategies oriented toward strengthening free-standing mutual help groups

   1. Provide technical counseling services to mutual helpers on group management and administrative procedures.

   2. Present workshops to mutual helpers on publicity, public relations, etc.

   3. Support and initiate network building among mutual helpers.

   4. Support and initiate continuing education in new techniques and information among mutual helpers.

   5. Provide social work personnel as resource persons and community linkage agents.

   6. Assign roving personnel as resource persons with specific technical expertise such as needs of dying.

7. Provide assertiveness training for mutual helpers.

8. Provide grantsmanship materials and training to mutual helpers.

9. Allocate agency funds and persons to assist mutual help groups as needed.

10. Provide seed money for new mutual help programs.

C. Strategies oriented to link mutual help groups and other natural helping systems

1. Develop resource files on mutual help groups and other forms of lay helping.

2. Initiate and advocate mutual help representation on agency boards, including health and welfare planning councils, churches, volunteer organizations.

3. Develop agency personnel competent in explaining mutual help to "outsiders."

4. Develop agency personnel to train lay volunteers who will assume liaison between agency "clients," mutual help groups and other established community resources.

5. Initiate and support local, regional and national conferences on mutual help.

6. Encourage church groups, PTA and other community and civic organizations to develop home visiting and telephone network services and provide these networks with information on mutual help.

7. Encourage volunteer community and civic organizations to "sponsor" mutual help groups -- i.e., to offer facilities, pay for mutual help training and/or transportation costs, provide seed money, etc.

OTHER RECOMMENDATIONS

The Interface Model is based upon the premise that teaching must be coordinated in both the field setting and integrative seminar. Here (A) policy issues, (B) field work issues, and (C) research issues need to be discussed.

A. Policy Issues

Among the policy issues which must be dealt with in the classroom and the field are:

1. Differential definition of problems/conditions defined as requiring remediation. The experiences of the self-help groups of the 1970's indicates the existence of endemic policy differences between professional and self-help providers in terms of the range of life space issues defined as appropriate to each caregiver's sphere of influence. In general, professionals have tended to narrowly define both problem areas and self-help contributions. In contrast, self-help members have tended to opt for broader definitions of the self-help function, and to query institutional restrictions placed on client-related services.

Policy students need to be sensitive to the need to elucidate and negotiate the "problems" boundaries, and to make manifest implicit demand factors for altered staffing patterns and deployment of institutional resources inherent in many self-help frames of reference.

2. The centrality of self-help as a dynamic for promoting change. Policy students must be sensitized to the political paradoxes inherent in attempting to "help the self-helpers," and must learn to avoid the pitfalls implicit in inappropriate funding and staff liaison to the self-help group. Alternatives to direct grants and professional staff services need to be creatively determined; as must be issues related to timely effort and self-help autonomy.

3. Definition of target populations. Recent research indicates that self-help populations tend to internally stratify themselves according to criteria not often apparent to the external observer. Commonalities in terms of acuteness, complexity and specific types of experienced problems are among those shared factors which promote self-help group cohesiveness. Policy-administration students must develop skills in exploring the self-help population's "interior" in determining whether the target population is homogeneous or heterogeneous; and in evaluating the potential successfulness of umbrella versus custom designed approaches.

4. Definition of constituencies. Within the target population it may be sensible to distinguish between the person who is the focus of the problem (e.g., the alcoholic, the ostomate, the former mental patient) and significant others (e.g., spouses, children, parents, friends). Alcoholics Anonymous, Al-a-Teen and Al-a-Non are obvious examples of different constituencies affected by the alcoholic problem. Policy students need to learn how to conduct needs analyses relating to this issue in which such factors as neighborhood demographic composition, the existence of other community-based age-graded social network services, community mobility and age, and the neighborhood's overall record of support for volunteer groups are taken into account.

5. Definition of staffing patterns, including varying levels relevant to differential roles and functions. For example, a policy-administration student must examine the issues of advocacy to determine whether advocates can best serve from within an organizational structure or outside of that structure. Policy students must also learn not only how to identify unmet needs, but also how to evaluate whether the initiation of a service is more effective if a mutual-help group carries this out. If service is to be initiated vis-a-vis mutual-help units, the policy student must learn how to identify leadership, establish a mediating relationship, how to overcome distrust and how to provide competent technical assistance, without taking over or controlling the entire process. These are complex skills that not only require an adequate level of knowledge but also supportive and open attitudes and a series of skills in the general area of negotiation and mediation.

B. Implications for Field Work

Field work for the development of a high level of learning in this area is particularly complicated. Such placements require either that a trust level be built with mutual-help groups (with field work supervision provided by a faculty-based instructor for the social work component), or that enough field placements in traditional structures can be found where the latter will have enough openness to permit for the development of major reliance on mutual-help approaches to service delivery. Since social work students will be engaged in developmental activities in many settings, the school must assume major responsibility for the accomplishment of learning. Such major responsibility includes interested and effective faculty members, time (probably in excess of that more commonly required in more traditional settings), and integrative seminars where all students gaining this experience are able to share their knowledge and feelings so that maximum learning can be accomplished. Faculty should also develop explicit strategies to include self-help members within the components of the integrative seminars so that mutual learning and educational feedback can be accomplished.

These approaches and faculty time requirements are, of course, not distinctive to this field approach, but are probably more basic to its success than in many of the field placements currently used in schools of social work. In addition, the faculty person(s) involved in this type of innovative approach may also miss the usual collegial supports provided within the traditional field placement structures. For this reason it is vital that the school administration and faculty provide strong support and some of the collegial interchange that is available in established settings.

C. <u>Research</u>

The approaches being recommended need to be tested and evaluated. It is therefore vital that a major component of both the knowledge and skills taught to students include an emphasis on linking the research skills development of the student to the class and field learning.

The need to conduct ongoing research while developing innovative educational designs is made even more problematic because of the nature of the setting. It should be noted that many mutual-help groups may be somewhat resistant to research endeavors because of their ideological commitments and suspicion of the "guinea pig syndrome." As many writers point out: Most active members of self-help groups seem to find questions about their group's effectiveness difficult to comprehend--they <u>know</u> their group works--so it is difficult to enlist their cooperation in the kind of systematic effort that would be necessary to satisfy scientific standards (Borman, 1975). In other instances, too, mutual helpers may find the abstract criteria and questioning stance assumed by social work researchers to be antithetical to the pragmatism inherent in mutual-help involvement. It should, however, be noted that traditional agencies who tend to express overt support for research are often equally resistant to the research enterprise. The difference is that traditional structures have often learned the professional rhetoric that supports the need for scientific study, although the research performance often is equally resistive. The research endeavor requires trust-building, non-intrusive measures and an ability to link the groups' concerns to the research questions. Students can learn greatly from this effort.

The social work researcher must be prepared to develop new attitudes and research skills associated with mutual-help research. Obviously, there is often a need to create measuring tools and language which is compatible with the mutual-help framework. Since there is considerable evidence that mutual helpers consciously pre-select themselves into this modality, assessment

100

according to traditional across-the-board service populations may be in-appropriate. Finally, in still other instances, the social work researcher must be prepared to accept the mutual-help group's request to be a valid partner in the very design and assessment of research. As this requires negotiating and humanistic skills often not highlighted in research teaching (which may view this sharing as a form of "dirty" research) the area of mutual-help research requirements must be added as a module or emphasis in research teaching. One approach to the research activity could well be a group endeavor, using the faculty coordinator as mentor. Because of the innovative nature of the mutual help field setting, and that setting's reported resistance to research, the following research issues need to be confronted: (a) developing non-intrusive research measures; (b) learning to link the mutual help group's concerns to the research questions; (c) the mutual help group as a research partner; (d) using outcome measures compatible with mutual help frameworks; (e) sharing and ownership of research-derived information; (f) member "anonymity"; and (g) linking research and policy roles (Borman, 1975; Kleiber and Light, 1978; Leiberman and Bond, 1978).

SUMMARY

This article has focused on the development of an interface model for repre-senting and analyzing the various helping sector of networks and/or support groups that may be called upon for preventing and/or ameliorating mental illness, and for providing supports for maximum social and emotional function-ing. It then applies this model to social work curriculum, in order to provide maximum development of knowledge and skill to the support and extension of networks and support groups that can enhance the mental health of target persons and populations.

Notes

1. By "natural helping sectors," we refer to those support systems which are part of people's primary institutional life, including their lay networks. These systems are the primary needs-meeting environments in which ordinary people are embedded. The absence of such natural helping systems tends to propel people into accessing more formal organizations and "regular" health and welfare arrangements.

2. By "alternative agencies" we refer to those arrangements which have developed in protest to formal structures and/or as a differentiated way of attempting to provide for unmet human needs. Alternative structures are frequently associated with an advocacy stance. They may incorporate mutual-help approaches (although, unlike the former, they are often more eclectic in their preferred modes of treatment).

REFERENCES

Antze, Paul
   1976   "The Role of Ideologies in Peer Psychotherapy Organizations: Some Theoretical Considerations and Three Case Studies," Journal of Applied Behavioral Science, 12: 323-346.

Borkman, Thomasina
  1976   "Experiential Knowledge: A New Concept for the Analysis of Self-Help
         Groups," Social Service Review, 50 (September):445-456.

Borman, Leonard
  1975   Explorations in Self Help and Mutual Aid, Evanston, Ill.: Center for
         Urban Affairs, Northwestern University.

Borman, Leonard B.
  1979   "Characteristics of Development and Growth." In Morton A. Lieberman,
         Leonard B. Borman and Associates, Self Help Groups for Coping with
         Crisis, San Francisco, Calif.: Jossey Bass.

Bowles, Elinor
  1978   Self-Help Groups: Perspectives and Directions: An Instructional
         Guide for Developing Self-Help Mutual Aid Groups, New York:
         New Careers Training Laboratory/CUNY.

Caplan, Gerald
  1974   "Support Systems." In Support Systems and Community Mental Health,
         New York: Behavioral Publication, pp. 1-40.

Collins, Marilyn C.
  1978   Child Abuser: A Study of Child Abusers in Self-Help Group Therapy,
         Massachusetts: Publishing Sciences Group, Inc., pp. 75-78.

Gartner, Alan and Frank Riessman
  1964   Self-Help in the Human Services, San Francisco, Calif.: Jossey-Bass.

Kleiber, Nancy and Linda Light
  1978   Caring for Ourselves: An Alternative Structure for Health Care:
         Report of the Vancouver Women's Health Collective, Vancouver, B.C.
         School of Nursing.

Lieberman, Morton and Gary Bond
  1978   "Self-Help Groups: Problems of Measuring Outcome." In Small Group
         Behavior, 9:221-241.

Silverman, Phyllis
  1978   Mutual Help Groups: A Guide for Mental Health Workers, Rockville,
         Md.: DHEW.

Silverman, Phyllis
  1978   op. cit.

Vinokur-Kaplan, Diane
  1975   "The Relevance of Self-Help Groups to Social Work Education,"
         forthcoming in Contemporary Social Work Education.

Wittman, Milton
  1977   "New Directions for Social Work in Mental Health." In Changing
         Roles in Social Work Practice, Francine Sobey (ed.), Philadelphia:
         Pa.: Temple University Press, pp. 72-91.

Wittman, Milton
1978   The President's Commission on Mental Health, <u>Report to the President
        from the President's Commission on Mental Health</u>, Washington, D.C.:
        Government Printing Office.

SELF-HELP SYSTEMS AND THE PROFESSIONAL AS VOLUNTEER: THREAT OR SOLUTION?

Cynthia S. Pincus
Yale University

and

Evie Hermann-Keeling
Parents Anonymous of Connecticut, Inc.

Many voluntary organizations directly reflect social trends. A current noticeable trend in the United States is that of Self-Help. Examples are abundant at the present time in many cities, such as Food Co-ops, Women's Centers, Credit Unions, Divorced Men's Associations and a growing number of individuals who barter services or goods. All are reflective of a contemporary national movement in the direction of mutual support and assistance. These new organizations tend to be built on the basis of co-operation rather than the exchange of money, and to involve people as peers regardless of their social roles. When professionals are involved, they give their time and work as one of a group of peer participants.

This trend may be accelerated in a time when severe budget cuts in health and social services are being advocated. A good model of a self-help resource is "P.A." -- short for Parents Anonymous, in which the author serves in a volunteer capacity as a professional sponsor or resource person. The focus of this paper is on this model and an examination of the conflicts and rewards encountered by professionals assisting such a group which demands new roles, behaviors and philosophy.

HISTORY OF THE SELF-HELP PHENOMENON

Supportive mutual aid societies proliferated in England during the Industrial Revolution. The Friendly Societies were the best known, and reportedly still numbered 18,000 as late as 1945. In our own country, guilds and trade unions, ethnic associations and political wards of the cities all cared for their own in the 19th and 20th century. The Washingtonian Movement, founded in 1840 to combat the evils of rum, was a religiously flavored effort to help individuals overcome temptation, clearly a forerunner to the highly successful Alcoholics Anonymous of our own era.

During the Depression many co-operative efforts sprang up to help with massive social problems. The federally funded programs of this time, such as the WPA, were modelled after self-help groups, as were many federal programs since developed to increase opportunity for specific groups, such as CETA.

Possibly the best known of all, AA, was founded in Akron, Ohio by a physician and a man in difficulty who collaborated to find a solution that would speak directly to the afflicted. Today this organization has 30,000 groups in 92 nations and has earned the respect of professionals all over the world for its impressive "track record" in helping alcoholics recover through self-help support systems. The "al-non" groups for spouses and children often attract members for years. One client told me that her mother has attended for 20 years, weekly, while she has been divorced from the problem drinker most of this time. Around the time that AA was getting underway, the Association for Retarded Children, and the United Cerebral Palsy Foundation were organized. In 1933 Recovery, for former mental patients, was organized by a doctor who found groups had been exceptionally helpful to his own patients.

The current wave of self-help is attributed by many to Martin Luther King's Southern Christian Leadership Conference. Under charismatic leadership, the Black community mobilized for social change with dramatic results. Support and consensus led to change through non-violent actions. Many groups followed the model: Chicano, Indian, Hispanic, women's and homosexuals' groups all used similar approaches. There was such a tremendous impact on the establishment-- the government, legislation, traditional institutions and the professional community--that the reinforcement to continue was strong. Seeing visible results led others to organize. Individuals came together in the 60's in anti-war activity, welfare rights, labor boycotts, civil rights actions, and the Women's Movement. These groups tended to have goals in common: the development of human potential, the demystification of bureaucracies and professionals, participation of individuals in matters affecting themselves, and consumer rights (Katz and Bender, 1976; Evans, 1979).

CONSUMERISM IN RELATION TO HEALTH SERVICES

At the same time that self-help systems have developed in relation to specific target problems, consumerism as an attitude toward health care has become conspicuous throughout the population. This entails the positive aspects, such as the recognition that individuals have a responsibility in maintaining their health through a total regime of diet, exercise, absence of destructive habits and intelligent use of resources both professional and pertaining to life-style. This has led to an increasing interest in the concept of health maintainance and holistic health or the use of varied practices ranging from diet to stress management to promote well being. There is also a critique aspect to the trend. Many professionals and patients reacted critically to an era in which recipients of care were left out of the decision-making process, had no access to vital information which would effect them and felt like passive, helpless recipients. Evidence of both sides of the response is abundant in a multiplication of Health Maintainance Organizations, in which a fee is paid annually (harking back to the ancient Oriental concept of paying the physician to keep one well), holistic clinics and centers, and the inclusion of client or patient advocacy in planning boards at hospitals, social agencies, etc. One organization, the Association of Feminist Therapists (which grew out of the Women's Movement's thrust toward a more effective use of political and advocacy power), promotes the recipient's right to knowledge of treatment alternatives, to evaluate the treatment process in terms of goals sought by the client, and to encourage the creation of new structures to protect the rights of mental patients in institutions where there may be no objective evaluation process which is not a part of the system delivering the treatment (Association of Feminist Therapists Newsletter, 1980).

VOLUNTEERS AND PROFESSIONALS

As a mental health practicioner in this era, one continuously encounters this trend toward self-help systems. Marilyn Ferguson, a commentator on science and health in general, has commented in her broad review, the Aquarian Conspiracy, that these ways of doing things are a future reality, not a counter-culture any longer so much as the next culture (1981). At the same time voluntarism is evolving.

In the 60's as a fledgling social worker, I learned quickly to regard volunteers as a separate category of people from myself, "the professional." Our teaching, our reading and our supervisors all tended to reinforce this distance. I found it common in child guidance clinics, hospitals and other agencies for staff to be separated from volunteers both structurally, as in separate orientations and meetings, and attitudinally; "we are doing the really important work here, -- they are 'just' volunteering."

Not many years later volunteers began to become a more integral part of responsive systems. The Civil Rights movement, like most political movements, depended on voluntarism. In the aftermath of the Women's Movement, there was an explosion of services for women created by the individuals who felt the needs themselves, blurring the lines between worker and client and forming powerful alliances between the two. An example was the career focused counseling services for women which developed in the 60's, estimated to be well over a thousand in the 1970's, and still multiplying across the country (U.S. Labor Dept., 1969).

As the professional director of one such counseling service--typical of the self-help trend--I was exposed to the cross-fertilization of ideas and energies that results from the growth of an agency structure in which volunteers and professionals work as a team, each bringing their unique perspectives and emphasis (Pincus et al., 1974). In this type of collaboration, volunteers become respected as having experiences and ideas of value.

During the same period of the 1960's and 70's, "Professional Volunteers" have been recognized as individuals who give their time, and have extensive experience in a field. They make a profession of their volunteerism, and are quite different from short term volunteers. They are committed, as deeply or more deeply than many of their paid colleagues. Another distinct trend in volunteering has been the extent to which it is career-oriented (Pincus, 1978). One director of a medical center volunteer department has estimated that 80% of her 800 current volunteers have a career-related reason for their placement. Many professionals have volunteered on Boards where there are clear agendas and an established inter-group process among professionals and non-professionals. All of these images are components of voluntarism. Only recently, as part of the self-help trend, vast numbers of professional psychologists, psychiatrists, counselors and social workers have become volunteer resource people in direct service positions with clients.

PARENTS ANONYMOUS

P.A. is characteristic of numbers of groups springing up to help individuals cope with problems related to alcohol, drugs, eating, gambling, anorexia and others. The particular problem addressed by P.A. is child abuse. It is a national self-help organization for parents who define themselves as abusive to their children. With over 10,000 members, and well over 800 chapters in the United States, it is developing rapidly as a national consumer organization (Hall, 1980a).

THE P.A. MODEL

Dedicated to the prevention of child abuse, P.A. is basically a consumer operated service offered free of charge to its members (MacFarlane and Lieber, 1978). There is a continuing major effort at promoting the availability of this service through local weekly meetings. Radio and commercial spots and posters and fliers are distributed on a monthly basis in continuous outreach. Many parents respond directly to this message, others are referred by public and private agencies, the clergy, friends, etc.

Like most self-help systems, P.A. provides a group experience, meeting weekly at a free accessible location, such as a church, community center or YMCA. Members share only first names and only need speak as much and when they want to. Phone numbers are exchanged, and members encourage each other to call at times of crisis.

The telephone is an important resource in the P.A. System. The national WATS line, and state-wide toll-free P.A. lines are offered to the public. Parents concerned about their emotions or behavior can call any hour of the day or night and speak to an understanding volunteer, trained to handle such situations. Many in P.A. groups return to the "Stress Line" as an adjunct resource when under pressure. P.A. members also call one another when they feel tension rising. In addition, the Stress Line or P.A. chapter may refer the parent to other local resources, such as child care facilities or therapists. Often, the professional sponsor or one of the group members will call a parent repeatedly if he/she feels the parent needs encouragement to get to the group. This becomes an out-reach practice and often an effective one; parents do come in and get help.

EVALUATION

Until recently, the professional and public response to child abuse was mainly a punitive one. In the last decade there has been a growing sense that many abusive parents can be helped. In 1974, an evaluation of treatment interventions was undertaken among 1724 parents by Berkeley Planning Associates with funds from the National Center on Child Abuse and Neglect. Of the parents provided with lay services such as P.A., 53% were judged "improved" as compared with 40% of those receiving professional and other types of service. This was attributed partially to the increase in self-esteem and independence which grows out of the self-help experience (Cohn, 1979).

The problem of abuse is far more widespread than is generally understood, even by professionals. The incidence of child abuse, wife beating, and more recently, attention to the problem of abuse of the elderly, suggest that the response of individuals to stress with the pattern of abuse to dependents is very widespread in our society. The P.A. model and understanding of the abuser should be applicable to all categories of abusers.

Research suggests that nine out of ten parents who abuse are not emotionally disturbed, but under severe stress at the time. A number of factors contribute to abusive behavior: the parent's background, social problems, financial and living conditions, isolation, other problems such as drug or alcohol addiction, and the age and personality of the child.

Research has shown that most parents who abuse, were themselves abused as children. Most are isolated from supportive systems, such as family, school and religious influences of a positive behavior-limiting nature. Most have a poor self-image and a lack of self-confidence. Many have had little or no exposure to positive parenting, either through modeling by their own parents or information about what to expect from children at different ages. Conservative estimates are that at least 2,000 children die each year as a result of child abuse. Many who survive have permanent resulting physical disabilities. Because children under age three are especially vulnerable to the effects of abuse, efforts are being made to alert the community services, emergency room staff and others in a position to spot such children, to identify and intervene in such situations. Sexual abuse and exploitation may be less easily detected, but can result in serious emotional and physical trauma (Connecticut Child Welfare Association, undated).

Less difficult to identify, but exceedingly widespread, are neglect and emotional maltreatment. Many children live for years with inadequate clothing, food, shelter and supervision. Many are insulted and rejected and as a result have difficulties in school and in personal relationships. Neglect and emotional abuse are prevalent in middle-class and even affluent communities and may be almost invisible. Suburban families with dual career life styles, in an age of stress and individualism, may be just as subject to this type of abuse as the families with physical/financial deprivations (Pincus et al., 1980). The subtlety of some forms of abuse was well described by this letter, sent by a P.A. member to three different newspapers recently:

> I and other members of my P.A. Chapter were very pleased to see your article calling child abuse to the public attention. However, the article emphasized what we feel is a misrepresentation of the situation.
>
> To the best of my knowledge, the majority of child abuse is far more pervasive and subtle than your article indicated. Probably all parents, at one time or another, will abuse their children, whether intentionally or not. The day-to-day abuse that goes on, such as hitting or verbal abuse, often is not evident outside the home. Many times it is only the parents who know that they hurt the child, whether or not they admit it. Looking at any child of the parents in my P.A. group, you would not know that we feel we abuse them. Many times it is because the parents are experiencing so much stress from coping with daily pressures, children that are hard to deal with, and any number of other factors that get in the way of dealing lovingly and non-hurtingly with their kids. I know that for those of us in my group it is just because we do love our kids that it hurts so much when we hurt them....we would have liked to see you point out how common child abuse is, even in many "nice" homes....P.A. is there for any parent who hurts their child or is even afraid that they might...

THE P.A. INTERVENTION MODEL

P.A. groups, like most self-help systems, "seem to have the key to problems their people face" (Gartner and Reissman, 1977). The reason for this lies in the fact that the program was designed by someone in the midst of the problem as has been the case with most of these groups.

In the case of P.A., it was a young mother, Jolly K, who went to ten different agencies without success in controlling her own abusive behavior. She became increasingly angry and frustrated that there were no resources that seemed to 'fit.' With the help of a psychiatric social worker, Leonard Lieber, she started her own self-help system which grew from three mothers meeting together for support to a nationally active organization with 1,300 chapters and over 10,000 members (Lieber and Wheat, 1979).

Significantly, the main headquarters were in Jolly K's kitchen. A number of authors have recognized the value of service that is spontaneous, focused and available when and where the problems are. Consumer oriented service is often an unplanned response to a crisis life situation. Meeting parents in a kitchen or church may make help far more accessible; the help is available simply by dropping in any week (Hall, 1980). The telephone network -- so vital to every P.A. group is also ever present -- and just a step away. Other parents, professional sponsors and the 24-hour-a-day stress line are all available by telephone.

When a self-help meeting is in progress, it is a moving thing to witness. As individuals share their problems, a tremendous rapport is developed. No time is wasted on the formalities of social exchange, making impressions, introductions or bureaucratic functions. Men and women meet as individuals with a common problem and this problem becomes a unifying force. P.A. parents are violently anti-abuse, so much so that they will travel -- as one mother did -- an hour in the rain, walking and taking several buses -- to get to the nearest meeting. Their feelings prompt them to want to confess in an atmosphere of understanding and acceptance; this then leads to more opening up.

As needs are met, there is more sharing of personal history and problems. Most P.A. parents have inherited abuse from parents who had marginal abilities to nurture at best, or were openly abusive at worst. Many are unwed mothers whose search for nurturing and acceptance led directly to early responsibilities for unplanned babies. Negative feelings about self are projected onto the children by parents and grandparents alike. Where the parent is alone, often the negative feelings toward the other parent contribute to the rejection of the child: "he's exactly like his father -- I can see it already."

Some parents are able to work on their own depressions, their personal problems with self-esteem, their social problems. Some are literally trapped by poverty like the young woman who had no money, no car, and no space for her two young children to play as she shared a house with her landlady and an additional boarder taken in to make ends meet, who was dying of a terminal illness on the living room couch.

As the group relates on this personal level, the parents' deeper needs are met. Dramatic changes occur in some. Parents speak of feeling accepted for the first time. As one woman put it, "I hear my words coming out of someone else's mouth!" Many have experienced a baffling array of responses from professionals, ranging from a total lack of concern -- like the pediatrician who said, "Forget it - I don't know what you're worrying about" to the stigma, even abhorrence of the problem which comes through in many peoples' responses to the thought of abuse of a helpless child.

In the group process parents band together in mutual acceptance and support in changing the behavior. As this happens, many show dramatic changes in morale, expression, grooming and living skills. Some lose weight, dress more neatly; many go to work or move up on jobs; babysitters are found and other resources researched. As their needs are met, a number of parents begin to see their children more positively and enjoy time with them, as opposed to the character- istic power struggles and tension of past experience. The group is a vehicle for the tapping of members' own resources. Through the support system, parents share insights and experiences. They also share practical hints for bad times:

    Take a bath
    Sing a song loudly
    Do push-ups
    Jump rope
    Call a P.A. Friend ... (No-Name Newsletter, April, 1981)

Many new therapies are based on the premise that a client's own resource will be most valuable in developing solutions (Lankton, 1980). Neurolinguistic programming taps resources the client has used successfully in the past and applies them to present situations. Feminist therapy and assertiveness therapy help individuals reclaim power over their own lives. Holistic health counsel- ing emphasizes the ability of the individual to know what is best to maintain his/her health using a combination of personal awareness about individual needs, and a variety of practices aimed at developing personal resources such as diet, exercise, stress reduction, etc. Social Work has traditionally defined itself as a field devoted to helping people help themselves.

Helper therapy is a demonstrated phenomenon familiar to us all (Reissman, 1965). How often we see clients, or acquaintances transformed after they have found a role in which they are needed and can contribute: the widow who feels useless discovers a work role in which she can make a contribution; the ex-mental patient starts to give help to someone else in a volunteer placement and changes a whole set of attitudes and behaviors. As the individual works, his strengths are reinforced, he receives positive feedback from others and social support for the task. This creates new ego strengths and helps the person move into new constructive coping roles. It is an age old truth of most of the world's religions that in giving we receive and in healing we are healed.

                    THE ROLE OF THE PROFESSIONAL

In self-help groups it is made clear that the members make the decisions and run the group meetings. P.A. parents help one another with transportation, trade strategies, make decisions about babysitting and other details. As the weeks go by, many are transformed, showing increasing amounts of energy and motiva- tion, leadership ability and self-knowledge. The professional's role must be clearly related to this process and neither distract from it or sabotage it. The parents select, or at least approve of, the professional sponsor. The sponsor's role does not involve being a therapist, keeping an agenda, making notes or records, or leading the discussion. It is not a professional activity allied to any institution or agency, and sponsorship is not a part of one's day to day job. One does it on one's own time and for one's own reasons; there is no reimbursement for professional services. The professional is, in fact, a volunteer.

The professional is thoroughly oriented by the P.A. staff, literature and contact with others in the system. Attitudes and acceptance of the peer model are essential to the process. These fundamentals are very important to the parents' sense of freedom of disclosure and trust. Like the room, the babysitter and the play materials, the professional's time is given, and what is said and done remains in this one place.

What then does the professional sponsor do? He or she must measure up to certain criteria, must have experience with group dynamics to offer help with problems as they arise, must be sensitive and non-judgemental concerning the issues of abusive parents, such as guilt and lack of self-esteem and must see through to the causes.

An initial task for the professional is a kind of "demasking" process. The professional role or mask must be dropped, and with it, off comes the whole machinery of policy, procedure and even ways of thinking, categorizing, conceptualization and jargon. Professionals spend so much time acting, feeling and thinking "professional" we are often not conscious of how programmed we have become. In these groups, no money is exchanged, no appointments made, no policies or procedures explained. There is, in fact, nothing to do but concentrate on the human issues at hand. We are back to the original helping model: that of the family. Every professional sitting down with a self-help group for the first time experiences a degree of anxiety over this shedding of the professional exterior. "What will I contribute? How will I serve here? How much should I intervene?"

As the initial anxiety is worked through, a fascinating realization emerges. In helping, people truly "help themselves", using their own resources; none of this complexity is necessary. Inside the professional, there is a body of experience, knowledge and understanding, gained through practice, that is sufficient and can be relied upon. It is a liberating experience to be able to contribute solely on this basis, person to person. What results is a true growth experience for the sponsor--the very reason so many individuals have volunteered over the centuries, and will continue to do so!

At the present time there are fifty-six active P.A. sponsors in Connecticut. They come from a vareity of professional backgrounds, including counseling, social work, education, medicine and the clergy. Some of their comments about their roles as sponsors include the following:

> "It's the one thing I do professionally that I don't get paid for, and it's the thing I enjoy the most..."

> (Keeling, 1980)

> "Being (a P.A. sponsor)...has been an incredibly rewarding enriching experience for me. I have watched parents grow, become articulate, positive and loving in their daily living...I am now deeply committed to the idea (of this type of support group) having been given the

opportunity to both help and to see this concept in action."

(Interchange, 1980)

The year and a half that I have spent as a P.A. sponsor...has
been a rewarding and gratifying experience to me...

(Interchange, 1980)

There are, undeniably, tensions between the professional community, and the
self-help system. Professionals are accused by some authors of elitism,
coming as we do predominately from educated and middle class backgrounds
(Gartner and Reissman, 1977). Professionals tend to regard themselves as the
holders of secret insights which are used as a form of power and status -- an
accusation frequently leveled at physicians, lawyers and mental health professionals.

Many professionals avoid referring clients to self-help groups, and knowledge
of their availability and specific purpose and function remains scarce. The
professional tendency to use the medical model, in which the client is seen as
"sick" and lacking in strategies to attack the problem, precludes many professionals from being able to see a self-help group as _having_ resources to make
available to its members.

Many are unaware that the experience has helped members utilize professional
help more easily. Ultimately, the two modes of treatment are quite compatible
and can reinforce each other.

The P.A. sponsor may feel rather alone in the face of what is still considerable
resistance in the professional community. He or she needs to know where the
community supports are and be able to lean on them when problems arise. The
support of community groups such as the Parents Anonymous Resource Association
(P.A.R.A.) in Connecticut, a back-up supportive group for parents and sponsors
which functions state-wide, and individual key staff such as the state coordinator, are of great importance to the professional giving time to such a
cause, providing reinforcement for difficulties that come up in the role.

The professional sponsor must work through anxiety and then conquer a still
more difficult dragon: the "rescue fantasy." This desire to rescue children
and solve all problems leads many a professional to feelings of helplessness
when faced with chronic problems such as alcoholism, compulsive gambling and
abuse. If this continues for prolonged periods of time, many succumb to burn-
out that results from feelings of continuous failure to meet standards on the
job. Professionals working with this type of problem need to adjust their
sights, to redefine their goals (Cohn, 1979). Professionals need to stop
thinking in terms of our own successes or failures as P.A. families progress
and, rather, to relate to the effective group process. We need to give the
power and the responsibility back to the families themselves. Their improvement does not rest on our shoulders. Leonard Lieber's law is TRUST THE GROUP!!!

Some of the more distinctive group processes may not be observed in self-help
groups. The usual deposing of the leader is not directed in the same way at a
professional who is supporting, but not leading, a group. Transferences are
minimized as the professional is seen more as "one of us but with a difference"
and may share personal anecdotes and demystify him or herself as part of the
process of group membership. As the professional learns to help in the

mobilization of the group members' resources, he or she develops a profound trust in their process. This involves learning that they will persist in their anti-abuse tactics, they will come up with answers and strategies, they will remain available to one another. The professional serves as a source of insights about behavior, knowledge about resources and a powerful symbol of behavior-limiting expertise, but always as a background to the dynamic internal resources developing within the group (Lankton, 1980).

CONCLUSION

The blurring of lines between professional and volunteer can be a healthy, humanizing process -- one in which everyone gains something. Professionals, immersed in their own specialties, are exposed to new perspectives and greater spontaneity in working with individuals with other experiences. The association helps to counteract the tendencies toward isolation and self-importance which are latent risks in professional life especially in careers of many years' evolution. In volunteering to self-help systems, professionals have an opportunity to perform a valuable service as facilitators, not leading or teaching but supplementing lay individuals bent on promoting their own strengths in ways that are of urgent importance. Professionals can derive satisfaction both from giving their time and expertise, and also from discovering the freedom of letting go of the professional mystique simply to serve on a human-to-human basis -- an enriching experience. All participants in self-help systems know the unique sense of empathy which stimulates the unfolding of personal resources in the individual.

Support systems are clearly here to stay. As professionals, we combat burn-out by relying on our own support systems, and sharing concerns with colleagues through courses, networking and training experiences and associations. In all fields networking is a marked trend, providing both contacts and mutual support.

Self-help groups are multiplying in agencies, churches and synagogues for many categories of human difficulty, from over-eating to divorce. At a time when funding is being withdrawn from many established areas of social service, the rediscovery of person-to-person helping chains is a welcome step in combating the isolation of a fragmented society. The professional community needs to recognize the values of this approach, and to integrate it into the larger total picture of contemporary resources for individuals.

REFERENCES

Association of Feminist Therapists Newsletter
   1980   April.

Borman, Leonard D.
   1979   As quoted in The Family Circle Guide to Self-Help, Glen Evans (ed), New York: Ballantine Books.

Cohn, Anne H.
   1979   "Effective Treatment of Child Abuse and Neglect," Social Work, Journal of the National Association of Social Workers 24 (November): 513-519.

Connecticut Child Welfare Association
  Undated Fact Sheet

Ferguson, Marilyn
  1981   The Aquarian Conspiracy, Los Angeles, Calif.: J. F. Turcher.

Gartner, Alan and Frank Reissman
  1977   Self-Help in Human Services, San Francisco, Calif.: Jossey-Bass.

Hall, Julian C.
  1980   "Encounters Where People Are: A Consumer-Oriented Strategy,"
         Social Work, Journal of the National Association of Social Workers
         25 (January):61-63.

Interchange: New England Resource Center for Protective Services Newsletter
  1980   4, 5.

Katz, Alfred and E. Bender
  1976   The Strength in Us: Self-Help Groups in the Modern World, New York:
         New Viewpoints.

Keeling, Rev. Robert
  1980   Personal communication.

Lankton, Steve
  1980   Practical Magic, Cupertino, Calif.: Meta Press.

MacFarlane, Kee and Leonard Lieber
  1978   "Parents Anonymous; the Growth of an Idea," National Center on Child
         Abuse and Neglect, Washington, D.C.

No Name Newsletter
  1980   Parents Anonymous of Connecticut
  1981   Parents Anonymous of Connecticut

Pincus, Cynthia, N. Radding, and R. Lawrence
  1974   "The Counseling Service for Women: Response to a New Need,"
         Social Work, Journal of the National Association of Social Workers,
         19 (March):187-194.

Pincus, Cynthia
  1978   Double Duties: An Action Plan for the Working Woman, New York:
         Chatham Square Press.

Pincus, Cynthia, L. Elliot, and T. Schlachter
  1980   The Roots of Success, Englewood Cliffs, N.J.: Prentice-Hall Publishers.

Reissman, Frank
  1965   "The 'Helper Therapy' Principle," Social Work, Journal of the National
         Association of Social Workers, 10:27-32.

U.S. Labor Department
  1969   Pamphlet No. 10, "Continuing Education and Related Services for
         Women."

Wheat, Patti and Leonard Lieber
    1979   <u>Hope for the Children</u>, Minneapolis, Minn.: Winston Press.

THE PROFESSIONALIZATION OF VOLUNTEER ADMINISTRATION

Felice Davidson Perlmutter
Temple University

Social administration[1] is a generic method which is practiced by social work executives in an array of social service settings including mental health, child welfare, aging, public assistance, among others. It is our thesis that volunteer programs can be considered an appropriate setting for the practice of social administration by an administrator who is a professional social worker.

This paper assumes that the arguments for volunteerism[2] have been cogently made elsewhere (Braithwaite, 1938; Ellis and Noyes, 1978; Naylor, 1973) and that the special contribution that volunteers can make to the social services is understood. It further assumes not only that the debates concerning volunteerism in the 1980's (e.g., the position of the National Organization for Women which does not accept the role of the volunteer as appropriate for the modern woman) are being addressed elsewhere (Haeuser and Schwartz, 1980), but that data concerning the relationship between social workers and volunteers are also available (Holme and Maizels, 1978).

We operate on the premise that volunteerism is an essential and vital activity with a long and valued tradition in the social services and that the charge for the social work profession is one of defining and refining the relationship between volunteerism and social work. That is what we are about.

THE CONTEXT OF VOLUNTEER ADMINISTRATION

As early as 1938, in her study of volunteerism in Great Britain, Braithwaite focussed on the role of the "voluntary administrator."

> The role of the voluntary worker in connection with the social services
> is not limited to the cases where he can participate in the actual

service rendered. Even when the service itself is performed entirely
by professional specialists the general administration and control
is in the hands of voluntary committee members (p. 56).

It is of historical interest to note Braithwaite's arguments for the unique
contribution of this position. First, she cites the value to the volunteer in
that the role provides "valuable training for citizenship." Second (and of
particular relevance to the above mentioned argument raised by NOW), there are
many capable women administrators who would not stand a chance at being elected
to public office on local government bodies, but who have the expertise regarding the social services and also "more time to devote to the work." Third, the
voluntary administrator is more in touch with public opinion than is the paid
functionary. Finally, the capacity for the public sector to hire "administrative personnel qualitatively and quantitatively" is limited and yet there are
many "public-spirited people [who] have specialized public interests and
specialized experience -- they would willingly serve as administrators of, for
example, hospitals or housing" on a voluntary basis (pp. 57-59).

While much has changed since that book was written, one pattern still persists.
That is the fact that there are numerous administrators of volunteer programs
who are themselves still volunteers. This is particularly true in small
organizational settings often found in homes for the aged, churches, among
others. This fact has several implications. It suggests that the organization
does not recognize the potential contribution that the volunteer administrator
can make to the program, especially in terms of cost-effectiveness. It also
suggests that the dependence on volunteer leadership may lead to a weaker program because of the problems of lack of continuity of leadership, lesser
organizational support and commitment.

A case illustration can best make the point. In 1960 The Human Relations
Commission (to be referred to as HRC) of the City of Champaign, Illinois was
concerned with racial tensions in the high school community. It sought the
services of a social worker, trained in intergroup relations and community
organization, to organize and administer a community program, but defined the
position as that of a volunteer. The social worker was willing to serve as a
volunteer but redefined the problem and the focus. The HRC accepted her interpretation that the complex community problem required a permanent, ongoing
commitment from the city and the HRC and could not depend on the unknown availability of volunteers with expertise in administration, race relations and
community work for the leadership role. Rather than volunteering to organize
a program which might be at risk because of the lack of continuous leadership,
the social worker spent the year developing community support for the program
as well as seeking external funding to get the program started with seed money.
Funds were obtained for this "Intergroup Activity for Youth" from the National
Institute of Mental Health for a three year community demonstration project
(Perlmutter, 1966). At the conclusion of the project, the City of Champaign
allocated funds for the position of administrator to continue the program as
part of the HRC's function. It should be noted that the program itself
depended completely on volunteer participation from teenagers, social workers,
adults and organized church groups (Perlmutter, 1965). The funding of one half-
time administrative position made possible the involvement of more than 100
participants.

In addition to the fact that administrators of volunteer programs are both paid
and unpaid, there are several other contextual factors which should be noted.

Of particular importance is the fact that the background, both in terms of education and experience, is very varied. There are no requirements that have been uniformly defined, either in terms of education, experience, or any other criteria. Usually the person comes up through the ranks and operates on an idiosyncratic, ad hoc basis. While this process does provide an opportunity for the creative individual with administrative proclivities to emerge and does also provide recognition of these abilities, the person usually operates in isolation and in a vacuum all too often feeling unsupported in his/her organization.

> Most of the people now employed in many fields to administer volunteer programs work quite alone or with very few associates who understand what conflicting pressures can build up. To survive, volunteer administrators (usually called directors or coordinators) must tread a fine line between administrative pressures to pick up a miscellany of tasks with community relations aspects and community pressures to serve the purposes of individuals or groups. Clarity about values and great skill are required to bring all goals into congruence with the idea of service to meet the real needs of persons for whom the services are intended. An organized profession could back up lonely practitioners when pressures mount from either their organization setting or community (Naylor, 1976, p. 47).

This lack of uniformity and an identifiable base is further exacerbated by the fact that directors of volunteer programs work in a broad array of settings. To cite churches, scouts, hospitals, settlement houses, mental health programs, child welfare agencies, services for the aging, and correctional programs is only to scratch the surface of the variety, found both in the public and the voluntary sectors. It is therefore not surprising that the cohort of administrators of volunteer programs is splintered into an array of professional associations. For example, in the greater Philadelphia area there are at least three associations (e.g., The Pennsylvania Association for Directors of Volunteer Services, The Delaware Valley Association of Directors of Volunteer Services and the S. E. Region (Pennsylvania state employees) of Volunteer Coordinators). While these numerous organizations are evidence of the urgent need for professional association, the lack of cohesiveness and unity weakens the capacity of these various groups to serve as a strong force.

One final contextual reality must be noted. Whereas historically volunteers came from the upper strata of society and reflected a noblesse-oblige orientation (Gurteen, 1882; Lubove, 1965; Seeley, 1957), this is no longer the case today (Manser and Cass, 1976). Volunteers come from all segments of society. One area of change which must be noted is the role of the black volunteer leader (Austin, 1970), which has dramatically increased since the 1960's. The involvement of volunteers in administrative positions is also increasing.

THE ROLE OF THE ADMINISTRATOR OF VOLUNTEER PROGRAMS

The role of the administrator of volunteer programs is almost without boundaries, ill-defined and oft amorphous. It encompasses both middle management and top management functions as it spans an array of administrative tasks. For example, the administrator of volunteer programs is usually involved in the more widely-known tasks of recruitment and placement. However, these two aspects are only part of what is conceived as a total approach to personnel management, which

119

includes staff development, in-service training and supervision to assure effective and satisfying performance on the part of the volunteer. These are functions frequently associated with middle management.

Richards (1978) describes this level of activity in detail in her discussion of one specific type of volunteer administration, that which typically takes place in the church setting. Richards emphasizes the importance of good administrative practice as being essential to the effective operation of a church program. This is interesting especially since churches are unique in that there is an enormous pool of potential volunteers in the organization which reduces the recruitment function. But the management principles from the business world nevertheless are sought here for a different set of problems surface which require managerial sophistication vis-a-vis appropriate system functioning and communication.

> ..., since all staff are as familiar with the potential volunteers as the Coordinator (administrator) of volunteers is, they can freely recruit volunteers themselves. In other agencies this volunteer service is somewhat removed from staff and they find it expedient to work through the volunteer office. In a church, where the function of the volunteer coordinator is somewhat foreign, staff tend to bypass the office to fill their own needs (Richards, 1978, p. 51).

MacBride (1979) focuses on a different set of competences needed by administrators of volunteer programs which is closely identified with executive functioning. These include financial management (including fund-raising and budgeting), public relations, public education, record keeping, program development, proposal writing and program evaluation. These are certainly technical areas of performance shared by top administrators in a wide array of settings, including profit and not-for-profit organizations.

Thus it is obvious that the position of administrator of volunteer programs cannot be readily categorized or defined; what is equally obvious is that it requires a broad set of skills and competences.

THE NEED FOR A PROFESSIONAL IDENTITY

A professional identity for volunteer administrators is identified as a priority need, as evident in the literature in the field (Althof, 1974; Anderson, 1976; Gowdey, et al., 1976; Naylor, 1976; Smith, 1976). Okin (1973) suggests that the single factor which can most determine the effectiveness-- the impact--of the masses of citizen volunteers is the appropriate training of the directors of volunteer programs.

Activity in this regard is occurring in many quarters. First, the professional associations are becoming stronger and more involved in the issue of professionalism.[3] Second, the U.S. Department of Labor's Division of Classification includes volunteer administrators as professional managers (Rehnberg, 1979). Third, a national certification plan is being developed and tested by the Association for Volunteer Administration (Boulder, Colorado), to articulate competence and provide societal sanction. Finally, occasional courses, workshops, and programs are offered in colleges and universities around the country.

The central question becomes, "what is the best route to take toward professionalism?" There is no answer to this question in the field and little evidence that the question has been directly addressed. In this proposal, we suggest an educational route, the route of professional education.

However, it is our view that it is necessary but not sufficient to focus only on the education of volunteer administrators since their capacity to function at an optimum level depends not only on their competence but equally on the organization's capacity to provide support and sanction for their office. Consequently, while it is necessary to strengthen the performance of the administrator, it is also necessary to build into the educational program content directed at key actors in the organization, including the executive directors and members of the Boards of Directors.

THE STATE OF THE ART: EDUCATION IN VOLUNTEER ADMINISTRATION

In 1979 a national survey of colleges offering programs in Volunteer Administration was conducted among a population of 35 colleges identified by the Association for Volunteer Administration. The findings were as follows: <u>not one academic degree was offered</u>; there were five certificate programs and two continuing education programs.[4] These findings support those of an earlier, more extensive study of "Higher Education Programs for Administrators of Volunteers" (Walker and Smith, 1977:3). Both studies highlight the undeveloped nature of the field, with a high turnover in courses. While the 1977 study did identify a few degree programs, it found that "masters degree programs that have any specialization in volunteer administration are quite rare (only two in our sample)."

Walker and Smith discuss some of the issues related to "program initiation, development and implementation." They identify both barriers and facilitators vis-a-vis degree programs. The barriers are primarily related to the university, where there is a reluctance to take on new programs unless there is "no financial risk to the institution." Furthermore, there does not seem to be a stake in this program area, and interest constantly waxes and wanes.

This issue of a "stake in the program," oft a barrier from the university perspective, is presented as a facilitator from the perspective of the field.

> The most significant success factor in program success seems to be the active, persistent and continuing committed involvement of one individual or a small group of individuals, involved themselves in or deeply concerned with the practice of volunteer administration (Walker and Smith, 1977:4).

A second facilitator is the participation of national or local organizations and leaders in the field of volunteer administration in the development of the educational program. This is based on the authors' assumption that college administrators and faculty usually have little knowledge or understanding of the field.

A third facilitator is finding an appropriate home for the program in the educational institution. Experience has shown that successful programs are usually located in "Human/Public/Social/Community Services or in Business/ Management Schools...." Fourth, the fear of the impact of the new program on the base unit should be dealt with, and discussion should include the program's implications for related departments in the institution. And finally, the pressure of a powerful and prominent local voluntary action coordinating group is important.

Winifred Brown, Director of the Mayor's Voluntary Action Center of the City of New York, has emphasized the need for professional education in Volunteer Administration, especially as the interest and activity in this arena increases.[5] Currently 30 states in our country have Offices for Volunteering, and a Federal Commission on Volunteerism is in the offing. The development of an effective cadre of professionals to meet these demands is a necessity. Brown's view is that the core of a graduate program should be in a standard professional school, such as social work, with a concentration in Volunteer Administration.

THE SOCIAL WORK MSW AS PROFESSIONAL BASE

(1) Rationale

The field of volunteer administration is rapidly emerging as one of major proportions. In the Delaware Valley area of Pennsylvania alone it is estimated that there are a minimum of 3,000 volunteer programs which would require 3,000 volunteer administrators.[6] There is a growing awareness on the part of this cohort on a national level that professional status is essential to provide them with the sanction and support they need in their workplace. It is keenly felt that the various workshops and continuing education programs are inadequate to meet this need. While a national certification program is being promulgated by the National Association for Volunteer Administrators in Boulder, Colorado, this is not enough. In addition to the issue of status and sanction is the issue of expanding the horizons and the job mobility of the individual volunteer administrator. As the situation is now, he/she is locked into this single job category. There is a need for transferability not only to paid employment but to other administrative roles in the social services. Similarly, MSW's could seek employment in the field of volunteer administration, thus encouraging a fluidity of movement.

It should be emphasized that the MSW degree should allow for the specification of "Concentration in Volunteer Administration" as a visible product.

There are many areas of compatibility between the profession of social work and the field of volunteerism. First, and perhaps foremost, is the dual concern of both fields not only with the delivery of services but also with advocacy for its client populations. Manser and Cass (1976) highlight this duality and Naylor (1976) gives emphasis to advocacy:

> The possibilities for strengthening programs by volunteer advocacy are growing out of experience in community action programs and governmental services as well as more traditional voluntary agencies. Acting as advocates or interpreters, volunteers serve clients directly, help people find appropriate services, or mobilize resources in their behalf.
>
> In all kinds of human services the volunteer serves as advocate for services with people and their families from the earliest prevention level throughout treatment, and continues to help persons to confidence and competence throughout the rehabilitation process.

It is interesting to compare this view with that of Slavin (1980:17) who writes about the role of the social work executive.

> Advocacy in social work....is normally seen as adversarial to administration, as a corrective action against arbitrary or destructive agency behavior. The target of advocacy action is most generally authority, the "powers", or organizational policy, the very aspects of the social agency with which the administrator is most centrally identified. On the one hand this makes it extremely difficult for the administrator to project a client advocacy posture. On the other hand, when deftly managed, the authority position of the administrator can facilitate advocacy behavior by staff members, clients, client organizations, and community consumer bodies. Easy access to board members both individually and collectively places the administrator in a strategic position of influence internally. Relationships with key persons of influence in the community, with organizations positively associated with advocacy goals, and with the media can be used to further client objectives.

A second area of compatability is that social work is practiced in a broad array of settings and fields of service, as is volunteerism. Third, many of these agencies already have large volunteer programs (e.g., Homes for the Aged, Hospitals, Women Organized Against Rape, etc.); not only are direct relationship possible with the administrators of the volunteer programs, but the development of field work interneships in volunteer administration is clearly feasible.

And finally, social administration is practiced at both the middle management level and the top management level. The administrative skills practiced by volunteer administrators which were identified earlier are also part of the expertise inherent in the MSW administration program. We will therefore explore the professionalization of volunteer administrators through the Masters in Social Work degree.

(2) Implementation

In this discussion of implementing an MSW program for volunteer administration we will address these topics: (a) criteria for admission, (b) curriculum design and (c) continuing education.

(a) Criteria for Admission

Schools of Social Work have always had flexible admissions criteria and have not only appreciated, but expected, diverse backgrounds among their applicants. Thus it has not been unusual to have an array of educational undergraduate degrees represented, ranging from English literature to mechanical engineering. It should also be noted that this diversity of background has also been found among directors of volunteer programs.

In addition to the educational requirements for admission, Schools of Social Work have paid attention to the life experience criterion of their applicants. The applications are always carefully read with a focus on the actual work of the applicant in some form of social service activity. Whether the experience has been for paid or volunteer performance has not been of concern; what has mattered is the nature of the experience and the commitment it represents to this field of service. Again we find a convergence between the experience of volunteerism and the interest of the Schools of Social Work.

In addition to the above criteria of interest to MSW programs are the qualifications often required by programs which offer a major or concentration in social administration. An added expectation for acceptance into these programs usually is that of experience in some form of direct service, usually with a minimum of two years. Volunteer activity equivalent to the full time experiential requirement is acceptable.

It is important to identify a special admissions issue which may exist for potential applicants who are already working as Directors of Volunteer Programs and who want to become MSW candidates. Schools of Social Work must recognize their special needs. If they are employed, they cannot easily leave their jobs for a full time degree program. In such situations, some schools offer extended degree programs which allow people in employment to retain their jobs while attending school for an extended time period. As part of the admissions process the employing organization must be involved in order to plan for the educational experience of their employee. Thus the criteria for admissions in these situations extend to include both the applicant and the employing organization. The employing organization must demonstrate its flexibility in meeting the School's criteria for the educational program in areas such as time for courses, field work requirements, among others.

(b) Curriculum Design[7]

Myers and Richards in 1979 did an extensive study of all appropriate professional programs in the greater Philadelphia area and concluded that "the administrative sequence of the School of Social Administration Graduate Department embodies many of the (areas of volunteer administration), and with the addition of specialized material regarding volunteerism seems a most appropriate 'home' for this sequence."[8]

The curriculum they were identifying as compatible with their needs includes courses which cover social work philosophy and ideology, social science knowledge and technical skills.[9] In addition to organization theory and social policy, the specific technical courses in administration include financial management, personnel management, grantsmanship and proposal writing, information handling and program evaluation.

However, several special needs of this cohort must be addressed. For example, a seminar on volunteerism is essential which provides an overview of that special field (history, personnel, programs, services, etc.). It should also be noted that excellent instructors are available from the field of volunteer administration who should be included in the teaching faculty, either for this seminar or for special mini-courses.

Finally, the design of field work for this group requires special attention. Several items are worth noting. First, an experienced administrator of volunteer programs could provide an excellent placement if this can be arranged. Second, if the administrator is also the student, there should be consideration given to allowing credit for life experiences and reducing field work hours. Third, if the student is working in the agency and using it as a field placement, supervision by another administrator should be arranged.

Since we are usually dealing with a mature and experienced adult student, special curriculum design and flexibility will be necessary if we are to meet the needs of the group of practitioners known as volunteer administrators.

(c) Continuing Education

While addressing the needs of the administrators of volunteer programs, another area requires urgent attention. All too often the volunteer administrators are left to carry the ball on their own, unsupported in their systems and under-resourced. It is essential that workshops, courses or any other appropriate format be developed for the executives of the organizations which contain volunteer programs in order to help these systems understand, value and support this vital manpower pool. In addition to the training for executives, schools should also address the continuing educational needs of the administrators of volunteer programs.

CONCLUSION

We are living in difficult and tumultuous times. Human services are at risk as are the human service professions. There may be a tendency for groups to close ranks, to become protective of their turf. This may especially be the case in relation to professional social workers and their reactions to volunteers at a time when jobs are harder to obtain. It, therefore, cannot be emphasized enough that volunteers do not replace professionals but rather perform functions that otherwise could not get done. And it is the administrator of volunteer programs who must serve the critical role of defining the roles, interpreting the functions and bridging the gap between the volunteers and the professionals. The necessity for professionalizing this cohort, important in any context, becomes all the more necessary in these complex times.

Notes

1. Also referred to as social work administration.

2. Volunteerism has been defined as a service provided without pay, through which the citizen who participates "is both a contributor to democratic solutions and a participant who is finding opportunity for personal growth and satisfaction" (Okin and Wiener, 1973:3).

3. The Association for Volunteer Administration, Boulder, Colorado, is very active and publishes several journals among its various educational and research activities.

4. The survey was conducted in November, 1979 by Cora Myers, Senior Consultant, The Consultant Community, and Janet Richards, Coordinator of Volunteers, Gloria Dei Lutheran Church, Huntingdon Valley, Pa.

5. Winifred Brown, Director, Mayor's Voluntary Action Center of New York City. Talk given at the Volunteer Action Council, Philadelphia, February, 1980.

6. Letter from Cora Meyers, November, 1979 to the School of Social Administration, Temple University.

7. Although many volunteer administrators do not have a first degree (BSW or BA), in this discussion we are focussing on the MSW.

8. Letter sent November, 1979.

9. The curriculum format is available upon request from the author.

REFERENCES

Althof, J. E.
  1974 "Going Academic: Move Your Program Into Service Learning," Synergist, 3(1974):9-12.

Anderson, R. M.
  1976 A Manual for Volunteer Coordinators, Los Angeles: Los Angeles Volunteer Action Center.

Austin, D. M.
  1970 The Black Civic Volunteer Leader: A New Era in Voluntarism, Waltham: Brandeis University.

Braithwaite, C.
  1938 The Voluntary Citizen, London: Methuen & Co., Ltd.

Ellis, S. J. and K. H. Noyes
  1978 By the People: A History of Americans as Volunteers, Philadelphia, Pa.: Engergize.

Gowdey, A. C., P. Cooper, and I. H. Scheier
  1976 Report on an Educational Needs Survey for the Leadership of Volunteers, Boulder, Colorado: National Information Center on Volunteerism.

Gurteen, S. H.
  1882 A Handbook of Charity Organization, Buffalo: Courier Company.

Haeuser, A. A. and F. S. Schwartz
  1980 "Developing Social Work Skills for Work with Volunteers," Social Casework, 61(December):595-601.

Holme, A. and J. Maizels
  1978 Social Workers and Volunteers, London: George Allen and Unwin, Ltd.

Lubove, R.
  1965 The Professional Altruist: The Emergence of Social Work as a Career, 1880-1930, Cambridge, Mass.: Harvard University Press.

MacBride, M.
  1979 Step by Step: Management of the Volunteer Program in Agencies, Bergen County, N.J.: Volunteer Bureau of Bergen County.

Manser, G. and R. H. Cass
  1976 Volunteerism at the Crossroads, New York: Family Service of America.

National Association of Social Workers
  1977   1977 Delegate Assembly Policy Statement, "Volunteers and Social
         Service Systems," NASW News, 22 (July 1977):39.

Naylor, H. H.
  1973   Volunteers Today - Finding, Training and Working With Them, New
         York: Dryden Associates.

Naylor, H. H.
  1976   Leadership for Volunteering, New York: Dryden Associates.

Okin, T. B. and C. K. Wiener
  1973   A Workshop for Directors of Volunteers, Washington, D.C.: National
         Center for Volunteer Action.

Okin, T. B.
  1973   Keynote Address, Association of Volunteer Bureaus Conference, May.

Perlmutter, F.
  1966   "An Intergroup Activity for Youth: A Case Study in Rancorous Conflict,"
         J. of Intergroup Relations, 5 (Autumn):65-74.

Perlmutter, F. and D. Durham
  1965   "Using Teenagers to Supplement Casework Service," Social Work,
         10 (April):41-46.

Rehnberg, S. J.
  1979   "A Brief Review of Learning Needs Surveys and Curriculum Development
         in Volunteer Services Administration," a paper prepared for the
         Association for Administration of Volunteer Services.

Richards, J.
  1978   "Church Volunteer Administration: Similarities and Differences,"
         Volunteer Administration, 11:49-52.

Seeley, J., et al.
  1957   Community Chest, Toronto: University of Toronto Press.

Slavin, S.
  1980   "A Theoretical Framework for Social Administration," Leadership in
         Social Administration, edited by F. Perlmutter and S. Slavin,
         Philadelphia, Pa.: Temple University Press, pp. 3-21.

Smith, D. H.
  1976   "Research," Voluntary Action Leadership, Spring-Summer:12-15.

Walker, J. M. and D. H. Smith
  1977   "Higher Education Programs for Administrators of Volunteers," Volunteer
         Administration, 10:1-9.

VOLUNTEERS AS ADVOCATES

Sally Y. Orr
The Association of Junior Leagues, Inc.

VOLUNTEER ADVOCACY - NEEDED FOR SOCIAL SERVICES

The current economic and social climate in the United States appears to be heavily weighted against social service programs. There is a determined effort to dismantle social services programs at the federal level, replacing them with block grants to the states which can be spent as the states wish. Even supporters of block grants fear that the drastic spending cuts proposed will make it impossible for states and localities to provide many essential services.

Unless public support can be rallied to resist these pressures, social service programs will continue to shrink, depriving many of this nation's neediest citizens of essential services. For this reason, it is critical that social workers learn to work with volunteer advocates--both to maintain existing services and to improve or create needed programs. This paper will address the need for heightened volunteer involvement in advocacy efforts as well as the ways in which social workers can work with volunteers to build effective networks of volunteer advocates.

Definition of Advocacy and Volunteers

According to Webster's New World dictionary, advocacy means the act of advocating, or speaking or writing in support of something. One may advocate for a case involving a single person or a cause involving many persons. The concept of advocacy considered in this paper is an adaptation of the definition of child advocacy developed by Kahn, et al. (1973: 10-11). Advocacy is defined as intervention on behalf of a group of persons such as children, families, the elderly, etc. in relation to those services and institutions that impinge on their lives. Many strategies may be utilized in this type of advocacy, e.g., planning and coordinating services, seeking changes in administrative procedures, lobbying for changes in existing legislation or the development of new laws, educating the public about existing services and needs or ensuring that various groups, e.g., the handicapped, children, obtain their legal rights.

Volunteers are defined as "individuals who freely contribute their services, without remuneration, to public or voluntary organizations engaged in all types of social welfare activities (Encyclopedia of Social Work, 1977: 1582). Although volunteers, as defined here, do not receive remuneration for their services, those working with volunteers must recognize that it may be necessary to reimburse volunteers for the expenses that they incur, i.e., travel, phone calls. Agencies or groups that work with large numbers of volunteers should have a budget item for volunteer expenses. If expenses are not covered, volunteering will increasingly become the province of the well-to-do, reducing the numbers and types of persons who are able to volunteer.

Using these delineations of advocacy and volunteer, a volunteer advocate may be defined as an individual who works without remuneration to intervene on behalf of a particular group to change those services and institutions which impinge on their lives. A wide variety of persons may serve as advocates, e.g., board members of a voluntary agency, direct service volunteers, members of public advisory boards, members of service organizations, clients served by individual programs or individual citizens interested in helping others. Direct service volunteers can be especially effective advocates because they have first-hand knowledge of the programs/institutions that they are trying to change.

The issue for social workers then is not whether volunteers can be used as advocates, but what type of volunteers are willing to serve and what role will they play? Or, as Hans Spiegel (undated) poses the question, "Which volunteer, doing what kind of volunteering vis-a-vis what governmental entity [or agency] and for what purpose?"

Accepting this type of reasoning, it is apparent that there is a role for all types of lay persons to act as advocates. As one observer points out:

> The 'poor power' concept of OEO, like the 'money power' or 'affluent power' of most older community councils, United Appeal, and philanthropic foundation approaches, are equally exclusive and elitist and have been marginally successful. While continuing to support organization of the poor and encouraging giving by the affluent, our conclusion in relation to the American ideal of helping all in need is that any citizen involvement or community organization effort that aims at less than genuine action, collectively undertaken by 'all citizens', will prove devisive and limited in effectiveness (Rya, 1977-78).

According to this interpretation, the terms "volunteer advocacy," "citizen participation," and "citizen involvement" are very similar.

Reasons for Involving Volunteers as Advocates

Unless they have widespread public support, social service programs will be the first to be cut when budget revisions are made. The swift Congressional rejection of President Reagan's proposal to cut Social Security benefits demonstrates the importance of the broad-based constituency that exists for this program. The elderly vote in large numbers; politicians try to avoid making cuts that will invite retaliation at the polls. Consequently, Congress rejected the President's proposal to reduce early retirement benefits.

The quick reversal on Social Security is just one illustration of the fact that the controversy over the Reagan Administration's proposals will be decided in large part by the reaction at the grass-roots level. The word from Washington nowadays is "get to the grass roots." Lobbyists for national organizations are often ignored unless they can produce evidence of support at the local level. For this reason, national organizations are working with networks of volunteer advocates to convince Congress that certain programs must be saved.

The decision in 1981 of Congress to refuse to place the Adoption Assistance and Child Welfare Act of 1980 (P.L. 96-272) in a social services block grant was heavily influenced by volunteers across the country who sent mailgrams, wrote letters, telephoned and visited their Congressmen to urge that the legislation not be placed in the block grant.

Constituents who are volunteers sometimes can receive a more sympathetic hearing from a Senator or Representative than the social worker who is perceived as lobbying to save his/her job, even if that job serves a very important purpose in the community. Constituents who are clients can be effective advocates if they can personally relate how the proposed cuts will harm them and their families. At the same time, it is essential that citizens who are perceived as "non-partisan," without any vested interest in a program, support threatened programs. As Senator Daniel Moynihan (D-NY) said when a volunteer from Kansas appeared in support of P.L. 96-272 before the Senate Finance Committee (chaired by Senator Robert Dole [R-KS]), "It is not the easiest thing to have a friend and constituent from Kansas come in here and tell you 'stop that crazy Administration before it does all those awful things.'"[1]

Celebrities who have a knowledge of, and commitment to, a particular cause also can serve as effective advocates. For instance, film star Jane Russell, who founded WAIF, an advocacy agency that seeks to find permanent homes for children, was an eloquent and effective advocate for P.L. 96-272. Her appearance before a subcommittee of the House Ways and Means Committee was televised on at least one national evening news show, and reports of her testimony appeared in such major papers as The New York Times and the Washington Post. She also was able to meet individually with several Senators and Representatives.

The block grants passed by Congress in 1981 may create a critical need for informed volunteer advocates at the state and local level. Most of the block grants do not mandate any special services or maintenance of effort on the part of the states and local communities. Social workers and their clients cannot alone hope to save needed programs. Broad-based citizen participation support is needed if programs are to be saved. For this reason, it is essential that social workers develop effective methods of working with volunteer advocates.

While the need to use volunteers as advocates is especially apparent during this period of shrinking resources at the national level, there are several other reasons for enlisting volunteers as advocates for social services. As social work has become increasingly professionalized, the opportunities for meaningful voluntary activity have diminished. Volunteers at all levels, including members of voluntary agency boards and government advisory groups, often have infrequent direct contact with an agency's operation. As volunteers have become increasingly divorced from direct participation, their interest and commitment to the delivery of services has decreased. Consequently, there often is little general support for social service programs. By providing volunteer advocates with a sense of involvement in social service programs, social workers can build on-going support for programs.

Volunteer advocates also often act as catalysts for effective change in programs whose personnel have developed a certain myopia that prevents them from perceiving weak spots in their programs. Even if the social workers have identified the weak spots, he/she (whether employed by a voluntary or public agency) may be afraid to speak out because he/she might lose his/her job or create controversy at the office. Volunteers do not face these impediments. They often have a broader outlook that allows them to perceive difficulties not apparent to a person more closely involved with an agency or government activity.

In fact, many of the most innovative changes in social services have been initiated by volunteers, working with social workers either within or outside the "system." For instance, volunteer service organizations such as the Association of Junior Leagues and the National Council of Jewish Women played key roles in achieving passage of legislation mandating citizen foster care review boards, revisions of state juvenile codes and passage of the Juvenile Justice and Delinquency Prevention Act of 1974.

Volunteers also sometimes can serve as "bridge persons" - those who can make contact with another group, even if the two groups officially are not collaborating or, in fact, are in conflict. Often, an informal contact such as a phone call or informal meeting can be handled effectively by a volunteer in a manner not possible by the social worker who is identified as an employee of an agency opposed to the positions of the agency or group to be contacted.

Obstacles to Use of Volunteers by Social Workers

Despite the clear need of the social services for support from volunteer advocates, social workers traditionally have been reluctant to work with a wide variety of volunteers. In fact, one observer charges that "the single greatest impediment to the full and effective involvement of citizens in social services is the resistance of the 'helping establishment'" (Allen, 1980).

There appear to be several reasons for the reluctance of social workers (and other professionals) to work with volunteers. One is that many social workers feel uncomfortable working with volunteers; they have not been trained to work with citizen policy-making groups or other volunteers. Another, very important, reason is that, in a period of budget cutbacks, there is a perception that volunteers will be used to replace professionals (Encyclopedia of Social Work 1977: 1583). However, the development of advocacy programs often provides new, challenging professional opportunities for social workers. Increasingly, the literature pertaining to such groups speaks of the need for "well-staffed" organizations (Spiegel, 1981; Perlman, 1978). Advocacy groups such as the

Children's Defense Fund employ a substantial number of professionals, including social workers. Volunteer organizations such as the National Council of Jewish Women and the Association of Junior Leagues also employ social workers. In fact, any substantial advocacy effort will create employment opportunities for social workers, especially those trained in planning, policy analysis and organization.

The "covert and overt conscious and unconscious resistance of professional paid staff" also can be traced to the reluctance of professional social workers to be judged by "non-professionals" (Haeuser-Schwartz, 1978). In addition, there is a widespread belief among some social workers that volunteers are "elites" who cannot understand or sympathize with the needs of the poor and other deprived groups. This type of mistrust of volunteers can be traced to the aversion to the "lady bountiful" image of volunteers of a bygone era and the widespread tendency to consider volunteerism and citizen participation as two separate activities.

Delineation of Roles

In developing any type of advocacy program, it is important to delineate the roles of the social worker and the volunteer. Social workers can work as lobbyists, coordinators of legislative activities, administrators or program developers, policy analysts and organizers. Their role varies according to the type of task they have to perform, the type of organization or agency and the type of volunteers with whom they are working.[2] For instance, the job required of the social worker differs if he/she is working with a voluntary agency, a government advisory group, grass-roots organizations, e.g., consumer groups, block associations, or self-help groups, mutual benefit organizations or membership organizations.

The traditional perspective that the board, i.e., volunteers are "instrumentalities primarily concerned with the fiscal operation of the agency while the agency's technical competence is viewed as the professional's appropriate concern" (Auerbach, 1961 as quoted in Perlmutter, 1978) will not succeed in developing effective advocates either for the agency or for the clients they serve. To be effective as an advocate, all volunteers, including board members, must understand the structure and mission of the area of social services their agency serves (Gratch, 1980); therefore, the social worker must develop ways of effectively informing board members about the agency's program. The appropriate role of social worker in educating a board of a voluntary agency will be quite different from that of the social worker employed by self-help groups where technical experts are used for specific problems as determined by the membership (Katz, 1965, 1970 as quoted in Perlmutter). A similar role is played by the social worker employed by coalitions of grass-roots organizations that were not initiated by outside groups such as government agencies or private national groups. In such coalitions, social workers can provide research capability and knowledge (Spiegel, 1981) as well as day-to-day administration. Regardless of the type of advocacy project, no effort can succeed without day-to-day administrative supervision (Brager and Specht, 1973). Very often, a lobbying campaign or administrative appeal has been lost because no one was "minding the store" on a day-to-day basis.

The tasks required of social workers working with a formal organization of volunteers are very similar to those required of the social worker employed by self-help groups of grass-roots coalitions. A social worker staffing the public policy committee of a national volunteer organization may analyze legislation and recommend policy options, provide day-to-day administration, write testimony to present before legislative committees, develop and maintain contacts with outside organizations, and mobilize grass-roots support for legislation supported by the organization. For instance, the Director of Public Policy of the Association of Junior Leagues, a social worker with training in organization, planning and policy development, sends regular mailings to members of the Association's legislative network. The mailings inform network members about developments in the child welfare and child health legislation supported by the Association and urge members to take specific action relating to the legislation, e.g., contact a Congressman, write letters, etc. Members of the network then contact their Congressmen to urge support for legislation backed by the Association. The expertise and knowledge gained by individual Junior Leagues from their projects in child welfare and child health often enhance their lobbying efforts at the national level.

Developing Effective Advocates

In developing effective volunteer advocates, the social worker also must recognize the need for the same types of development required in any other type of organizing. The important tasks of socialization, developing a sense of belonging and organization building are all necessary (Brager and Specht, 1973). To ignore any of these stages of development, or to insist on the role of the professional versus the volunteer, is to court defeat. All studies stress the fact that volunteers work best if they have a feeling of belonging and possess an understanding of the problems of the agency with which they are working. If the volunteer is made to feel like an outsider, or ignored except in times of emergency, no successful advocacy program will emerge.

Membership organizations, of course, already often have instilled a sense of "belonging" in their members. Often, however, only a small proportion of the members are engaged in a particular advocacy effort. For this reason, it is very important that the general membership be informed of actions taken in the name of the organization. If the advocacy efforts are successful, the membership generally will be supportive of the advocacy efforts. If the advocacy initiative fails or becomes controversial, however, the members not involved may insist that the organization withdraw support of the advocacy initiative. For this reason, large membership organizations often employ professional staff to provide continuity, handle day-to-day administrative details and inform the volunteer leadership of developments in the legislature and/or administrative agency pertaining to the advocacy efforts.

Among those volunteers engaged in advocacy, there are several levels of involvement. Brager and Specht (1973) have identified four types of participants in organizing: executive, active, occasional and supportive. This type of layered participation is especially evident in large membership organizations such as the Association of Junior Leagues and the National Council of Jewish Women or service organizations with large memberships such as the YW and YMCA. In such organizations, members of the Board and its Public Affairs or Public Policy Committee are clearly executive participants. Individual affiliates that have submitted testimony to Congress, commented on regulations pertaining to legislation supported by the national organization or written to individual Congressmen are active participants.

Generally, the most involved supporters of the "active" affiliates are likely to be individual members who have a first-hand knowledge of the program that prompted the national organization's involvement. There also are occasional participants, e.g., those who respond to a phone call for support, as well as supportive participants, e.g., affiliates that inform their members about the progress of legislation supported by the national organization but are not ready to take action on behalf of the legislation.

STRUCTURE IN ADVOCACY WORK

Whatever the type of activity, an identifiable structure is needed in working with volunteer advocates to expand the involvement of volunteers as well as to support effective relationships (Brager and Specht, 1973). Regardless of the structure developed, successful advocacy depends on the establishment of goals and objectives (Gratch, 1980; Langton, 1978). There are many ways in which a structure can be helpful in establishing a framework for advocacy. For instance, training programs can be used to expand and improve volunteer involvement. Committees, in addition to serving as work vehicles, also provide a way of developing affective relationships among members, especially among volunteers who have little or no contact with each other outside committee meetings.

Different Strcutures for Different Types of Organizations

Most importantly, it is essential that social workers involved with volunteers analyze the type of volunteer activity with which they are engaged and determine what type of organization is best for what occasion. The types of advocacy activities mentioned in this paper seldom fit under the general supervision of a volunteer coordinator. For example, members of a board of directors may relate better to the Executive Director or the staff responsible for particular committees. Service volunteers or clients may work better with an individual worker responsible for a specific activity. Sometimes, members of a committee can function as advocates for specific issues with backup from the staff of the committee. The structure should be designed to meet an organization's awareness of the need for advocacy, the type of volunteer, and the type of advocacy. This is especially true when one is working with non-traditional groups such as self-help organizations, grass-root coalitions, or large-member organizations whose interests and activities are not restricted to social services. This does not mean that structure should be haphazard or non-existent. A carefully developed, well-financed and well-staffed program is needed for a successful advocacy effort.

> Advocacy must have a discrete budget, adequate to meet the program's articulated goals. Advocacy fails when there is no explicit appropriation for the effort - when it is carried out by the diversion of staff and board members' time. The performance becomes mediocre, usually going to those persons whose other duties are flexible or few enough to embrace the involvement (Gratch, 1980: 24).

Difficulties in Working with Volunteers

Despite the clear advantages of working with volunteers, certain difficulties must be acknowledged. For example, there is a definite need for flexibility on the part of the social worker. Professional social workers working with volunteer advocates must recognize that the relationships between non-professionals and professional staff are not static and permanent. They change depending upon the role to be played by each in a particular situation (Perlmutter, 1969 as quoted in Perlmutter, 1978). The challenge for social workers in working with volunteer advocates is to develop ways of helping volunteers attain the knowledge and expertise needed to advocate effectively for social services. To achieve this goal, social workers should be able and willing to inform volunteers of the failures as well as the successes of their agency's (or department's) programs and to accept intelligent suggestions for change - including those that come from volunteers who are considered "non-professionals." A successful advocacy program involving volunteers is built on mutual respect and sharing of the "warts" as well as the good features of a program. Too often, social workers have expected volunteers, especially board members, to lend support uncritically, responding enthusiastically to appeals for funds even though they have been given little information about programs or been ignored when they raised questions about a program's quality.

Social workers involved with volunteer advocates should be willing to spend time in training and adjusting to working with a larger pool of personnel with each providing fewer hours of performance per person, as well as accepting the added costs to the agency of providing training programs and supervision for volunteers. The social worker employed by a volunteer organization also sometimes has to accept direction from "non-professionals." In addition, developing a core of volunteer advocates opens the traditional agency to questioning by non-professionals, sometimes resulting in substantial change to the agency.

The same problems pertain to legislatively-mandated advisory boards for government agencies. Many government agencies resist establishing advisory boards or openly manipulate them (Milbrath, 1981). However, those government agencies that provide adequate staff and allow citizens to fulfill the role of advisors often find needed support for innovative new programming as well as support when effective existing programs are criticized or threatened with cutbacks. In fact, the openness to critical examination created by an infusion of volunteers often is a blessing in disguise. Volunteers sometimes can identify problems not readily apparent to the "insider." They also can build support for making needed changes.

Notes

1. Hearing, Senate Finance Committee, March 26, 1981, Senator Moynihan in response to testimony presented by Jan Deering of Wichita, Kansas, Public Policy Chairman, Association of Junior Leagues.

2. Social workers and volunteers affiliated with voluntary agencies should be informed about the rules set by the Internal Revenue Service for lobbying by organizations which are classified as "public charities" under Section 501(c)(3) of the Internal Revenue Code. Until the passage of the Tax Reform Act of 1976, the law regulating the lobbying activities of public charities was unclear, stating only that "no substantial part of the activities" of the organization could be used to influence legislation. The penalty for violating this regulation was loss of tax-exempt status, something essential to the survival of voluntary agencies. Since "substantial part" was never defined by the I.R.S., many voluntary organizations were hesitant about lobbying. The passage of the Tax Reform Act

of 1976 encouraged lobbying by allowing every public charity (except church groups) to elect to come under an amendment which:

> ...defines lobbying;
>
> ...permits lobbying without penalty up to a certain percentage of the organization's total annual expenditures;
>
> ...penalizes minor infractions by taxing lobbying expenditures above that percentage;
>
> ...reserves the ultimate penalty - loss of tax-exempt status - for repeated excessive lobbying.

REFERENCES

Allen, Kerry Ken
   1980   "A Voluntary Agenda for the 1980s." Voluntary Action Leadership (Summer): 22-25.

Brager, George and Harry Specht
   1973   Community Organizing. USA: Columbia University Press.

Checkoway, Barry and Jon Van Til
   1978   "What Do We Know About Citizen Participation? A Selective Review of Research." In Stuart Langton (ed.) Citizen Participation in America. Lexington, Mass.: D. C. Heath and Company, 25-42.

Civic Action Institute
   1980   Community Organizing in a Partnership Institute. Washington, D.C.

Gold, Doris
   1977   "A Cognitive Minority: Feminists and Volunteering." (unpublished) (August) Revised August 1978.

Gratch, Alan S.
   1980   Board Members are Child Advocates. New York: Child Welfare League of America.

Grosser, Charles F.
   1979   "Participation and Practice." In Carol B. Germain (ed.) Social Work Practice. New York: Columbia University Press.

Haeuser, Adrienne Ahlgren and Florence S. Schwartz
   1978   "Developing Social Work Skills to Extend and Enrich Human Services in the 1980's with 1980's Volunteers." Presented at the Council on Social Work Education, Twenty-fifth Anniversary Annual Program Meeting, APM Session 171, New Orleans.

Kahn, Alfred J., Sheila B. Kamerman, and Brenda G. McGowan
   1973   Child Advocacy: Report of a Baseline Study. Washington, D.C.: U. S. Department of Health, Education and Welfare, Office of Child Development, Children's Bureau. DHEW Publication No. (OCD) 73-18.

Langton, Stuart
   1978   "What is Citizen Participation?" In Stuart Langton (ed.) _Citizen Participation in America_. Lexington, Mass.: D. C. Heath and Company, 13-24.

Langton, Stuart
   1980   "The New Voluntarism." Paper prepared for the Conference on Philosophical Issues in Voluntarism, Virginia Polytechnic Institute and State University, Blacksburg, Virginia (November).

Levin, Herman
   1977   "Voluntary Organizations in Social Welfare." In _Encyclopedia of Social Work_. New York: National Association of Social Workers, pp. 1573-1582.

Milbrath, Lester W.
   1981   "Citizen Surveys." Citizen Participation, 2 (March/April): 3-4, 16-17.

Perlman, Janice
   1978   "Grass Roots Participation from Neighborhood to Nation." In Stuart Langton (ed.) _Citizen Participation in America_. Lexington, Mass.: D. C. Heath and Company, 65-79.

Perlmutter, Felice
   1978   "Citizen Participation and Professionalism: A Developmental Relationship." In Simon Slavin (ed.) _Social Administration_, New York: Haworth Press.

Rosener, Judy B.
   1978   "Matching Method to Purpose: The Challenges of Planning Citizen Participation Activities." In Stuart Langton (ed.) _Citizen Participation in America_. Lexington, Mass.: D. C. Heath and Company, 109-115.

Ryan, William
   1977- "Philosophy of Citizen Involvement." Volunteer Administration,
   1978   Winter: 1-6.

Seider, Violet M. and Doris C. Kirshbaum
   1977   "Volunteers." In _Encyclopedia of Social Work_. New York: National Association of Social Workers, pp. 1582-1590.

Spiegel, Hans B. C.
   1981   "Coalitions of Grassroots Groups." Citizen Participation, 2 (March/April): 6-7, 10, 24.

Spiegel, Hans B. C.
           "Appropriate Role of Citizen Volunteers in the Federal System." (Undated)

MOTIVATION AND EXPECTATION IN SUCCESSFUL VOLUNTEERISM

Michael Phillips
Fordham University

The success of a program using volunteers is dependent upon the program's professional staff clearly understanding and supporting the motivations which lead people to volunteer. It is important to realize that the efforts to recruit volunteers must have a different focus from those efforts designed to keep the volunteers in a program. If volunteers are to remain part of the program, one needs to help them see the reality they are experiencing as congruent with their expectations of the program.

The literature on volunteerism has stressed the fact that there are many motivations for volunteering. Most often the motivations highlighted are altruistic ones such as: a desire for involvement in "in" activities, a concern for others, an opportunity for emotional association with others and a "service" focus (Schindler-Rainman, 1977). Most of the types of volunteer activities cited by Ellis and Noyes in their book on the history of volunteers in America are thought of as altruistically based. However, without in any way denigrating the altruistic aspect of volunteering, many professionals have long recognized that volunteering is also motivated partially by self-interest. Self-interest aspects of volunteerism have been identified as: learning, self-actualization, and increased status (Naylor, 1967). Increasingly programs are identified in terms of how they help the volunteer (Stanton, 1970) and professionals are including self-interest as an aspect of their recruitment procedures (Haeuser and Schwartz, 1980; Scheier, 1977; Lobb, 1979).

To bring altruistic and egoistic aspects of volunteerism into clearer focus, it is helpful to think of volunteering in terms of social exchange theory. Social exchange theory contends that all interactions are based upon an exchange of costs (what one gives - the altruistic aspect of volunteering) and rewards (what one receives - the egoistic aspect of volunteering). Schafer (1980) has pointed out that to sustain a volunteer effort over time the rewards to the volunteer must exceed or at least balance the costs. This principle is known as "equity" and serves as a means to help evaluate programs.

In volunteer activities, the relationships between the altruistic (cost) and egoistic (rewards) motivations are modified by: 1) the degree to which the expectations of the volunteer are met (Routh, 1977) and 2) the phase of the volunteer effort (Wolensky, 1980). For example, while the initial motivation to volunteer may be altruistic (to help someone else), that motivation may also be reassessed in terms of its return. Similarly, the decision to continue as a volunteer will be evaluated in terms of its costs and rewards.

This paper draws upon data collected as part of an evaluation of the Fresh Air Fund's Friendly Town Program. It explores these ideas and evolves practice principles for professionals in similar endeavors.

THE FRIENDLY TOWN PROGRAM

The Friendly Town Program is a largely volunteer effort guided by the professional Fresh Air Fund staff who coordinate the placement of some 11,000 deprived New York City Children in the homes of volunteer families. These host families live in 321 different communities from Maine to West Virginia.

As the reader will note in Chart 1, the program has six components. The Fresh Air Fund Friendly Town Department is made up of paid staff who administer and

CHART 1

FRESH AIR FUND FRIENDLY TOWN PROGRAM COMPONENTS

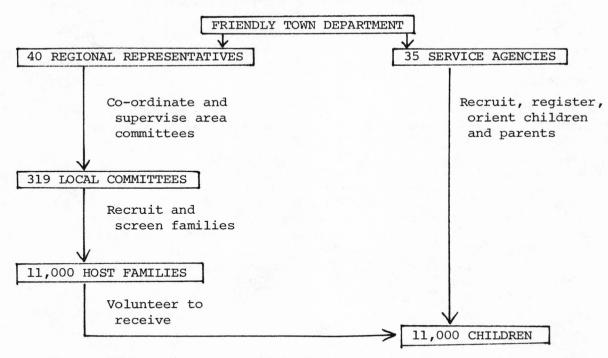

coordinate the entire program, provide consultation to other components, match the children with available hosts and schedule transportation. The children are located through a network of independent community service agencies. The Friendly Town recruiters, some paid by local agencies and some volunteers, recruit, register and orient the children to the program. Recruitment is done mainly by word of mouth since agencies have more children wishing to go to a

Friendly Town than hosts available.

The hosts are reached through a two-stage process. The coordinating of large geographic regions and supervision of local committees is done by a group of 40 volunteer Fund Representatives. These volunteers serve as the link between local committees and the Fresh Air Fund. All are or have been Friendly Town hosts.

On the local level there are the Friendly Town committees. These committees are made up of volunteers who handle local publicity, recruit and screen host families, schedule the local arrival and departures of children, and, with consultation from the Fund Representative and the Fresh Air Fund Office, handle any problem which the children or host encounter.

Finally, there are the host families who volunteer to take a city child into their home for at least two weeks.

The evaluation of the Friendly Town Program involved a random sample of interviews conducted during the summer and fall of 1979. The number of completed interviews were: children, 319; parents, 368; hosts, 305; community agency staff, 40; Fund Representatives, 38; and Friendly Town committee members, 90.

An overall review of the program indicates that it is highly personalized. The community agency staff know of the children and meet with their parents to discuss the program. Similarly the Fund Representatives are previous Friendly Town committee chairpersons and host families and personally know many of the host families, and the children who come. Recognizing this personal touch is important and the Fresh Air Fund staff makes special efforts to maintain personal contacts with all areas by visiting the community agencies and the Friendly town to which the children are sent. This personal contact appears to support the general principle which involves direct contact between volunteer host and child.

MOTIVATIONS OF HOSTS

To fully understand how a host becomes involved and is retained in the program as a volunteer, it is important to look at their involvement as a progression with certain identifiable stages. Note that the motivation of the volunteer at each stage is somewhat different: stage 1 - exposure to the idea that one might be a host, stage 2 - preliminary decision to be a host, stage 3 - final decision to become a host, stage 4 - child living with the host and finally, stage 5 - decision whether or not to have a child again the next summer. Awareness of the Friendly Town Program (phase one) is most often the result of an exposure to the program through newspapers or other media (42% of hosts). These reports tend to reflect the fact that persons in the community provide homes for deprived city children and that there are many children awaiting host family invitations. Whether exposed via the media or by friends who are hosts (about 1/3 of hosts) the primary motivation during this phase is altruistic.

Phase two involves the seeking of information about the program. During this phase, a prospective host is visited by a member of the Friendly Town committee who discusses the program in detail with the family. The committee members discuss the need for hosts and what supports there are for families. While technically a family may be dropped at this stage, this rarely happens in practice and few committee members indicated ever having had to actually refuse

a host. Families seem to select themselves and inappropriate families are unlikely to continue into the stage of actually taking a child. If a family is
clearly not suitable, the local Friendly Town visitor will attempt to help them
see that they do not meet the program criteria. For example, a mother who just
wants a babysitter to care for a young child would be asked to withdraw.

Phase two begins to move the host away from a position of total altruism since
the Friendly Town committee person also stresses the gains of having a child
visit for two weeks. At the same time, however, the prospective host begins to
see the value of being part of a group that will provide him/her with support
and help in times of difficulty. Despite this modest egoistic appeal, the primary
motivation during phase two remains altruism with the host most likely to remember
the interview as stressing the program's benefits to deprived city kids and the
fact that many children are awaiting hosts (45%).

Phase three represents a shift with hosts clearly considering the benefits and
costs of the exchange (the taking of a child). The decision becomes a family
decision discussed by the host mother with her husband 93% of the time and with
the children in the family 53% of the time. During these discussions non-
altruistic motivations appear to predominate. Self-interest becomes important
with almost 60% of the mothers indicating they decided to become hosts because
it would provide companionship or enjoyment for them or their children, or would
expose the family to a different lifestyle. Consideration of the benefits to the
host family is also reflected in the fact that 77% of the hosts request children
the same age or close to the same age as their own children. In the interview,
some families even mentioned that they made this choice in order to give their
child greater exposure to a different lifestyle. When hosts have made the
decision to take a child they appear to get support from others for their
decision. Only 7% indicated that friends were negative and 5% indicated that
neighbors were negative. This finding may mean that while few hosts indicated
that they had discussed the decision with friends or neighbors, they may have
considered the possible reactions of friends and neighbors to the child.

EXPECTATIONS OF HOSTS

During the fourth phase, when the child lives with the family, the expectations
of both host and child become an important dynamic in whether or not the visit
succeeds and the volunteer remains in the program. The host, out of his/her
own motivations, both altruistic and egoistic, had developed a set of expectations about what the child will be like. If that expectation is met or exceeded
and a similar expectation of the host on the part of the child is met, the visit
will be a success. This fact was most clearly highlighted in a sub-study of 52
hosts who did not re-invite children the following summer. Of the group of 35
who were not prevented from taking a child by such problems as divorce, illness
and employment, 26 indicated that the child was "different from what they had
expected." The differences included children who wanted to stay in the house
all day, children who had "bad habits," "bad language" and children who did not
get along with the hosts' children. It is of note that in the latter cases the
hosts tended to blame their own children for the difficulty. It was the im-
pression of the interviewers that the hosts were attempting to reinforce the
idea that their altruism was not ill-founded and that the city children were
truly worthy. Similarly families' sense of altruism asserted itself in the two-
thirds of the non-repeating hosts who indicated that they wished to be hosts
again in the future.

Another way to explore whether the expectations were met is to look at what the children and their parents expected from the visit and see if that met the hosts' hopes and expectations. The children's parents indicated that they expected their children to get from the experience the opportunity to:

learn about a different way of life	61%
see a new environment	12%
become more independent	12%
do things they could not do in the city	3%
all other	12%

It is important to note that the differences in "way of life" and environment were often described by parents not as "Country vs. City," but as exposure to a different race, class and family which included a husband/father. These perceptions were probably reinforced by the fact that the local agency recruiters saw exposure to cultural differences as a major benefit of the program.

Perhaps because many of the children are quite young when they first go to a Friendly Town host, they are less likely to identify the same reasons as their parents. Nonetheless when asked why they had gone, 53% indicated "to have a good time," 31% "because their mother wanted them to," 30% "to go to the country," 27% "to make new friends," 17% "to do things can't do at home," and 12% "to be on one's own."

For both parents and children, having new experiences was important. Interviews with parents and children indicated that this expectation had been met, including new relationships with other people (22% and 9% respectively), new outdoor and farming skills (20% and 61%), a special visit somewhere (6% and 25%), improving or learning a sport (27% and 67%) and a new confidence or independence (9% and 7%). Thus, it is not surprising that about 95% of both parents and children indicated they felt positively about the visit and 87% wished to return the next summer.

Since the children came expecting to have new experiences, to be more independent, to make new friends, and to have new exposures, and hosts expected the child to expose them to a different lifestyle and provide companionship, a question arises: Did these two expectations mesh? Already noted above is the fact that the children did have a variety of new experiences and formed strong relationships with the host families. The hosts indicated that for their family the best things about having had the child visit were:

The child was enjoyed by family members	72%
The companionship the child provided the family	64%
The mutual education provided by having the child present	50%
The child's having enjoyed himself/herself	31%
The child becoming like part of the family	12%

Similarly on a question about what the host family had gotten out of the visit the responses were:

Exposure to a different lifestyle	52%
Having a good time with the child	34%
Having another family member/children learn to share	13%

The above reasons clearly reflect the degree to which the experience had benefits to the family and the degree to which the hosts' expectations were met.

In fact, in another question, asking whether the visit turned out as they expected, 69% of the hosts indicated it had, and another 25% indicated that it turned out better than they had expected. Only six percent of the host mothers indicated it was worse than they expected. This is remarkably similar to the 96% of the children who indicated they had a positive relationship with the host mothers.

One final note needs to be made about the "fit" between hosts and the Friendly Town child's background. While about 95% of the host families are white, 96% include a father in the household and their median income is slightly over $19,000, the City child's family is radically different. The families from whom the children come are among the more deprived families in New York City. Sixty-six percent of the children come from families in which only the mother is present and in only 23 percent is the child's father part of the household. The average income is $300 or less monthly; many are receiving public assistance and the maximum family income is $9,600 a year. The families tend to be larger than average with 60% having three or more children. Racially, 54% are Black, 22% Hispanic, 12% White, 2% Oriental.

Interestingly these cultural differences appear to be an asset rather than a hindrance in the recruitment of both children and hosts. Many mothers indicated that one reason for sending their children was the opportunity for their child to be exposed to a different culture. For example, one mother said: "seeing a world different from my own is important...at least he knows it's out there" and another said: "I think they should travel and learn how to cope with not only black people." Some children also spontaneously indicated that the cultural differences were a benefit of the Friendly Town Program. Three examples are: "they will learn a different way of life," "I already know all the people on this block and wanted to meet other people," and "because I saw a world different from my own."

As with the children and their parents, hosts saw the exposure to another culture as an important benefit of the program to them. Fifty-two percent of the hosts, as was noted earlier, cited exposure to a different lifestyle as the reward for the child being with the family. Such a cultural exchange does not automatically go well. Local agency people must prepare children for the visit. For example, city children are frightened in the country because they do not know that it is dark and quiet, that there are bugs, and that they may sleep in a room alone. Similarly, the hosts need information on such things as how to care for a young black girl's hair.

Information on general differences in lifestyles is also important. Many a host feels disappointed when a child arrives with new clothes. They think this means the child is not "deprived" and do not understand how important it is to the parents to present their child positively. Another common occurrence is that a child is frightened because he/she has never lived somewhere where the doors are not locked. Not knowing this, a host may misinterpret the child's fright as rejection.

Hosts may also have trouble because they expect too much of the "cultural exchange." Hosts are often troubled that the child does not wish to talk about his/her life in the city until he/she knows the host well, believing that their comments will reflect badly on their own family. The professional has a responsibility to see to it that hosts understand such differences. Early clarification of different expectations helps hosts who are not comfortable with

144

these differences to withdraw. Those who choose to take a child do so because they have a clearer set of expectations of what the visit will be like. This convergence of expectations, in turn, supports productive cross-cultural relationships.

PRACTICE PRINCIPLES

This presentation of the findings of the Friendly Town study suggests a number of practice principles for similar programs utilizing volunteers. These principles are:

1. When a volunteer program requires highly personal involvement between volunteer and recipient, the program's publicity needs to be personalized. It is necessary to provide detailed descriptions of actual volunteers' experience including rewards and expectations on both sides.

2. In cross cultural volunteer programs, while the first exposure is likely to occur via the media, personal follow-up contacts are necessary. When such contacts are with persons who have themselves been volunteers, the applicants sense that there is a support group to whom they can turn in time of difficulty. Sharing between current volunteers (hosts) and applicants helps prepare the volunteer for the cultural shock which is a common experience in such programs.

3. At various phases in the volunteer experience, different motivations appear to predominate. While altruism may be the initial motivator, the decision to volunteer at a later phase is re-evaluated in terms of an exchange model where the volunteer assesses the rewards of the experience against its cost. Enlightened self-interest is clearly one aspect of volunteer relationships. The professional must identify with the volunteers, what they have to gain from the relationship and define the limits of what they are expected to give.

4. The purpose of any volunteer program must be clearly stated. Citing the benefits of the program to the volunteer should not obscure the basic purpose of the program. In clearly stating the purpose, one has the opportunity to show why the volunteer is important to the purpose and has something special to contribute to the effort. It also helps the volunteers see the limits of the task so they can assess whether they can give what is needed.

5. In highly personalized programs, it is extremely important to define clearly what the volunteer can expect from the program (Gallup, 1980). In all volunteer programs which are highly personalized and include culturally diverse groups, it is extremely important that the volunteer receive very clear and detailed statements of expectations, problems, cultural differences and goals of the program, etc. All contribute to more successful coping and gratification on the part of the volunteer. Such specificity can be provided through 1-2 interviews and/or through training sessions.

6. For a volunteer relationship to be sustained, it must have clearly defined parameters, including a specification of the time limits. Within these parameters, volunteers will make a long term decision on what level of rewards they will need to balance out the costs to them of maintaining their volunteer commitment.

CONCLUSION

The Friendly Town Program has been successful because the rewards to the volunteer turn out to be larger than anticipated. The hosts' initial altruism which is reinforced by the benefits the host families receive, leads to the establishment of long term relationships between host and child.

Notes

1. A summary of The Fresh Air Fund Friendly Town evaluation study is available from The Fresh Air Fund, 70 West 40th Street, New York 10018.

REFERENCES

Ellis, J. and K. H. Noyes
   1978   By the People: A History of Americans as Volunteers. Philadelphia: Energize.

Gallup, G.
   1980   "Volunteerism, America's Best Hope for the Future." Voluntary Action Leadership, Fall: 23-28.

Haeuser, A. A. and F. S. Schwartz
   1980   "Developing Social Work Skills for the Future." Social Casework, 61 (December): 595-601.

Lobb, C.
   1979   Exploring Careers Through Volunteerism. New York: Richard Rosen.

Naylor, H. H.
   1967   Volunteers Today. New York: Associated Press.

Routh, T. A.
   1977   The Volunteer and Community Agencies, Springfield. Illinois: Charles C. Thomas

Schafer, R. B.
   1980   "Equity in a Relationship Between Individuals and a Fraternal Organization." Journal of Voluntary Action Research, 8 (July-October): 12-20.

Scheier, I. H.
   1977   People Approach. National Information Center on Volunteerism.

Schindler-Rainman, E. and R. Lippett
   1977   The Volunteer Community. La Jolla, Calif.: University Associates.

Stanton, E.
   1970   Clients Come Last: Volunteers and Voluntary Organizations. Beverly Hills: Sage.

Wolensky, R. P.
   1980   "Toward a Broader Conceptualization of Volunteerism in Disaster." Journal of Voluntary Action Research, 8 (July-October): 43-50.

AN ALTERNATIVE THEORETICAL PERSPECTIVE ON RACE AND VOLUNTARY PARTICIPATION

King E. Davis
Norfolk State University

INTRODUCTION

Several previous studies on the voluntary participation of Black and White Americans have tended to focus on the individual as the primary unit of analysis. This research direction has identified individual motivation and socio-economic characteristics as the independent variables that explain racial differences in rates of voluntary participation (ACTION, 1975). However, the findings resulting from this motivational oriented research have tended to be contradictory over time and have not been reproduced when the studies have been replicated (Olsen, 1970; Orum, 1966; Babchuck, 1962). Several studies conclude that Black participation is considerably less frequent than Whites (Lenski, 1961; Wright, 1969; Campbell, 1960) while other studies have concluded that Blacks are exaggerated volunteers--participating at a rate far in excess of their expected frequency (Myrdal, 1944; Babchuck, 1962). The logic in this former line of reasoning leads one to hypothesize that lower motivation on the part of Blacks contributes to and is the major cause of their lower rates of voluntary participation. Assuming that there is a valid relationship between Black voluntary participation and motivation suggests that efforts to increase Black voluntary participation should be aimed primarily at the individual. Two approaches would seem feasible, given motivation as the key independent variable. For example, voluntary organizations could seek out highly motivated Blacks or simply respond to their requests and provide a vehicle for their self-stimulated participation. On the other hand, a much more difficult and costly process would require voluntary organizations to design special recruitment techniques to seek out poorly motivated Blacks and institute programs to increase their dormant motivation for voluntary activity (National Center, 1975). Obviously, there are a multiplicity of unknown factors at the base of these two approaches which reflect the paucity of the theoretical frameworks that undergrid the respective approaches.

The second major factor that is proposed in the literature as an explanation
for voluntary activity is socio-economic status (Drake, 1945; Rose, 1964;
ACTION, 1975). Governmental studies have indicated that higher income, education and social status are correlated with higher rates of voluntary participation (ACTION, 1975). Since a significant proportion of the Black population
has low median income, education, as well as status, one could predict and
expect infrequent voluntary participation. If this assumed relationship between socio-economic status and voluntary activity is valid, programs designed
to increase the rate of Black participation could achieve success when there was
a significant increase in the overall socio-economic status of the Black population (Orum, 1968; Olsen, 1970; Babchuck, 1962; ACTION, 1975) or, such programs
could identify and attract the small number of Blacks whose income and education
are approximate to those of the "average" volunteer (ACTION, 1975).

PROBLEM STATEMENT AND PURPOSE

Current social science literature does not explain the multiple contradictions
relative to the frequency of Black voluntary participation. As a result, our
collective understanding of how and why Black voluntary participation differs
from that of Whites is insufficient. The major conceptual frameworks, utilizing
individual characteristics as the independent variable, have not provided a
substantive basis for developing, implementing or evaluating approaches designed to increase Black voluntary participation.

The one conclusive finding from the literature appears to be that communities
are enhanced by broadscale voluntary participation (Stenzel & Feeney, 1976).
Therefore, increased voluntary participation by Black populations might be
instrumental in bringing about changes in policies, programs, services and
conditions that affect Black people. The problem for consideration in this
descriptive essay is to determine the extent to which, if any, organizational
variables are related to the frequency of voluntary participation by Blacks.

The purpose is to identify, describe and discuss alternative independent
variables that help explain the frequency and typology of Black voluntary participation. In addition, an effort is made to utilize these variables in a
conceptual framework of Black voluntary participation that clarifies their
interrelationships and thus reduces the polemical conflicts that have characterized the field for some time. Finally, the purpose here is to provide a
framework for approaches and efforts by social workers that are designed to
increase Black voluntary participation.

CONCEPTUAL FRAMEWORK

A partial explanation of the observed frequency of Black voluntary participation
may be obtained by utilizing a conceptual framework in which the unit of
analysis (independent variable) is organizational as opposed to the individual
(motivation), covered in several previous studies. What is hypothesized here
is that organizational characteristics or typology tend to be the major influence on the rate of Black voluntary participation in mediated organizations.
Furthermore, by not recognizing the significant role of these characteristics
and typologies, researchers have heretofore tended to erroneously attribute the
cause of low Black rates of participation to lower motivation.

The failure to recognize the decisive role that organizational typology plays in influencing actual rates of voluntary participation permits one to assume that racial differences in the frequency of voluntary activity are consistent across organizations, whereas it is hypothesized in this paper that racial differences in participation are significant only when specific organizational types and characteristics are studied. It is proposed that voluntary organizations, in which there is a significant racial difference in the frequency of participation, are recognizable and the processes that precipitate the less than expected frequency of Black participation are identifiable and therefore susceptible to change (see Chart 1).

DEFINITION OF TERMS

The major concepts in the theoretical framework proposed are heterogeneity, homogeneity, formal voluntary system and informal voluntary (helping) network. Definitions of these terms should prove useful in evaluating the theory:

Homogeneity: a term that refers to a characteristic of a voluntary organization in which the membership is drawn, appointed or accepted from only one group. Homogeneity could be based on such characteristics as race, religion, sex, age, education or income. While the process of selection of voluntary group members may be based on one of these variables, such a practice may not be reflected in organizational policies. The exclusionary practices may be maintained simply by precedent, appointive process, group will, prerequisites or community perception. The end result is that outgroup members are excluded, do not apply or are rejected if an application is made. Individual motivation is seen as of lesser significance when and where homogeneity exists--since these organizations are not seen as responsive to the most exaggerated levels of motivation. Homogeneity is not an apriori condition of permanency. It is believed that voluntary associations can and do shift their structural characteristics over time based on changes in group standards, legal suits that challenge the organization or economic forces that make such change profitable (Turner, et al. v. Fouche, et al., U. S. Supreme Court, 1970).

Heterogeneity: refers to a condition or characteristic of a voluntary association in which the membership is drawn, accepted or attracted from multiple groups. To some extent, diverse groups are publicly recruited, included in all levels of the organization and receive rewards that reinforce their participation and stimulates the participation of others with similar characteristics. Heterogeneous voluntary organizations, too, may shift from full heterogeneity (equal representation of the various groups involved) to partial heterogeneity (where one group holds a slight but significant numerical or authoritative advantage over another). Where partial heterogeneity exists and the process of majority rule prevails, specific interest groups have a tendency to control the activities of the organization and may tend to insure that its activities meet their needs as opposed to the needs of outgroup members or the community at large. The realization of such activity may tend to reduce the motivation of outgroup members and could eventuate in their withdrawal from participation, severely reducing the level of heterogeneity and balance of power. While heterogeneous organizations can, and actually do, shift or change their identifiable character over time, they tend to be relatively stable, constant and semi-permanent.

Formal Voluntary Systems: these are community organizations that have a systematic process for recruiting, utilizing, rewarding and maintaining

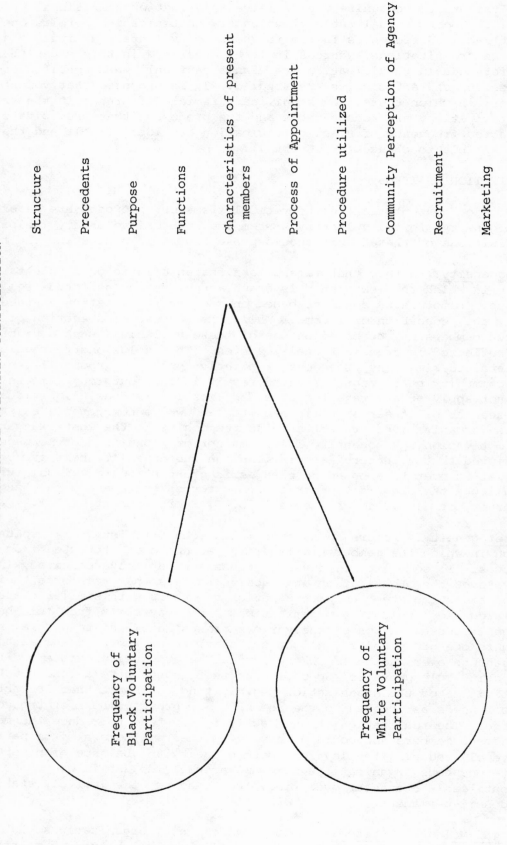

Chart 1

ORGANIZATIONAL VARIABLES THAT ARE BELIEVED
TO INFLUENCE VOLUNTARY PARTICIPATION

Structure

Precedents

Purpose

Functions

Characteristics of present
members

Process of Appointment

Procedure utilized

Community Perception of Agency

Recruitment

Marketing

Frequency of
Black Voluntary
Participation

Frequency of
White Voluntary
Participation

volunteers. They have policies, procedures and staff and tend to act as mediators (Tilden, 1977) or liaisons between persons of one socio-economic status (volunteers) and those in another who are recipients of some kind of agency service. Many community organizations are believed to have a preference for the formal voluntary systems in which there are historical differences in status and power between the volunteers and clientele. This preference is believed to be communicated publicly and acts as a deterrent to potential low income volunteers. Formal voluntary systems often tend to reflect the needs, perceptions, characteristics and race of higher income individuals and thus tend to decrease the probability of significant involvement by lower income or Black volunteers. Voluntary participation in formal systems tends to be non-spontaneous, mediated by organizations rather than individually arranged, reflects differences in socio-economic status between the volunteer and the recipient and is often motivated by a quest for control. Formal voluntary service rarely involves the transfer of funds in the form of salary, although indirect monetary benefits may accrue to the volunteer through tax advantages, and certain job advances may be dependent upon or enhanced by such activity.

Informal Volunteer (Helping) Networks: these are voluntary activities that usually take place without agency linkages or mediation between a receiver and a volunteer. This form of voluntary activity is arranged by individuals, families or by neighborhood or friendship ties. The participants usually are from the same or similar socio-economic class and the motivation for helping appears to be friendship, respect or communal values. Volunteers generally receive praise, thanks and small amounts of remuneration that reinforce helping behavior. Informal systems often carry with them the expectation (overt and covert) of reciprocity. In many instances, these voluntary services take place at the neighborhood level as opposed to more formal voluntary systems in which the services are mediated through a variety of agency structures (McClure, 1971). Because of the level at which such volunteer activities take place, the absence of formal agency ties and the absence of prestige, this type of activity is often not counted as volunteer although it may constitute the major type of volunteer activity in low income communities (McClure, 1971).

Discussion and Application: an interpretative analysis of current voluntary literature suggests the presence of two major types (and four sub-types) of voluntary organizations:

Type 1 -- Homogeneous (informal and formal);
Type 2 -- Heterogeneous (partial and full)

There does not appear to be an informal heterogeneous model. It may be that the nature or process of multi-interest, multi-racial or multi-sexual organizations in this society occurs only under formal or mediated auspices--perhaps owing to the historical differences in status between various groups. It also seems plausible that voluntary organizations of an informal heterogeneous nature may change rapidly from the informal in order to sustain the organization. While it is agreed theoretically that informal heterogeneous types are possible, more field research is necessary to add another dimension to the evolving theory.

Type I--organizations are racially homogeneous and consist of four distinctive sub-categories, that are also constituted along racial and formal/informal lines.

Sub-type (A) is comprised of those voluntary organizations that exclude, reject or do not reinforce the participation of non-Blacks. Sub-type (A) organizations

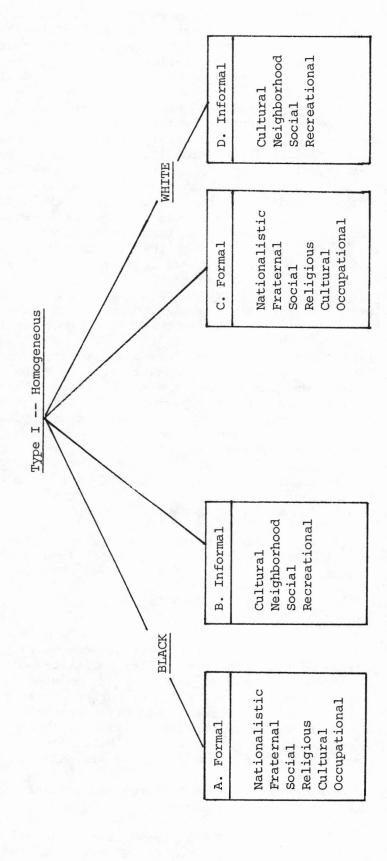

Chart 2

HOMOGENEOUS VOLUNTARY ORGANIZATIONS
BY STRUCTURE AND RACE

Type I -- Homogeneous

BLACK

A. Formal

Nationalistic
Fraternal
Social
Religious
Cultural
Occupational

B. Informal

Cultural
Neighborhood
Social
Recreational

WHITE

C. Formal

Nationalistic
Fraternal
Social
Religious
Cultural
Occupational

D. Informal

Cultural
Neighborhood
Social
Recreational

are characterized also by a formalized structure for volunteer activities. Sub-tupe (B) organizations àre differentiated from sub-type (A) by their informal structure, while racial closure remains an important part of the structure. Sub-type (C) organizations are those in which Blacks and other non-Whites are excluded, rejected or that do not reinforce the voluntary participation of Blacks. These organizations, too, seek closure for their members and bar admission to non-group members. Sub-type (D) is similar to sub-type (B) in that it is organized primarily along informal lines. On the other hand, sub-type (C), which also rejects Black membership or participants, is organized along more formal lines in which racial closure may be less overt.

In each of the four sub-types of homogeneous voluntary organizations, race is the predominant factor that determines whether one is acceptable or accepted as a volunteer in a particular organization. Actual discussion of race or racial prerequisites may take place only when the homogeneous character of Type I organizations is challenged through legal suits or conflict (Turner, et al. v. Fouche, et al., 1970, Educational Equality League, et al. v. Tate, et al., 1971). These organizations often do not view themselves as reflecting or utilizing racial designations as prerequisites for organizational membership. However, excluded participants are frequently sensitive to racial barriers and utilize various measures to challenge the organizations (U. S. District Court, 1980). Even when challenged by law or conflict, Type I organizations (particularly the formal) may not publicly disclose or discuss the significance the organization attaches to race as an entry variable. Previously, racial closure was more publicized overtly; however, heterogeneous civil rights organizations and legal suits have diminished the overt display of racial closure in public accommodations (Turner, et al. v. Fouche, 1970). Challenges to homogeneous organizations from highly motivated members of outside racial groups tends to coalesce the groups and solidifies their quest for closure. In some instances, identifiable Black homogeneous voluntary organizations (SCLC, CORE, SNCC, Black Panthers, Muslims) have been identified by the power structure as threats and have been subjected to governmental investigation and action that may have resulted in disruption of their formal structures. The informal structures, however, may continue intact at the neighborhood level where its activities are covert and beyond statistical quantification. White organizations, too, that have been identified as threats (Ku Klux Klan) are subject also to encounter governmental "concern" about their activities and be forced eventually to disband publicly and redevelop their activities on a less formal level.

Within Type II--voluntary organizations there are three distinct sub-types (A, B, and C). Sub-type (A) is the most racially heterogeneous of all the sub-types. It is characterized by a high degree of quantitative racial balance. In sub-type (A), Whites and Blacks participate with near equal frequency, with leadership positions spread throughout the membership, based primarily on ability or support, as opposed to race, sex, religion or nationality. One is reminded of some of the civil rights organizations that existed in the 1960's as approximate examples of this type. Social welfare organizations, social change movements, legel organizations and some union groups are approximations of this type. In reality, few pure sub-type (A) organizations are believed to exist over time. The life span of sub-type (A) groups seems limited and influenced greatly by changing societal patterns in the distribution of economic benefits, power and political advantage. Sub-type (B) organizations may be viewed publicly as more closely aligned with Black causes. These organizations may be the remnants of previous homogeneous groups, that have attracted a larger number

153

Chart 3

HETEROGENEOUS VOLUNTARY ORGANIZATIONS
BY RACIAL DOMINATION

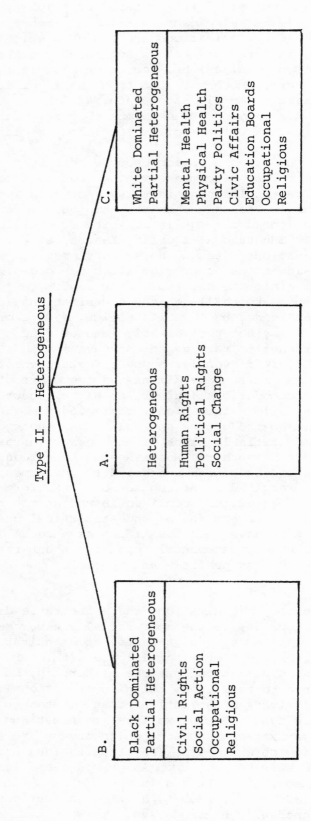

Type II -- Heterogeneous

A.

Heterogeneous

Human Rights
Political Rights
Social Change

B.

Black Dominated
Partial Heterogeneous

Civil Rights
Social Action
Occupational
Religious

C.

White Dominated
Partial Heterogeneous

Mental Health
Physical Health
Party Politics
Civic Affairs
Education Boards
Occupational
Religious

154

of White participants. Some civil rights groups that were previously fully heterogeneous may be falling into sub-type (B) (partial) organizations as their White participation rate has diminished drastically over the past ten years.

Sub-type (C) are those voluntary organizations which have lower rates of participation by Blacks. Such organizations as those in sub-type (C) may be those that have traditionally been viewed as racially homogeneous by policy and precedent, or they may be organizations that were previously homogeneous. Type (C) organizations could result as Blacks who previously held membership withdraw to homogeneous organizations. It is interesting to note here that numerous Black professionals withdrew from active participation in formal heterogeneous professional organizations in the late 1960's (social work, psychology, accountancy) and formulated a plethora of informal and formal homogeneous organizations in which racial closure was practiced and in which programs, policies, bylaws and governance structures reflected Black monopolization. This shift from active participation in heterogeneous professional organizations represented a significant alteration in a long term trend of Black participation in heterogeneous voluntary organizations towards more self-help homogeneous organizations. In some professional organizations, the withdrawal of Black membership left the organizations with a different organizational typology. Some groups like the AMA, that have minimal Black participation, have not been historically receptive to Black participation, thus leading to the development of the NMA, a Black voluntary organization of physicians (a homogeneous grouping). The Republican party is another example of sub-type (C) organizations with minimal current participation of Black Americans. While not totally a racially homogeneous organization, the participation of Black Americans is currently so minimal that the Republican party is on the fringe of the partial heterogeneous group. However, the recognition of this typological position by the party and its subsequent efforts to attract Blacks into the party may alter its typology over time. Some religious, health, mental health, civic and social welfare organizations also fall into the sub-type (C) category. While these organizations may profess racial heterogeneity, their organizational posture, policies and interracial variables may perpetuate only partial heterogeneity. Those Blacks who participate in these organizations typically have higher than average motivation and income and must withstand considerable pressure from within and from outside to maintain their participation status. The structure of these organizations, their meeting times, format, task selection, objectives and fiscal policies may tend to maintain relatively insignificant rates of Black voluntary participation. Because of the absence of meaningful Black participation and the absence of social consciousness that would insure the meeting of Black needs, Black Americans need to participate more frequently in sub-type (C) organizations. Few Blacks, high socio-economic status notwithstanding, will be willing to withstand the institutionalized barriers to gain participation in sub-type (C) organizations even though Black participation may be required by laws governing the organization (U. S. Senate, 1980).

Some previous studies of Black participation rates have compared Black and White participation rates within sub-type (C) organizations without a clear conceptualization of these organizational typologies which basically render them totally different organizations. Such studies will have a very high probability of producing extreme differences in participation rates owing to the presence of racial typology within the organizations, while the researchers basically assumed organizational similarity. On the other hand, studies of sub-type (B)

organizations would have an equally high probability of finding lower participation rates by Whites. Few studies, however, have been carried out on sub-
type (B) organizations, except as the organizations are seen as threats to
governmental security (Lincoln, 1973; Marine, 1969; Anthony, 1970; Bell, 1968).

Failure to control for organizational typology has resulted in efforts at
comparison of non-comparable variables that predictably yield consistently
lower rates for Black voluntary participation and excessive rates for Whites.
If a mixture of organizational types are compared or contrasted, one will find
extreme variation in the rates of Black participation.

As one moves from the racially homogeneous voluntary organizations, three
factors are noted: 1) the degree of racial exclusivity is by definition decreased; however, 2) the frequency of participation overall declines; and
3) the characteristics of the volunteers (sex, income and education) differ
from those found in racially homogeneous groups. Racially homogeneous groups
are believed to have a wider variety of income and other socio-economic
characteristics among members.

IMPLICATIONS: VOLUNTARY PARTICIPATION, COMMUNITY CONTROL AND SOCIAL POLICY

The conceptual framework proposed here, as an explanation of the observed low
frequency of Black voluntary participation, suggests that voluntary organizations are related significantly to the distribution of community power,
resources, decisions as well as to the formulation of social policies. Thus
the lowered participation (whether via organizational or individual factors)
of Black populations in these organizations has a very high probability of
perpetuating the historical maldistribution and concentration of power.
Obviously, change in the mal-distribution of power, resources and decisions is
a complex process but does appear to require change in the typological character of the voluntary sector that, as proposed here, has successfully delimited
Black participation to their own homogeneous and heterogeneous organizations.
However, one must not assume that the voluntary sector (Black or White) exudes a
readiness for change in its typology or functions. Let us examine two issues
that are related to the historical character of voluntary organizations and to
the factors that will hopefully bring about change: (1) monopolization of
voluntary leadership by heterogeneous organizations and (2) steps for precipi-
tating readiness for change.

(1) In general, early volunteer leaders were appointed or selected by
members of their own upper income classes whose wealth and income were generated
primarily from private business (Austin, 1970). Lower income populations have
been excluded historically from positions of leadership in community-wide
voluntary organizations (Austin, 1970) and subsequently were forced to develop
alternative voluntary structures which had an insubstantial relationship to the
formulation or modification of social policy. Low income groups appear to have
developed alternative voluntary organizations that were engaged primarily in
expressive functions as opposed to economic or political functions (Rose, 1964).
As a result, low income voluntary participation was less effective in securing
or guaranteeing rights or access.

The circular pattern of the American voluntary structure permitted higher socio-
economic classes to become the primary formulators of social policies for
numerous health, welfare, educational and social service agencies in the

Chart 4

VOLUNTARY PARTICIPATION BY RACE AND ORGANIZATIONAL TYPOLOGY

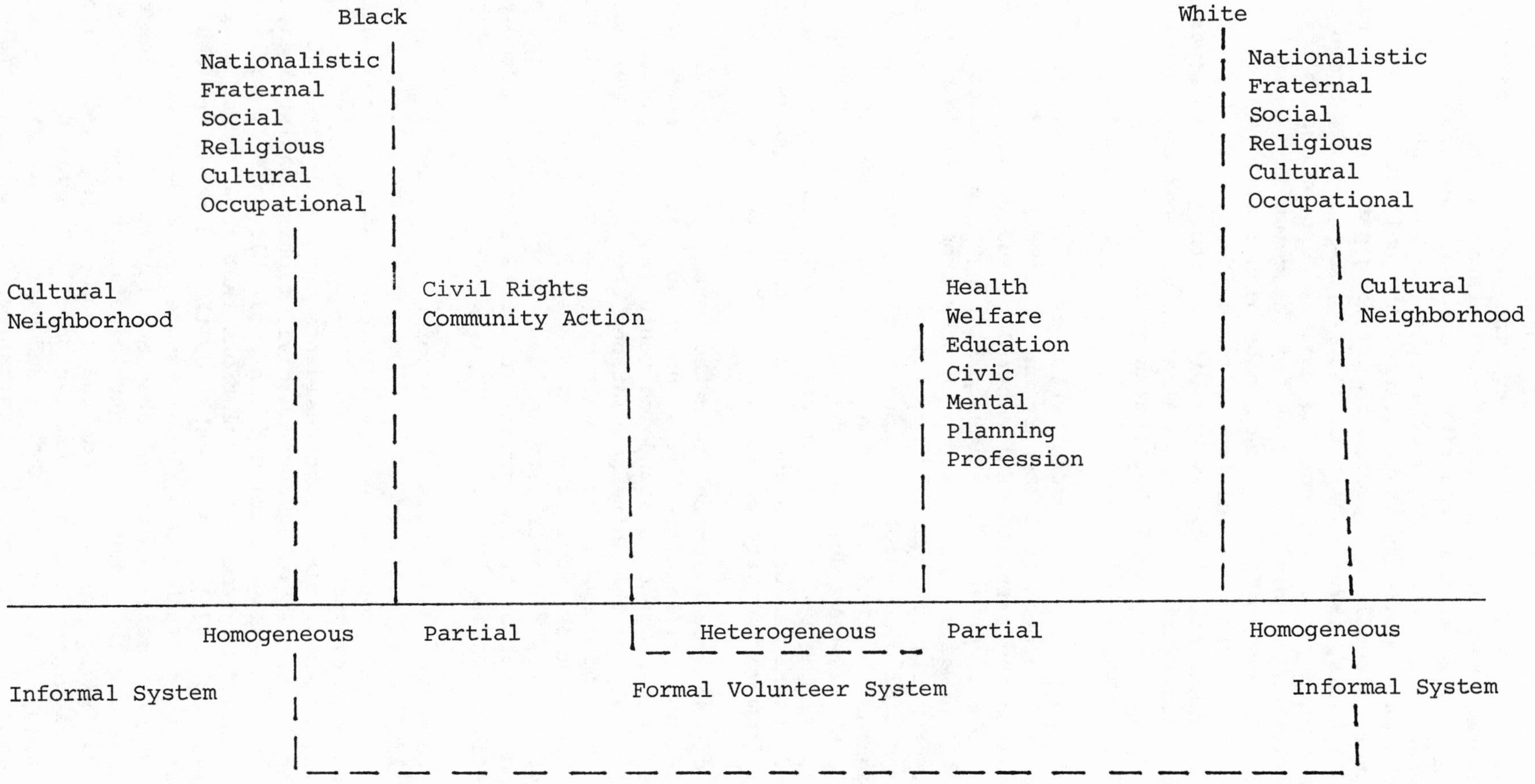

charitable as well as the public sector. The new markets for these agency services, however, had racial, economic and ethnic characteristics that were antithetical to those of the traditional volunteer leadership cadre. Business-men, professionals and their wives dominated early voluntary activity and formulated the major policies that governed the collection and distribution of community funds, direction of programs, staffing patterns and administration (Austin, 1970; Davis, 1976). As a result of this control, human services in many major American cities reflect the values, perceptions, priorities, needs and characteristics of only one segment of the community (Austin, 1970; Davis, 1976). Because of the domination by higher socio-economic classes of the three processes that are related to community closure (Neuwirth, 1969), volunteer leadership became synonymous with wealth. The idea was propagated also that voluntary participation required or was somehow enhanced by the specialized skills and values that characterized private proprietary business (Austin, 1970; Davis, 1976).

As the racial and economic characteristics of urban areas underwent significant changes from 1940 through 1970 (Department of Commerce, 1974), higher income groups maintained their traditional control of the voluntary sector (Austin, 1970; Davis, 1976). One of the ubiquitous changes in America in the period from 1940 to 1970 was the migration of Blacks from rural counties into major urban areas, primarily in search of positions in the labor force and some respite from racial oppression (Department of Commerce, 1974). Coupled with this interregional migration has been an enigmatic trend in which higher and middle income Whites have deserted the center city for contiguous areas in subur-ban counties. As the racial characteristics of populations in urban areas have been reversed, there has been a concomitant demand for human services (public and private) from varied income segments of the Black community.

As a result of the population shifts noted here, some agencies altered their service programs to reflect the needs and priorities of these new market seg-ments, whereas other agencies abandoned their inner city offices and relocated in closer proximity to the White populations they formerly served. While the potential markets of many of these inner city agencies changed, the control of programs, policy, funds, administration and staffing remained virtually un-changed (Davis, 1976). Former city residents continued to exert a monopoly or authority and control of human services networks that now served predominantly Black populations (Davis, 1976).

Some of the tumultuous upheavals that occurred in a number of major urban cen-ters in the 1960's are believed to have been precipitated, in part, by a demand for greater community control and involvement in the decision making apparatus by Black residents of the city (Millett, 1977; Ransford, 1967). Similar to immigrants before them, Black city residents and their alternative voluntary organizations (primarily religious and civil rights) insisted that their constituents were legally entitled to an equitable role in decisions about funding, services, programs and regulations that impacted on their lives and communities (Davis, 1975). As a result of these demands and the rise of violent voluntary action by Black youth, local, state and Federal governments (as well as some private foundations) established and funded new policies and programs aimed at increasing the non-violent participation of the Black poor (Austin, 1970; Millett, 1977). Community control became an issue, a goal and a strategy for changing the former complexion of voluntary urban organizations. This new strategy, however, had to contend with an inveterate pattern of con-trol and domination of voluntary organizations by higher income groups with significant linkages in government and business.

Since the 1960's community control and the variety of voluntary agencies that were spawned have not appreciably increased the frequency of Black participation in key social policy decisions at the local level. Many of the voluntary organizations that were ostensibly designed to be vehicles for Black participation in policy formulation have been dismantled as the funding and legislation which supported them have expired (Millett, 1977).

(2) There seems to be no doubt that participation in voluntary organizations is a significant process for influencing the policy decisions of health, welfare, educational as well as other human service organizations (public and private). The activities of voluntary organizations in many American communities parallel and reinforce the activities of elected officials, who have delegated specific authority and responsibility to the voluntary sector. Participation can be the decisive means for insuring that the goals, resources, services and practices of human service agencies are consistent with and representative of the varied segments of the community. Social Workers are aware, however, that voluntary participation is not spread equitably across all segments of the community. Studies by ACTION have documented that the most frequent volunteers are Whites (females) and the most infrequent volunteers are Blacks. While these and other studies have documented the lower than expected frequency of voluntary participation within the Black populations, the theoretical frameworks for increasing our understanding of this phenomena have focused almost entirely on motivation as the key independent variable. As a result, social workers and volunteer organizations interested in increasing greater equity in the voluntary sector have directed their programs towards increasing motivation, while ignoring the more vital role of organizational variables and characteristics. Such efforts have not resulted in a profluence of Black volunteers. In fact, aspects of the voluntary sector remains as trifurcated by race, sex and income in 1981 as in 1968, when ACTION conducted its initial National surveys.

To alter the historical pattern of homogeneous volunteer organizations seems to require a combination of a number of interrelated steps:

a) First, research needs to be conducted on voluntary organizations at the local level to determine the racial composition of their membership, the equity of procedures and processes that are utilized to acquire or appoint members, the activities members engage in (the skills required) and the system of reinforcement used to reward participation. Studies of the voluntary sector have been conducted successfully by a number of researchers and have been used as the basis of petitions for change. An analysis of the characteristics of the voluntary sector and the processes for appointment can also be critical in defining issues. For example, in the historic Brown vs. the Board of Education case, the primary issue that was debated was the equity of educational opportunities and facilities for Black children. An equally important issue that was not given sufficient emphasis was the homogeneous composition of the volunteer school board and the procedures that denied Black citizens their right to participate in school decisions.

b) A second factor for stimulating change is public exposure of the racial characteristics of voluntary organizations, the processes that permit the continuation of homogeneity and the significant relationship between voluntary organizations and the distribution of community power. Efforts need to be made to insure that local groups recognize the important roles played by voluntary organizations and the organizational factors and climate that delimit or discourage equitable cross-racial participation.

c) Pressure, protest and negotiation have been the most successful strategies utilized by Black groups that were seeking change in predominantly White social institutions. Black organizations have not utilized protestive strategies to exact change within the voluntary sector to the extent such strategies were used to bring about an increase in public accommodations.

d) Legal challenges have proven to be a successful mechanism for altering the composition of and access to minorities to a variety of voluntary organizations. Resort to legal means has also been useful in altering the various practices and procedures that maintain the extant characteristics of such organizations (Turner, et al. v. Fouche, 1970; Educational Equality League, 1971; U. S. District Court, 1980).

e) Finally, a variety of public laws (Public Law 94-63), have been shown to have brought about a greater balance in the composition of voluntary boards associated with community mental health centers funded by Federal dollars. Such laws, while not requiring specific numerical representation, do require centers to have governing boards whose characteristics are roughly approximate to or "representative" of the population in the service area of the center. Studies of the composition of these boards have shown that they are representative of the population, and that Blacks have played significant roles. One aspect of these public laws that may be related to their success is the linkage of compliance with the continuation of financial support and Federal sanction.

CONCLUSION

Historically, participation in voluntary organizations has been one of three mutually reciprocal processes for insuring that individual, group and community needs are met. Voluntary participation has been utilized by individuals and groups to increase the probability that their communities and their special interests were represented and protected (Austin, 1970). Two other reciprocal processes for obtaining similar assurances include representative input into policy formulation of government and control of significant resources and decision-making within the private business sector of the economy. For groups with delimited access to socio-economic resources and political representation, voluntary participation can be the decisive reciprocal process for involvement in the prevailing system and a mechanism for exacting a measure of equity or redistribution of rights and privileges (Yearwood, 1977).

Groups and communities that lack equitable apportion in all three processes cited here are much more likely to be characterized by unmet needs and a deficiency of power to alter their circumstances. Hence, the historical and current dilemma of Black populations in America: needs and problems exceed resources and power.

Since unmet needs and insufficient resources tend (up to a point) to act as powerful stimuli for individual and group behavior (aimed at social change), one would expect and predict that participation in voluntary organizations and social movements would be more frequent among such groups and infrequent among groups whose primary and secondary needs are met. On the surface, the relatively consistent finding that low income Black populations participate in instrumental organizations far less frequently than higher income Whites, is illogical and inconsistent. One could, without critical thought, conclude that Blacks are less motivated than Whites. However, more substantive theorizing begins to provide the rudiments of an explanation that reduces the apparent inconsistency.

The finding that Blacks are infrequent participants in instrumental organizations raises more significant questions about the functions, typology and procedures of these organizations than about the motivations of Blacks for voluntary activity. It seems apparent that one major function of instrumental organizations, as found in most American communities, is the maintenance of the established distribution of power, resources and decision-making that characterize the community. Thus groups who profit from the current distribution pattern are more likely to dominate such organizations and establish procedures to lower the probability of rapid or structural social change. Organizational typology, procedures, appointive requirements, as well as activities are designed to insure that new members assist in its social maintenance functions.

One can conclude from this perspective that the typology and major functions of many instrumental organizations that operate in local communities are incongruous with the needs of the majority of the Black population. Black populations and communities need major alterations in the distribution of resources, opportunities, power and decision making. Black populations, too, require organizations that will not only petition for social change but for equity and justice. As a result, there appears to be a substantive conflict in the purpose for participation in and expectations of voluntary organizations between Blacks and Whites. Such conflict may find expression in the expanded development of extreme homogeneous organizations, a return to more conservative policies, a distortion of the extent of social change or an increase in the effort to promote change as well as an increase in the resistance to change.

The major point that needs to be underscored here is that organizational variables are significantly related to the frequency of Black voluntary participation. In addition, it should be clear that these organizational variables are more significant than individual or group motivation or socio-economic characteristics. To increase Black participation in voluntary organizations that make critical social policy decisions, one must find ways to bring about change in these organizational variables: functions, typology, procedures and activities. Without change here voluntary organizations will continue to reflect the typological character cited in this essay.

Organizational functions and typology tend to be relatively enduring characteristics and thus increase the resistance of organizations to change. Since these characteristics add stability to an organization, there is likely to be opposition to change and in some instances an inability to change. Thus one should not anticipate that voluntary organizations will respond readily to efforts to alter their homogeneous or heterogeneous character or their social change or maintenance functions. To bring about change in these organizations requires a complex mixture of strategies, incentives, resources, legal challenge, protest and negotiations.

REFERENCES

ACTION
  1975   Americans Volunteer, Washington, D.C.: U. S. Government Printing
          Office (February).

Anthony, Earl
  1970   Picking Up the Gun: A Report on the Black Panthers. New York:
          Dial Press.

Austin, David M.
  1970   "The Black Civic Volunteer: A New Era in Voluntarism." Harriett
          Goldstein Series, Issue #5, The Volunteer in America. Waltham:
          Brandeis University.

Babchuck, Nicholas and Gordan Wayne
  1962   The Voluntary Association in the Slum. Lincoln: University of
          Nebraska Studies New Series #27.

Bell, Inge
  1968   Core and the Strategy of Non-Violence. New York: Basic Books.

Campbell, Angus
  1960   The American Voter. New York: John Wiley.

Davis, King E.
  1975   The United Way of Atlanta: A Sixteen Year Review. Washington, D.C.:
          The Youth Foundation.

Department of Commerce
  1974   The Social and Economic Status of the Black Population. Washington,
          D.C.: U. S. Government Printing Office.

Drake, St. Clair and Horace Clayton
  1945   Black Metropolis. New York: Harper.

Educational Equality League
  1971   Educational Equality League et al. v. Tate et al., U. S. District
          Court, E. D. Pa. Judge Broderick, No. 71-1938, Nov. 8, 1971, 333,
          f. Sapp. 1202.

Lenski, Gerhard
  1961   The Religious Factor: A Sociological Inquiry. New York: Doubleday
          and Company.

Lincoln, C. Eric
  1973   The Black Muslims in America. Boston: Beacon Press.

Marine, Gene
  1969   The Black Panthers. New York: Signet.

McClure, Jessie
  1971   "Participation in Voluntary Organizations: A Study of Biracial
          Voluntary Associations." (Unpublished) Boston: Brandeis
          University.

Millett, Ricardo
    1977   Examination of Widespread Citizen Participation in the Model Cities
            Program and the Demands of Ethnic Minorities for a Greater Decision-
            Making Role in American Cities. Pablo Alto: R. & E. Research
            Association.

Myrdal, Gunnar
    1944   On American Dilemma. New York: Harper.

National Center for Voluntary Action
    1975   Recruiting Low Income Volunteers. Washington, D.C.: NCVA.

Neuwirth, Gertrude
    1969   "A Weberian Outline of a Theory of Community: Its Application to the
            Dark Ghetto." British Journal of Sociology.

Olsen, Marvin
    1970   "Social and Political Participation of Blacks." American Sociological
            Review. 35 (August).

Orum, A. M.
    1966   "A Reappraisal of the Social and Political Participation of Negroes."
            American Journal of Sociology. 72 (July).

Ransford, H. E.
    1967   "Isolation, Powerlessness and Violence: A Study of Attitudes and
            Participation in the Watts Riot." American Journal of Sociology.
            75 (March): 581-91.

Rose, Arnold
    1964   The Negro in America. New York: Harper.

Stenzel, Anne R. and Helen M. Feeney
    1976   Volunteer Training and Development. New York: Seabury Press.

Tildon, C. G. and J. C. Thompson
    1977   "Forms and Formalization of Volunteerism: An Historical Perspective."
            (Unpublished Paper), Blacksburg: VPI, April 27, 1977.

Turner, et al.
    1970   Turner et al. v. Fouche, et al., U. S. Supreme Court Justice Stewart,
            No. 23, January 19, 1970, 90 Supreme Court 532.

U. S. District Court
    1980   National Black United Fund, Inc. v. Alan Campbell and United Way of
            America, Civil Action, No. 76-1431, U. S. District Court, July 1,
            1980, Barrington Parker Presiding.

U. S. Senate
    1980   Public Law 96-398. Mental Health Systems Act.

Wright, R.
    1908   Philadelphia Colored Directory. Philadelphia: Nostrand.

Yearwood, Lennox
    1977   "National Black Organizations in American Urban Communities." (Un-
            published Dissertation), Buffalo State University.

VOLUNTEER TRAINING FOR NON-BUREAUCRATIC AGENCIES: UTILIZING SOCIAL WORK ROLES TO INCREASE VOLUNTEER SKILLS

Patricia S. Potter-Efron
Buffalo Memorial Adolescent Treatment Center
Mondovi, Wisconsin

Ronald T. Potter-Efron
University of Wisconsin-Eau Claire, Wisconsin

THE VOLUNTEER AS A MEMBER OF THE TREATMENT TEAM

Volunteers are frequently sought by human service agencies to meet the needs created by chronic understaffing and funding problems. As an example, fifteen volunteers working six hours a week for six months will contribute 2340 hours to an agency. However, developing an effective program that allows for coordination of volunteer duties and staff responsibilities may be difficult to achieve. Shortages of staff time, lack of clear direction, and bureaucratic limitations all can produce a situation in which volunteers are not efficiently utilized as a part of the treatment approach of the organization, although several studies have demonstrated that quality volunteer training is the key to solving the problem of how to make volunteers part of the treatment team. Such training must be geared to the exact nature of the service organization and to the background of persons recruited as volunteers. When done appropriately this training greatly increases the skills of volunteers and thus their value to the organization.

The training program presented here has been designed to be used in relatively informal, non-bureaucratic agencies such as many shelters for domestic abuse, homes for runaways, ex-offender centers, and halfway houses. These agencies have particular characteristics and needs, as will be explained; and they offer the volunteer an excellent opportunity for maximum positive involvement because of their relative lack of formal barriers to participation.

THE NATURE OF INFORMAL, NON-BUREAUCRATIC AGENCIES

Western society has become increasingly rationalized and bureaucratized since the Industrial Revolution. Nowhere is this trend more evident than in the area of social services, in which individual charity and family responsibility for the unfortunate have gradually been superceded by formal governmental agencies such as Departments of Human Services and large institutions for developmentally disabled and emotionally disturbed persons.

Etzioni (1964: 53-54) clearly summarizes the characteristics of formal organizations: these agencies are based on the principle of rationality; continuity depends on the existence of rules that result in all persons being treated similarly; each worker has a specific sphere of competence; the organization is structured vertically, in a clear hierarchy of authority and control; specialized training is necessary to learn the technical codes and rules of conduct of the organization; writing is the method by which information is transmitted; and the organization is composed of individuals in standardized official positions.

Not all helping organizations, however, have become formalized. Some shelter homes for battered spouses, ex-offender centers, telephone crisis lines, alcohol treatment facilities, adolescent runaway centers, and other groups adhere to a fundamentally different, more informal structure. The basic characteristics of these agencies are: 1) relatively small size - these organizations often employ fewer than ten individuals so that more daily communication is face to face; 2) non-mainstream target groups - they tend to serve relatively socially "invisible" clients, such as battered women, for whom the society has neither devoted sufficient resources nor created bureaucratic "professional" services; 3) minimal division of labor - workers in these groups tend not to have clear, specialized roles. For example, there may be a stated belief that "whatever needs to be done around here should be done by whoever is available to do it"; 4) minimal hierarchy - there are few levels of status and power. Staff members are considered equals and the agency director is normally visible and available to the staff; 5) informality - workers in these organizations rely upon word of mouth instead of memos, often dress more casually than do workers in more formal agencies, and address each other and clients in relaxed, informal style; 6) recruitment from personal experience - staff is often drawn in part from the target group itself. For example, many alcohol and drug centers tend to employ only those who are recovering alcoholics and/or active members of Alcoholics Anonymous or Alanon; 7) "family" beliefs about role performance - members of the group "belong" to the organization not only because of their official duties but with their entire personality. Loyalty to the organization is intense and personalized and the whole organization is designed and run as much like a family as possible. Frequently such agencies are located in converted houses instead of office buildings.

Helping agencies actually exist on a continuum from most to least bureaucratized.[1] The primary focus of this report is on the utilization and training of volunteers in relatively informal, non-bureaucratic agencies.

IMPLICATIONS FOR USE OF VOLUNTEERS AT INFORMAL AGENCIES

At informal agencies there are both advantages and disadvantages for the volunteer who wishes to become deeply involved in challenging and socially valuable tasks.

Advantages

Probably the single most positive aspect for a volunteer in an informal agency is the opportunity for maximum involvement available in such organizations. Because there are few formal barriers to participation, such as official performances that can only be carried out by credentialled employees, and because

166

role definitions are vague and global rather than specific, a volunteer can theoretically and sometimes in practice enter completely into the tasks of the organization. For example, the authors have observed full time volunteers taking regular shifts at several of these agencies, sometimes for extended periods of time. On occasion the distinction between staff and volunteers becomes minimal.

Other advantages for the volunteer reflect the basically egalitarian structure of the informal agency. An important gain is that the volunteer has greater flexibility to create his or her own unique place in the agency than s/he has in more highly bureaucratized organizations. Because each volunteer is treated and valued as an individual, it is feasible for several volunteers to design for themselves separate and distinct duties (e.g., public speaker, peer counselor, fund raiser) even though they are all of similar status. This flexibility is often unavailable in larger organizations because of the relatively restricted functions reserved for volunteers.

Fewer status concerns is another advantage for volunteers at informal agencies. Status relates to the presence of vertical layers of power within an organization. The relative lack of such layers in informal organizations allows the volunteer easier access to staff and supervisory personnel. Nor are positive ideas likely to be blocked or disregarded simply because they were conceived by volunteers, a problem common in formal organizations. Since status is a minor concern in non-bureaucratic organizations the volunteer is less likely to be burdened with the label of low status.

A fourth advantage is the opportunity for immediate feedback at these agencies. The smallness and intimacy of non-bureaucratic organizations allows the volunteer to receive quick, relevant feedback from staff, supervisors and clients concerning the quality and direction of the volunteer's effort. Plans can be made and implemented rapidly, mistakes can be corrected when discovered, and equally importantly, the volunteer can be rewarded with praise and appreciation for a job well done by persons who are in a position to recognize such achievements as they occur.

Similarly, the informal agency provides the volunteer with an opportunity to learn vital skills. Comparatively free from paper work and other bureaucratic functions, the informal agency is likely to be deeply concerned with the survival of its clients. Whether answering the call of a potential suicide, helping a battered woman and her children obtain a court order against her husband, or discussing the use of narcotics with a runaway teenager, the volunteer is likely to find himself or herself passionately concerned with the well-being of the client. The skills volunteers must develop to cope with these problems are intimate, profound, and unique to each person. Bureaucratic agencies can seldom match the depth of challenge offered to the volunteer at informal agencies in this regard.

Another advantage for certain volunteers is the possibility to become employed after a period of volunteerism. Although not the purpose for volunteering, persons who devote time and energy to informal agencies may be hired when opportunities arise because of their high visibility and value to the organization. This possibility for employment is particularly relevant for previous clients of the agency who may be able to make a transition from client to volunteer to staff member as part of their own healing process. Since roles are less inflexible at informal agencies, it is unlikely that a person will be viewed as a permanent volunteer simply because he or she begins a relationship with an agency in that capacity.

In summary, the principal advantages of non-bureaucratic agencies for the volunteer occur because these agencies are particularly open to the time, energy, ideas, and interests of the volunteer. When successful, the volunteer is likely to become highly involved with such agencies, to be and to feel deeply appreciated, and to learn valuable skills in a number of crucial areas.

Disadvantages

Non-bureaucratic agencies can provide excellent volunteer experiences. However, certain structural properties of these organizations can also lead to frustration and disappointment for the volunteer. These issues are described below.

One substantial problem is the relative lack of guidance and guidelines for the volunteer. Because the staff needs to be flexible and because new and unpredictable crises occur with regularity in these agencies, the volunteer may find himself or herself placed into situations without any advance notice or preparation. For example, an angry spouse might appear at a spouse assault center, demanding immediate entrance, and confront a volunteer who has been left alone at the center for a few hours while the regular staff person on duty attends to a crisis in the family of another client. The volunteer may not have received training to deal with this problem and may not have anyone to consult with during the emergency. Although many non-bureaucratic agencies do designate one individual as volunteer coordinator, these persons may not have been specifically trained for this responsibility; other agencies lacking a specified volunteer coordinator may have difficulty in scheduling and use of volunteers.

Lack of role clarity for volunteers can be disadvantageous when it leads to confusion. A volunteer who enters a formal bureaucracy will usually be given specific, limited tasks. In contrast, the volunteer at an informal organization may have no designated responsibilities. At worst, some volunteers will find themselves sitting around aimlessly while around them staff are busily working, too involved to help the volunteers locate a productive task.

Limited opportunity to learn certain professional skills. For the volunteer wanting a professional challenge the informal agency may offer limited opportunities. Paper work such as case summaries may be minimized, relationships with other agencies may be less developed, and staff loyalty may be to paraprofessional groups such as Alcoholics Anonymous rather than to professional organizations. These limitations will feel restrictive to some volunteers.

Another possible problem is the danger of exploitation of volunteers. Two kinds of exploitation are possible: volunteers may be expected to act as "gofers," performing non-challenging tasks such as raking the yard, or they may be given great responsibilities equivalent to those of full-time workers without commensurate reward.

In sum, unclear roles, lack of guidelines, little professional training and the dangers of exploitation must be recognized and combatted to help make the volunteer experience most valuable at informal agencies.

INFORMAL AGENCY NEEDS AND FOUNDATION VOLUNTEER TRAINING

There are important advantages to agencies which invest in extensive volunteer training. Counseling skills can be effectively enhanced by short-term training (Bailey and Crage, 1980; Becker and Zarit, 1978); even short training programs can positively alter relatively strong and consistent personal response patterns (Beale, Payton and Zachary, 1978). Avery (1978) found that significantly higher empathy skills from short term training were maintained over time, as well. But in addition to having personnel who are more highly skilled available for patient and client care, trained volunteers in our experience with agencies have been more willing to make longer and more intensive commitments to their agencies. The agencies offering training have had a greater number of persons volunteer, and they had had a long-term result of increased interest, support and respectability within their communities. This seems quite reasonable in view of Wiehe and Isenhour's (1977) finding that personal satisfaction and self-improvement were the most important motivations for volunteer work. Training provides skills improvement and increases both one's competence and one's confidence.

The problem of developing a training program where there is none may seem major, however, since in many informal agencies the staff is already overworked and volunteer training is viewed as essentially different from other staff activities: we have developed a foundation training schedule, as well as a plan for setting priorities in advanced training, which we believe will be useful in resolving these problems.

An agency must, in order to use volunteer help confidently, have volunteers available who:

A) Are knowledgeable about the problem or problems being dealt with, and are informed about what goes on in the agency;

B) Are able to listen and hear what clients, staff and other volunteers are communicating;

C) Understand agency methods, rules and goals and have a commitment to maintaining them;

D) Are able to gather information and record it accurately in the proper manner;

E) Are able to adequately perform all the responsibilities assigned to them;

F) Can understand and maintain confidentiality where relevant;

G) Are clear about their own values and biases with reference to a client group.

In addition, informal agencies must develop a training format that reflects both in process and content the special characteristics and needs of non-bureaucratic organizations noted previously. This means that the training process should emphasize immediate and informal participation by staff and volunteers rather than a highly structured role-specific format and that training be designed to produce flexible generalists who can take initiative and responsibility in many areas and who can respond with caring and reason in a difficult situation should a staff supervisor not be immediately available.[2] For example, volunteer training, even if limited in time, needs to introduce volunteers to the areas of empathy, valuing, and problem-solving, whereas trainers in a more formal agency where volunteer roles tend to be more specified and less global, might focus on only one of these.

A basic training schedule must touch on each of these matters, although a final evaluation of the volunteer will depend on what s/he actually does after training. Here we wish to provide a general outline of a 16-20 hour basic volunteer training, and an example of how such an outline can be adapted to meet a program's specific needs.

The following design is a generalized summary of the amount of training required for an agency staff to feel confident in extensive use of its volunteers in paraprofessional capacities of many kinds. Although we have seen agencies which required as much basic training as 45 hours, most we have worked with have found a more limited program of 15-20 hours quite adequate. To make this amount of training worth providing, however, a six month minimum commitment is required of the volunteers who take the training, and a minimum number of hours of service per week is demanded by the agency (generally from 3 to 6 per week). The training sessions themselves appear to work best for most groups if all hours are taken in a period of 2 days to 2 weeks--volunteers become confident sooner and staff needn't train again for several months.

A training program does demand the time and energy of volunteers, especially if this training is scheduled in the relatively large blocks necessary for efficient use of staff. However, we have found that most volunteers are able to adapt their schedules to block training and that recruitment of skilled volunteers is directly proportionate to the quality and intensity of the training program. Additionally, scheduling a major part of the training before volunteers make contact with clients facilitates screening to exclude those whose motivation or skills level is inappropriate. For these reasons we suggest that training programs be scheduled at 3-6 month intervals and that new volunteers be expected to "pass" the training prior to extensive client contact.

BEGINNING THE TRAINING PROCESS

Special care needs to be taken when introducing a foundation training plan to volunteers who have been contributing to a program for some time. Training programs do work best for both staff and volunteers when they are required for all volunteers. Even a long term volunteer can benefit from a review of the agency process--and s/he may have a need to clarify biases and values (Winn, 1978), especially if s/he was initially part of a client population, such as a recovering substance abuser, former victim of abuse, long reformed ex-offender or runaway. (Stratton, 1976, notes the danger of assuming sole competence on the basis of past experiences.) One excellent way to insure that everyone gets useful training experience with a common base is to require the training and give long-term volunteers some role in the training design. This increases the range of volunteer interaction, encourages volunteers to be resources for each other, and can provide both new experience and a good basis for later use of volunteers as volunteer trainers. Careful planning the first time, when major staff participation is important, will take time; but once "off the ground" in most settings, one staff person and one skilled volunteer can supervise/implement future trainings with a minimum of time and bother. The system which uses and stretches volunteer capacities will often generate higher levels of commitment, enthusiasm, and activity on the part of its volunteers, for having one's talents recognized and used well is rewarding.

An example of specifically adapted training is the following program, constructed from the basic design by trainer volunteers and staff at Refuge House, a shelter for battered women in Eau Claire, Wisconsin. This initial eight hour session was designed to be followed by one focusing heavily in the area of practice skills. The trainee group was thirty volunteers.

TABLE I: FOUNDATION TRAINING DESIGN

Content	Competencies*	Activities	Hours
I. Issue Information	A	The issue in social context	4
	A	Client identity and behavior	
	A, B	Client group and individual needs	
	A	Legal, medical, economic aspects of problem	
II. Program Setting	A, B	Introduction of staff and roles	4
	F	Confidentiality	
	A, B	Volunteer in the setting--main issues	
	C, D	Rules, regulations and rationale of agency	
III. Practice Skills	C, D	Telephone/Intake procedure for the volunteer	6-8
	C, D	Record keeping for the volunteer	
	E, A	Volunteer and emergency action	
	E, B	How to listen and hear	
	E, B	Practice in empathy	
	E, C	Practice in problem solving	
IV. Valuing Process	G	Structured values clarification exercises	2
	A, C	Common myths about issue/client group	
V. Special Problems	A, E	Any additional training in perspectives necessary to function well with the agency, including community relations, modelling, special procedures	1-4

*Letters refer to competencies listed on page , "Agency Needs and Foundation Volunteer Training."

TABLE II: EIGHT HOUR SHELTER TRAINING, REFUGE HOUSE

CONTENT SEQUENCE	ACTIVITIES	HOURS
I. Valuing Processes	Forced choice values, values clarification exercise on violence, victims and batterers.	½
II. Issue Information	Film on battering as a social problem.	1
III. Issue Information	Presentations--Who is the battered woman? Who is the batterer?	45 min.
IV. Issue Information	Presentation and discussion of the cycle of violence and theory of learned helplessness.	45 min.
V. Valuing	Structured exercises enabling trainees to experience helplessness, power, and awareness of self.	1
VI. Program Setting	Small group work on agency management of five aspects of program-- small groups report to training session as a whole.	1½
VII. Program Setting/ Practice Skills	Staff and volunteer role plays of usual and emergency situations while watching volunteers do appropriate record-keeping for each situation.	1½
VIII. Program Setting	Rules, regulations, and rationale of program, including volunteer roles and contributions.	1

A subsequent 8-hour training session for this agency will focus on Issue Information--1½ hours (content areas begun in small group work); Valuing--30 minutes (additional values clarification exercise); Practice Skills--5 hours (intensive training in listening, empathy and problem-solving); and Special Problems--1 hour (teaching and modelling of parenting skills).

All of the material presented is within the range of the staff of most informal agencies, some of which regularly provide public education for the community or other agencies. When a limited staff setup does not include someone with specific training skills, there are at least two alternatives: first, staff can meet and assess their ability to create a training as a group. We have seen "untrained trainers" do good jobs by dividing tasks, inventing "typical situation" role-plays, brain-storming the training they themselves would like to have had. This process can have a very invigorating effect on the staff as a whole, and each staff person gains investment in the volunteer program. We have even seen some staff persons volunteer extra time to bring off a training. A training evaluation will help revise the first offering for future groups. Secondly, where this is impossible, trainers may be recruited as volunteers. A teacher who knows values clarification or uses role-playing, a former client with empathy and confidence, a college professor, or a professional social worker with another agency may all be willing to help design and implement training. The best approach is to directly state your need for their expertise and request that they volunteer. A busy person will often accept a creative challenge.

In any extended training, lecture presentations and films should be alternated with more experiential techniques. Bell and Margolis (1978) advise the use of lecture/demonstration when knowledge is to be provided, and role-playing, case discussion and other interactive methods when the training goal is to enhance discovery. Use of modelling and role-playing have also been shown to result in significantly better counseling skills for parapropfessional trainees, than the lecture-discussion method (Teeran and Gabel, 1978). Providing training participants time to practice skills they have just seen demonstrated has also resulted in significantly higher use of interviewing/interaction skills (O'Toole, 1979). We have found that the best training demonstrations and role plays emerge clearly from consideration of two questions: (1) What are the most typical situations encountered here? and (2) What two emergencies do we want each volunteer to be capable of handling should they arise?[2]

A basic volunteer training such as that outlined above is foundation knowledge for training of volunteers in advanced skills. Clearly, all volunteers are not going to be qualified or able to perform advanced functions and variation in personal abilities suits some persons for one activity more than another. Consistent, thoughtful staff supervision of the basic volunteer training will enable a staff to better evaluate the unique abilities and potential of their volunteers.

ADVANCED VOLUNTEER TRAINING

Thoughtful, well planned volunteer training programs are becoming increasingly necessary in less bureaucratized agencies, most of which are limited in size and facing both a burgeoning client population and losses in federal and state funding. In some agencies, volunteers may begin to assume functions which agency staff have most often performed until now (see Table III, task levels 2, 3, and 4). Those agencies which cannot or choose not to use volunteers in advanced skills capacities could lose important portions of their client service programs.

Those agencies who do use volunteers in advanced capacities will need to train their volunteers thoroughly and well.

In the supervisory process, a role-oriented perspective on skills is especially helpful in identifying persons who may "naturally" take to certain advanced volunteer activities. Compton and Galaway (1979: 339-343) indicate five major roles to be played by professional social workers: Broker, Enabler, Teacher, Mediator, and Advocate. As they define these roles, the skills required to perform them are quite distinct. We have found this definitional system useful in helping agency personnel to establish priorities; in determining appropriate training modules for both basic and advanced volunteer training programs; and in explaining staff and volunteer functions clearly to incoming persons.

The function of the social BROKER is to connect people with services, services with other services, and aid in negotiating the by-ways of the social service system. The ENABLER assists others in developing and using coping skills of many types. The TEACHER provides both new information and a model for learning and using alternative behaviors. The MEDIATOR uses persuasion and conciliation to resolve disputes in a system (i.e., the family) or between systems. The ADVOCATE manipulates the environment on behalf of the client. Using these terms, we can divide the normal activities within an agency or program and establish a hierarchy of responsibilities in each area--responsibilities which can quite capably be performed under staff supervision by well-trained volunteers. Table III provides examples of activities appropriate to each of these roles at four skills levels.[3]

Generally it is practical to train volunteers in small groups through Step 2 activity. In Steps 3 and 4, however, we believe the most effective training occurs on a one-to-one basis through two primary methods, modelling and assisting. Modelling: A staff member invites a volunteer to accompany him/her while s/he performs a particular program activity and afterwards takes the time to explain just what was involved and the steps s/he executed in doing it. Assisting: The staff person invites a volunteer to help perform an activity, in which the volunteer takes actual responsibility for a portion of the program. As with modelling, a debriefing and evaluation process is essential, if the ultimate goal is to enable the advanced volunteer to perform the function by him/herself in the future. The point of the process is to integrate the training with daily activity of staff so that advanced training is both on-going and individualized to meet agency/volunteer needs. Outside of the debriefing process, the remainder of the training activity (modelling and assisting) is integrated into everyday staff planning and implementation. Siddall and Bosma (1976) offer further insight into the dynamics of training someone to function as a co-therapist.

The agency gain, once a volunteer has been trained and is performing Step 3 and 4 activity on a regular basis, is substantial: For example, each trained volunteer working three hours a week with a six-month commitment past training will contribute 72 paraprofessional hours to an agency--an equivalent of nine days of productive activity if s/he has been well-trained by agency personnel. Such a volunteer, working in capacities where s/he feels competent and challenged, is highly likely to contribute for a period longer than six months--contributing commitment and ideas as well as simple energy over a long period of time. A volunteer who has been trained and judged to be reliable by staff will require less supervisory time and vigilance, be more easily integrated into the agency "community" and contribute more of his or her talents to the organization.

TABLE III. ADVANCED SKILLS OPPORTUNITIES FOR VOLUNTEERS

ROLE	SKILLS LEVEL			
	STEP 1 - BASIC	STEP 2	STEP 3	STEP 4
BROKER	Referral of client to other community agencies (e.g., to Salvation Army, Department of Social Services)	Referral of community resources into agency (e.g., help organize special program in parenting)	Act as liaison between agency and community individuals (e.g., client intake and scheduling volunteers)	Development of new resources (e.g., research new funding sources)
ENABLER	Empathic listening and support (child care and residential support)	Empathic listening and problem solving (e.g., some types of peer counseling)	Individual or group co-counseling with staff member	Individual or group counseling with reporting to staff member
TEACHER	Provide basic information about program to clients	Public education	Teach specific information or skills to clients	Train new volunteers
MEDIATOR	Empathic day to day contacts (e.g., modeling effective parenting skills with parents and children)	Modeling conflict resolution skills (e.g., help with conflict management in residential setting on a daily basis)	Mediate between client and other systems (e.g., helping detail a restitution agreement between offender and victim)	Train new volunteers in mediative skills
ADVOCATE	Personal advocacy (e.g., accompany clients to doctor, bank, and other personal activities)	Systems advocacy (e.g., support clients in court and social service interviews)	Community advocacy (e.g., attend city, county, and state meetings and hearings with specific advocacy assignment)	Advocacy management (e.g., help organize and implement advocacy programming as a whole)

175

SUMMARY

Informal, non-bureaucratic agencies such as shelter homes, ex-offender centers and half-way houses, are generally of relatively small size, serve non-mainstream target groups, and function with a minimal division of labor, and minimal hierarchy. Communication in such agencies is often informal, workers are frequently recruited from the client target group, and members of the group belong as whole persons. There are distinct advantages and disadvantages to volunteering in such agency settings. It is often both possible and practical for a volunteer to become part of the treatment team or to perform other skilled functions.

In order to use volunteer help with confidence, a staff must educate its volunteers in five areas: Issue Information, Program Setting, Practice Skills, Valuing Processes and Special Problems. Specific activities to promote and increase specific skills are suggested in a 16-20 hour design format for basic volunteer training. An example of how this design was adapted to the needs of a particular shelter for battered women is provided.

Duties which may be performed by volunteers in the informal, non-bureaucratic agency setting are divided into four levels on the basis of five functions of social work practice: Broker, Enabler, Teacher, Mediator, and Advocate. Advanced training, a more highly individualized process based on structured use of modelling and assisting, is both more personalized and more integrated into daily agency process than is basic training.

The increase in staff confidence and volunteer reliability and commitment resulting from well-designed volunteer training at foundation and advanced levels is substantial, and often results in a volunteer becoming an effective member of the treatment team in the non-bureaucratic agency.

Notes

1. A simple management profile instrument useful for evaluating formality, bureaucracy and freedom of communication between volunteers and staff in a specific agency is included in Wilson (1976, pp. 69-74).

2. Further information on setting, training details and use of specific presentational methods is available in Wilson (1976), "Chapter VIII: Training: Designing Creative Learning Experiences," in Stenzel and Feeney (1968) "Sample L: Leadership Skill Practice in Group Training" and in Naylor (1967).

3. A useful alternative method of looking at advanced training roles may be found in Austin (1978), where professional roles are broken into 12 categories, including those of Brokerage and Advocacy. Austin labels his classifications as "Generalist Worker Roles."

REFERENCES

Austin, Michael
   1978   Professionals and Paraprofessionals. New York: Human Sciences Press.

Avery, Arthur W.
    1978   "Communication skills training for paraprofessional helpers."
            American Journal of Community Psychology, Vol. 6, No. 6, 489-591.

Bailey, Roy D. and Andrew Crage
    1980   "Nursing assistants as co-therapists." Child Care, Health and
            Development, Vol. 6, No. 1, 17-24.

Barnett, Ola
    1978   "Nonprofessionals in the rehabilitation of mentally disordered sex
            offenders." Community Mental Health Journal, Vol. 14, No. 2, 110-115.

Beale, Andrew V., Otto D. Payton, and Ingrid G. Zachary
    1978   "The effects of a communications course for health professionals on
            empathy discrimination." Journal of Applied Rehabilitation Counseling,
            Vol. 9, No. 2, 46-49.

Becker, Francoise S. and Steven H. Zarit
    1978   "Training older adults as peer counselors." Educational Gerontology,
            Vol. 3, No. 3, 241-250.

Bell, Chip R. and Fredric H. Margolis
    1978   "Blending didactic and experiential learning methods." Training and
            Development Journal, Vol. 32, No. 8, 16-21.

Compton, Beulah and Bert Galaway
    1979   Social Work Processes, Rev. ed., Homewood, Ill.: Dorsey Press.

Etzioni, Amitai
    1964   Modern Organizations. Englewood Cliffs, New Jersey: Prentice-Hall.

Naylor, Harriet H.
    1967   Volunteers Today: Finding, Training, and Working with Them. Dryden,
            N.Y.: Dryden Associates.

O'Toole, William M.
    1979   "Effects of Practice and Some Methodological Considerations in Training
            Counseling Interviewing Skills." Journal of Counseling Psychology,
            Vol. 26, No. 5, 419-426.

Siddall, Lawrence B. and Barbara J. Bosma
    1976   "Co-therapy as a training process." Psychotherapy: Theory, Research
            and Practice, Vol. 13, No. 3, 209-213.

Stenzel, Anne K. and Helen M. Feeney
    1968   Volunteer Training and Development: A Manual for Community Groups.
            New York: Seabury Press.

Stratton, Ray
    1976   "Stratton's Disease: an ailment of alcohologists." Alcohol Health
            and Research World, Vol. 1976(Summer), 27-28.

Teevan, Katherine Grady and Harris Gabel
    1978   "Evaluation of Modelling--Role-Playing and Lecture-Discussion Training
            Techniques for College Student Mental Health Paraprofessionals."
            Journal of Counseling Psychology, Vol. 25, No. 2, 169-171.

Wiehe, Vernon R. and Lenora Isenhour
  1977   "Motivation of Volunteers." Journal of Social Welfare, Vol. 4, No. 2,
         73-79.

Wilson, Marlene
  1976   The Effective Management of Volunteer Programs. Boulder, Colorado:
         Johnson Publishing.

Winn, Francis J.
  1978   "Staff Attitudes Toward the Aged in Nursing Homes: A Review and
         Suggestions for an Alternative Approach to Training." Educational
         Gerontology, Vol. 3, No. 3, 231-239.

A FRAMEWORK FOR THE ANALYSIS OF BOARD-EXECUTIVES RELATIONSHIPS IN VOLUNTARY AGENCIES

Ralph M. Kramer
University of California, Berkeley

Despite its centrality in the governance and management of voluntary nonprofit organizations, the board-executive relationship has not received much critical analysis nor has it often been the subject of empirical research. Most of the practice wisdom is normative and relies heavily on evocative metaphors such as "partnership" or "leadership team" which assume consensual, coequal collaboration with little attention given to the existence of a power dimension or conflict between the two partners (Trecker, 1970; Glen & Conrad, 1976; O'Connell, 1976; Weber, 1976).

Even in organization theory where power emerged in the 1970s as a leading theme in conflict and political economy models (Zald, 1973; Gummer, 1980; Hasenfeld, 1983), few attempts have been made to conceptualize the board-executive relationship as one of the key variables controlling policy making and the allocation of organizational resources. Even when the governance of voluntary agencies has been studied, the focus has been more on issues pertaining to representation, elitism, or "minority rule"

179

and other such lapses from democratic norms (Fayence, 1977; Steckler & Herzog, 1970; Marmor & Marone, 1981). There has been relatively little follow-up on a group of findings published in the 1960s which pointed up the unequal distribution of power between board and executive, as well as sharp differences in their status, values, reference groups, agency identification and other relevant social-psychological attributes. Indeed, similar findings by independent investigators of opposing welfare ideologies even raised the question how the voluntary agency could operate in the face of such sharp disparities in values between policy makers and managers who were structurally and functionally bound together (Nettler, 1958; Stein, 1961; Senor, 1965; Kramer, 1965). The failure to pursue some of these leads also reflects the underdevelopment of practice theory for professional interpersonal encounters that are socio-political rather than clinical in content (Bolan, 1980; Specht, 1983).

In this paper we attempt to update and build on previous studies of board-executive relationships in voluntary social service agencies. The approach here is primarily analytical rather than prescriptive and proposes a conceptual framework shown in Table 1 which can be used for the description and explanation of board-executive relationships and ultimately for research which can contribute to practice theory. In the process, we shall draw mainly on concepts from social exchange, role and symbolic interaction theories within the context of a political economy model of organizational behavior. Instead of the mystique of partnership, we shall utilize the six concepts of status, norm, role, authority, responsibility, and power as summarized in Table 2. Because roles are based on status and norms, the latter two will be discussed first.

Status

Status refers to one's position in a social system and enables a person to anticipate how they will be perceived and treated. Intrinsically a social process, status - like power - exists only in relation to others who recognize it and who therefore approach one in a mutually understood way (Homans, 1961: 145-153).

It has been recognized that board members and executives each have contrasting statuses within the social system of a human service organization. Board members are part-time volunteers who serve without monetary compensation and who contribute their time, funds, support and other resources, while the executive is a full time professional, a paid employee of the organization who may also have the status of an expert.

Board members may have a higher socio-economic status than the executive, particularly if they are community notables or

TABLE 1

Elements of An Analytic Framework for the Study of Board-Executive Relations

Organization
<u>Organization</u>

structure, size, age, type
fiscal system

Executive

Professional status, expertise,
interpersonal competence,
ideology, self-image, reference
groups, role repetoire, self-role
congruence, duration of employment,
personal attributes and
leadership style

Board Member

SES, prestige, duration of
service, knowledge, skills,
access to resources, financial
support, service beneficiary,
other loyalties, welfare
ideology and commitment, self-
image and reference groups

Interpersonal Role Relationships

History, status differentials, definitions
of role and situation, power/dependency,
tradeoffs and resource exchange

Issue

Substantive character,
salience and controversy-
potential

Situation

Crisis/routine,
time constraints

TABLE 2

Comparison of Board Members and Executives on Six Attributes

	Board of Directors	Executive
Social Status	Volunteer Trustee Employer Community notable	Professional/expert Full time employee Director of social agency
Behavioral Norms	Altruism and best interests of community Proscription of self-dealing and conflicts of interests Collaborative partnership with executive and stewardship Participation in and support of the agency	Ethical, professional performance Subordination of personal interests to those of the agency and the decisions of the Board Helping relationship to board members, including leadership development
Roles	Policy maker/trustee Employer Interpreter, supporter & advocate	Multiple & diverse: enabler, guide, manager, educator, expert, etc.
Responsibility for	Governance: policy making/adoption Resource acquisition, allocation and control Appointment of executive & adoption of personnel policies Community relations *	Implementation of policy via administration of program Appointment & supervision of staff Assisting the board & liaison between it and the staff *
Responsibility to	Community (membership, contributions & constituencies) & clientele	Board of Directors, clientele, staff, community & professional interests

TABLE 2 (continued)

Types of Authority	
Legal (formal/official) right as trustees to govern, receive and allocate funds	Hierarchical – delegated by Board to implement policy (administer program), employ & supervise & evaluate staff
Hierarchical – over executive	Professional expertise

Power (resources for influence)	
Status & authority as a corporate trustee	Status as a professional with expertise
Prestige as a community notable	Administrative authority & responsibilities
Legitimation of the organization	Full-time commitment; duration & continuity of service
Access to resources	Access to organizational information
Personal knowledge, skill, time energy	Informal relationships with key persons
Duration of service and intensity of commitment	

183

economic influentials. Other status differences relate to gender, profession, ethnicity, or being a beneficiary of the agency's services.

One consequence of the volunteer status of the board member is a weaker attachment to the agency which generally is time-limited, marginal, avocational (i.e., a leisure-time activity) and episodic, in contrast to the executive's full time, continuing commitment to a daily job. Yet the board's corporate status as the employer of the executive can serve as a powerful, counter-vailing factor. Here, as in other instances, the attributes of the board member have a dialectical character whereby "that which enables also disables, and for precisely the same reason." The social status of the board member is simultaneously the source of his[1] ability to legitimate the agency by demonstrating that it has the support of respectable citizens who do not derive any monetary benefit from their participation. But at the same time, the volunteer's status is the source of different values, reference groups, and commitments from those of the executive. That board members do not hold the same welfare ideology as the executive and the staff is a recurrent finding since it was first noted over twenty years ago (Nettler, 1958; Kramer, 1965; Knight, 1968; Robins & Blackburn, 1974), although the significance of these disparate belief systems for policy making and administration is still unclear.

While board-executive status differences are noteworthy, there is greater similarity in the behavioral norms pertaining to their respective duties, privileges, rewards and rights.

Norms

Norms are socially sanctioned beliefs and expectations which guide behavior, reducing uncertainty, and which lead to social tradeoffs. Agency board members are influenced by norms associated with service as a corporate trustee, responsible for the steward-ship of a community non-profit organization. Board members are expected to be motivated primarily by altruism and not derive any personal, financial, or tangible gain from their service to the community. Consequently, self-dealing and conflicts-of-interests are proscribed. Board members are expected to receive "psychic benefits" and to be rewarded primarily through community and organizational recognition of their "doing good" and ful-filling their own sense of obligation. There are also more specific behavioral norms which require attendance and partici-pation in board meetings; being objective and rational in decision-making, willing to contribute time and money and to be a loyal supporter of the agency.

The norms pertaining to the obligations, privileges and rights of executive behavior are essentially those expected of an employed

184

professional (i.e., ethical, competent performance, devotion to the organization, and subordination of personal interests to the organization and the prerogatives of the board of directors.

Another related professional norm, espoused more often by social workers, is that the executive should be engaged in a "helping relationship" with a board member, assisting him to carry out his organizational responsibilities, and, in the process, to help him develop his leadership capabilities (Levy, 1982: 103-107). This view, together with the conception of the relationship with the board as a partnership or team, working together harmoniously to accomplish the goals of the organization, is the model most frequently found in the professional literature.

Role

Role refers to reciprocal social behavior which is located in a system or network of social relations, based upon status and associated with a set of norms. The concept of organizational role, which includes attitudes and values as well as behavior ascribed to any and all persons occupying a specific position, is especially useful in describing the division of tasks, power and other resources (Turner, 1968: 552-557).

The roles of board member and executive consist of mutual, socially defined behavioral expectations toward each other which include their respective responsibilities, privileges, authority, etc. These patterns of reciprocal behavior which can be viewed as an exchange, a trade-off or a contract, involve obligations, rewards, inducements and contributions. Examples of roles some-what analogous to that of board-executive are: client-social worker; client-planner; student-teacher; congregation-minister; and school board-school superintendent (Gross, 1958). There are at least four patterns of such role relationships whereby the executive interacts with: individual board members; the president and members of the executive committee; informal sub-groups including factions and/or cliques; and to the board of directors as a collectivity. These relationships may be formal or informal, and occur before, during and after meetings.

There are numerous concepts derived from role, symbolic inter-action and social exchange theory which can provide a vocabulary for the analysis of board-executive relationships and which could contribute to the development of practice theory. These include: self-image, definition of the situation, role episode and role taking, role conflict, and exchange of resources.

The basic idea of a role implies the existence of a self-image which is influenced by the process of role taking, i.e., seeing ourselves through the eyes of others. Thus, board members and

the executive serve as Significant Others for each other whereby
they adjust their behavior in accordance with their view of how
they think they are or will be perceived by the other. This
process of role taking--described by Katz and Kahn (1966: 182-197)
as the "role episode"--is also influenced by organizational,
situational, interpersonal and personality factors.

Self-images are reinforced through recurring social relationships
when the anticipated interaction takes place, although there are
possibilities for change and replacement as well as new
definitions of the situation or strategies to alter an extant
role (Bolan, 1971). Board members and executives do not simply
conform to each other's expectations, but instead they seek to
play roles which are consistent with their self-images (Argyris
and Schon, 1974: 206-207). For example, power and status
differentials can be reflected in self-images which may influence the expectation of their respective role performance.
A board member may have a poor image of himself when comparing
himself with the executive's apparently greater knowledge, or he
may feel considerably superior to the executive whose social
status and salary is lower. In the latter case, the executive
may be expected to be quite deferential in his demeanor. This
could be reinforced because the executive may be uncomfortable
in working with people with higher social status.

This two-way influence system consisting of reciprocal self-
images, definition of situation and role expectations is depicted
below:

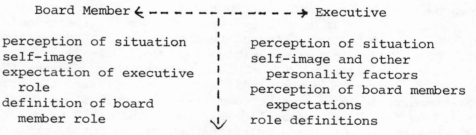

Shared role conceptions are particularly important in a joint
enterprise such as the board-executive relationship where
continuing collaboration is required for the good of the
organization. What are the reciprocal role expectations of
board members and executives? Compared to the multiplicity of
behaviors expected of an executive, the roles ascribed to board
members are relatively few in number and include: trustee/
steward, policy maker, supporter-contributor, employer, advocate,
advice-giver, legitimator, buffer, representative, task
performer.

There is no agreement on a single role for the executive except that it should be "helpful." Instead, there are dozens of somewhat diffuse, often conflicting and ambiguous roles. The following list contains the most frequently cited roles for the executive:

activator	grantsman
administrator	guide
advocate	initiator
analyst	interpreter
catalyst	leader
consultant	manager
coordinator	mediator
developer	organizer
director	planner
educator	resource person
enabler	staff
entrepreneur	stimulator
expert	synthesizer
facilitator	"technipol"

Given this diversity and the absence of guidelines regarding when to perform which role,[2] it is not surprising that there is considerable confusion, lack of consensus, as well as a high potential for role strain and conflict. A sharp divergence of opinion regarding the major responsibilities of executives was found in a 1974 study of United Way agencies in New York City involving over 200 agency executives, presidents, and over 1600 board members (Schoderbek, 1979). Presidents and board members saw the primary role of the executive much more as an administrator rather than someone responsible for policy. For example, while presidents and board members regarded the hiring and firing of staff as the highest ranking executive responsibility, it was ninth out of thirty functions for the executives for whom policy recommendations to the board was their second most frequently cited role. The findings are summarized in Table 3.

TABLE 3

Comparative Ranking of Executive Responsibilities

	Executives	Presidents	Board Members
Hire and supervise staff	9	1	2
Recommend policy to the board	2	8	4
Administer all phases of agency operations	7	2	3
Plan program policies	5	9	9

Role conflict can occur under a wide variety of conditions:
when there is a lack of congruence between self and role, or a
poor fit between either capacity or the individual's own conception of his role; between opposing conceptions of the
executive role by different board members (e.g., between advocate
and mediator, enabler and activator; or conflicting role expectations by the same board member). Other sources of role conflict
are a double-bind, lack of necessary knowledge or skill, lack
of clarity regarding expective behavior, and lack of resources
such as time and energy. Role theory suggests other role
dysfunctions such as role ambiguity, role incompatibility,
excessive expectations, unfulfilled roles, and role abandonment.
Roles can also be described as descriptive (what they are); as
probabilistic (what they will be); modal (what they can be or
what is possible) and prescriptive (what they ought to be)
(Biddle, 1979; Bates, 1962).

To further analyze the role relationships between board and
executive we must shift from the level of the individual board
member to that of the board as a collectivity, and examine the
character of their respective responsibilities, authority and
power. These three concepts can be regarded as sides of a triangle
whereby changes in one always affect one or both of the other
sides of the triangle (Gross, 1968: 74-100).

Responsibility

There are two dimensions of responsibility: (1) as an obligation
for the performance of certain functions or services; and
(2) responsibility to one's self and others for certain actions,
which is a form of accountability. Illustrative of (1) is the
following typical division of responsibility for board and
executive:

Board Members	Executive
1. policy making and long-range planning	1. implementing policy and programs
2. hire/fire executive	2. hiring staff
3. legal responsibilities	3. fund raising
4. fiscal management	4. educating board
5. public relations	5. supervise and evaluate staff
6. evaluation of programs and executive	6. public relations
7. personnel policies	7. liaison between board and staff
	8. budget development and control

The major internal and external responsibilities of the board
can be reduced to four: (1) governance which includes decision-
making, policy-making, adoption, and authorization; (2) resource

188

acquisition, allocation and control; (3) personnel-hiring/ firing the executive and personnel practices; (4) community relations and support (Rosenthal and Young, 1980: 96). The accountability of the board of directors is expressed in their responsibility to the membership, the donors, the clientele, the staff and the community at-large together with its various constituencies.

The major responsibilities of the executive can be reduced to the typical management functions summed up in the acronym POSDCORBE; developing and assisting the board, and serving as liaison between it and the staff, and resource mobilization. The accountability of the executive is manifested in his responsibilities to the board, clientele, staff and to various community and professional constituencies. Beyond this, executives should be advocates for their clientele, social entrepreneurs, and humanizers of institutions (Caiden, 1969: 14).

Attempts to delineate a suitable division of responsibility between board and executive by distinguishing between policy and administration are increasingly regarded as unrealistic because of lack of conformity to actual practice. A more dynamic conceptualization is required to describe the interpenetration, the fluid and shifting role of professionals in policy-making, which is probably much greater than board members' involvement in administration.

While both share some aspects of policy making, as a practical matter it is usually the executive who defines what is a policy matter, even though only the board can adopt policy (Kramer, 1981: 119). Executives generally have considerable discretion to define an issue as administrative, technical-clinical or professional, and thus avoid the involvement of the board in its settlement. In this way, the substantive character of the issue may affect the jurisdiction and the division of responsibility between board and executive. As reported in a survey of board members:

> "Although in theory both director (in profit-making organizations) and trustee board members of nonprofits should make policy decisions, chief executive officers and executive directors have control of strategic management even though their power is derived differently." ..."many trustees ignore the task of discussing policy and accept the de facto decisions of the executive director, though such neglect and acceptance seems to vary with the size of the organization" (Unterman and Davis, 1982: 36).

Authority

Authority is an accepted right, a form of potential power to make certain kinds of decisions, initiate action, allocate resources, reward and sanction, receive requests, and to transmit certain kinds of information (Gross, 1968: 87-94). The board has both legal and hierarchical authority to govern the organization derived from their official status as trustees of a corporation which, e.g., authorizes them to receive and allocate funds. One portion of its hierarchical authority is vested in its right to hire and fire the executive; the rest is delegated to the executive to implement policy, administer the program and to employ the staff.

The executive has hierarchical authority over the staff, as well as the authority of professional expertise. All three types of authority are needed by the agency. The lines of authority are generally between people of the same status, i.e., board member to board member and executive to staff. Consequently, board members do not have any authority over the staff except over the executive director; nor does the latter have any authority over the board members.

While authority is a more visible form of power, the influence of a board member or executive is not restricted to their respective authority. As we shall see next, changes in authority or responsibility affect the extent of power, i.e., the ability to influence the behavior of the board member of executive in a desired direction. The relationship is asymmetrical because one can have considerable power with relatively little authority and responsibility, or vice versa, one can have considerable authority and/or responsibility, like many board members, and relatively little power.

Power

As noted earlier, discussions of power in the board-executive relationships are rare, despite the recent finding that "... conflict between executive directors and trustees is all too common in not for profit organizations, especially in middle size and small non-profit organizations where differences may become personal" (Unterman and Davis, 1982: 36). Perhaps the reluctance to recognize openly the existence of power in such social relations exists because "to unmask the actual distribution of power may serve to reduce the power of those operating behind the mask" (Gross, 1968: 77).

It is true that there are a number of conceptual problems in estimating power because of its multiple sources and effects. To avoid some of these difficulties, power can be viewed as a reciprocal relationship where the power of one derives from the dependency of another, i.e., the greater the dependency of one person, the broader the influence of the other (Hasenfeld, 1983: 178-185). As a synonym for power and to avoid some of its pejorative character, we shall refer to resources for influence and distinguish it from the notion of control. As Zald points out, board member and executive each bring to bear on their relationship distinctive resources, varying in importance and "it is the balance of resources in specific situations and decisions that determines the attribution of relative power in the encounter between boards and executives" (Zald, 1968: 98).

What are some of these resources for influence accruing to boards and executives by virtue of their respective status? It is first necessary to distinguish between the resources of the board as a group with its corporate, legal authority which serves to legitimate the organization, and the board member as a person who has other resources for influence. The individual board member may have prestige as a community notable, and hence his name is a resource. He may have access to funds, his own and others, or to other volunteers or goodwill for the agency. By means of peer and other interpersonal relationships, board members can form coalitions which can exert influence within the board or in the community. Apart from their community connections, board members can have knowledge, skill, time, energy, as well as the duration and intensity of their commitment to the agency.

Sources and determinants of executive influence

The power of the executive stems largely from his status as a professional, his administrative authority and responsibilities, and his informal relationships. As a professional he is presumed to be knowledgeable about the agency and its operation as well as the field of service in which it functions. His professionalism also implies a full time if not a lifelong career commitment. There is also the influence based on continuity and presumably the longer the duration of his service, the greater his influence.

> ...the executive is in many ways invested with virtually unlimited power over many things and persons. The larger and more bureaucratic the organization, and the more autonomous the executive, the greater the opportunity to exploit or abuse such power with relative impunity. The smaller the organization, ...the more direct than unsettling the experience for victims of such exploitation and abuse and the more personal the effects may be or may feel (Levy, 1982: 61).

Because of his location in the communication structure of the agency he has access to and control over information which can then be shared selectively with board members and staff (Brager and Specht, 1973: 223). The executive probably receives and gives more information than anyone else and he acts as a communication link between board and staff. As noted earlier in the discussion of responsibility for policy making, the executive's expertise and access to information makes it possible for him to identify, select and define the issues that eventually comprise the agenda for the board of directors. The executive helps define the situation for the board through his responsibility for the preparation of virtually all the written material they receive such as minutes, reports, budgets, memoranda, analyses of policy alternatives and their likely consequences, etc.

Apart from carrying out his professional responsibility "to inform, educate and guide the board," the extent of the executive's influence on the issues he selects for attention will also be affected by their substantive character, as well as the decision making situation. For example, board members' influence may be greater if issues are particularly salient for them such as the allocation of funds, facilities, and other tangible resources, or if an important policy precedent will be set, or if personnel practices or interorganizational or community relations are involved. If, however, an issue can be defined as clinical-technical, professional or administrative, then it is quite likely that board member opinions may not be sought or count for very much. Also, certain types of decision making situations will tend to optimize the power of one or the other. In times of crisis, when an organization is facing major changes or threats, or when the time has come for executive succession, then the board will probably be dominant (Zald, 1969: 107). On the other hand, when the situation is more routine or when there are severe time constraints, then the matter may well be left to the executive for his action.

In addition to the resources for influence that are essentially structural, i.e., inherent in the professional status and administrative position of the executive, power can be mobilized through his informal, interpersonal relationships with the chairman, individual board members and key persons in the community. As a gatekeeper the executive provides access to recognition and prestige for persons whose names can be proposed to nominating and other committees which continually seek volunteers for community service tasks. By suggesting names to various community and national bodies he is in a position to influence who may rise to leadership and who will sit in judgment and make decisions in the future (Kahn, 1978; Feldstein, 1982). By selective sharing of information to certain persons he can give them more status because of their possession of inside information. In addition, the executive has a form of "input control" whereby he can influence the selective recruitment and socialization of new board members who are required by the annual turnover of a portion of most boards of directors.

Other structural features of the board of directors reinforce the informal power of the executive including the relatively large size of many boards which are only nominally policy making:

> The large board is preferred because it satisfies volunteers' desires for nominal involvement while leaving the director in control...some trustees also prefer a large board because they enjoy the public platform, the business context, and the opportunity to avoid individual responsibility (Unterman and Davis, 1982: 30).

In addition, boards tend to meet infrequently and most board members give relatively little time to their tasks. Another consequence of a large board, apart from the marginal attachment and the limited, episodic participation of most board members, is "the maneuverability which comes from ambiguity" (Brager and Specht, 1973: 236). This refers to the diffuseness of the board of directors' collective control as employer of the executive, i.e., while the total board is responsible for hiring and firing the executive, no one member is, thus enabling a wily executive to maneuver among different factions.

The ways in which the executive utilizes his professional authority and responsibility in interpersonal relationships (i.e., his power) will be determined by his ethical commitments and professional philosophy. The extent to which he values open sharing and disclosure of information rather than its suppression; truthfulness, loyalty, justice, fairness, etc. will shape much of his use, non-use or abuse of power (Levy, 1982: 68-70; Forester, 1982). Guiding the executive's behavior may be a view of the board as a nuisance or unnecessary burden, a group to be overcome, rather than an indispensable resource whose development is an essential part of professional responsibility and which requires appropriate values, knowledge and skill. These two extremes reflect the strain between a technocratic and a democratic ideology found among voluntary agency executives. The former refers to the belief that experts or professionals should have most of the power in organizational policy making, and from this perspective a board member can contribute little to the agency except perhaps legitimation. On the other hand, a democratic ideology regards as a norm the professional obligation to deducate citizen volunteers to enable them to develop their

leadership abilities. There is some impressionistic evidence
that while the democratic ideology is officially promulgated,
the technocratic ideology is widespread even if it is not
publicly acknowledged (Kramer, 1981: 112).

While board-executive relationships are influenced by the
attributes of the actors and the situation in which they find
themselves, they are also shaped by the organizational context
in which the interaction takes place. The extent to which one
or the other may prevail is affected by such structural factors
as the size, degree of complexity, bureaucratization, professionalization, or decentralization of the organization.
One could hypothesize that the more these variables are
optimized, the more dependent will board members be on the
executive for information and assistance. The agency's fiscal
system will also operate in favor of one or the other. In
organizations dependent on many small donors rather than on a
few large donors, or where there is great reliance on governmental contracts and grants, the executive may be less dependent
on the board members' fund raising abilities. Also, the stage
of development of the organization, whether it is new, old,
growing or declining would also seem to have differential effects
on the power of the board or the executive, with the board more
influential in the early rather than in the later stages of an
organizational career (Senor, 1964; Zald, 1969).

Actually, power/dependency is a continuum which ranges from
authoritarian, leader, catalyst, supporter/enabler, interpreter/
informant, submissive, and servant (Bolan, 1971: 388) which could
be combined into a three point scale of control, facilitating or
laissez-faire. Each end of the continuum represents an extreme,
and it is rarely the case that executives are either authoritarians
or only note takers at meetings, servants scurrying to do whatever the board wishes. At the same time, it is not unknown that
with a very careful facade and appropriate posture, the clever
professional can maintain a democratic form but really run the
entire organization.

Who dominates when?

Actually, we have very little research evidence regarding the
conditions under which one or the other dominate. In the past
some sociologists have made broad generalizations claiming that
most of the time the professional dominates the board, while
others claim that the opposite is the case (Gouldner, 1963;
Wilensky and Lebeaux, 1965). In one of the few empirical studies,
four different patterns of power distribution were identified in
the governing boards of 15 Israeli agencies. They were arranged
on a continuum with power concentrated in a single person, either
the executive or the president, and at the other end, power was

dispersed with varying forms of professional leadership (Kramer, 1981: 120).

One Man Domination	Board Domination	
Executive or President	Strong Professional Leadership	Weak Professional Leadership

Concentrated Power ----------------------- Dispersed Power

The agencies were almost equally distributed between the patterns of concentrated and dispersed power, but these patterns did not seem to be associated with any particular set of interests, issues or values. For example, the type of power distribution was not related consistently to the degree of active participation on the board or the rate of turnover. Attempts to carry the analysis beyond this point were not productive because the concentration of power in the executive or the board does not always tell us when and how it will be used, on behalf of what interests, values, and issues. It is therefore difficult to avoid the pitfalls which have plagued studies of community decision-making which assume a stable, consistent and fixed distribution of power that persists despite the issue and the particular situation.

Consequently, the power/dependency relationship between board and executive is neither a constant nor a zero-sum game; rather, "it depends" i.e., it is contingent on the factors which have been previously identified and which are summarized below:

Conditions Conducive to Greater Power for the Executive

To the extent that these variables are optimized, there is a greater likelihood that the executive will have relatively more power than board members:

Organization	large size	professionalization
	complexity	technical knowledge base
	bureaucratization	many small donors
	decentralization	reliance on governmental funds

Board Members   large number
high turnover
infrequent meetings
little service utilization/benefit
multiple community loyalties
shared welfare ideology
relatively low knowledge, experience,
   status, prestige and access to resources

	weak agency identification
	low degree of financial support
Situation	severe time constraints
	routine, absence of crisis
Issue	substantively clinical, technical, professional or interorganizational
	less tangible, non-fiscal or community-related
	non-precedent setting, less policy
	low salience
	non-controversial
	programmatic

Conclusions: Conflict or Resource Exchange?

Although the preceding analysis has emphasized the power relationships between board and executive, it is intended to be more of a countervailing corrective to the prevailing view of a partnership, rather than to argue for a conflict model. Even though there may be a power struggle between board and executive --and in the last analysis the board has the right to fire the executive--in practice the system tends to suppress conflict. Despite the significant disparity in their respective authority, responsibility and power, as well as in their status, norms and roles, the system of board-executive relationships operates in an equilibrium based on interdependence, tradeoffs and an exchange of resources.

Each party has resources and incentives to minimize conflict. Under the conditions of lay policy control and professional guidance, controversial items likely to cause undesirable conflict can be screened out through the executive's control over the agenda so that only safe issues are presented for consideration. This helps explain why so many boards are almost exclusively policy ratifying or adopting bodies, a phenomenon which has been described as non-decision making in which many meetings characteristically consist of reports that serve to "educate" or "bring along" the board.

Other built-in factors from the standpoint of the board which tend to minimize conflict include the lower saliency of goals, i.e., the multiple community loyalties and the marginal attach-ment of most board members mean that some issues are simply not worth fighting about. Apart from the wish to avoid unpleasant strife and embittered social relations, board members are also hindered in some conflict situations by the absence in the social services of objective measures of organizational effectiveness and executive and professional staff performance.

196

Another view, of course, is that conflict is not necessarily dysfunctional and that there can be a "creative tension" between board and executive which can work to the advantage of the organization. Indeed, this is what seems to be the case. Analysis of the structure and dynamics of the board-executive relationship suggests that they are dependent on each other but for different resources: they both "need" each other to carry out their respective responsibilities and to derive the necessary satisfactions. There is a functional necessity for complementary collaboration between these two sets of self-interests in which resources are exchanged. The executive requires the sanction and support of the board for his authority and his responsibility, which includes his technical assistance to them, and in turn, the board legitimates the agency. In return for the resources they bring to the agency, the board members receive from the executive prestige and validation of their corporate status as trustees and as community leaders. In the governance and policy making of the organization, both functional and hierarchical authority are needed and complement each other. The board has both legal and hierarchical authority and the executive has hierarchical authority delegated to him as well as the authority of his own expertise. The board presumably attends to certain aspects of the external environment which they share with the executive, while the latter is more responsible for the internal management.

The input system also contributes to the equilibrium. The process of selective recruitment and socialization nurtured by the self-perpetuating character of the board of directors of most voluntary organizations means that new members tend to be chosen because of their similarity in values and status to the continuing board members so there is little disruption of the ongoing pattern of board-executive relationships.

Using the language of social exchange theory, we could conclude that board members and executives interact in a patterned series of transactions to exchange resources for their mutual benefit, i.e., they seek to optimize their respective interests and to avoid or minimize perceived costs. The behavioral and decisional outcomes of this interaction depend upon the power/ dependency relationship between them and their relative power depends upon the importance of the resources they control (Emerson, 1975; Foa and Foa, 1980). Most of the time there is a balance of power which may, of course, be tilted in the direction of one or the other when the relevant variables are in place.

Notes

1. Note that the use of masculine pronouns applies to both men and women; it is obviously not intended to imply the

exclusion of women from the roles of board member or
executive.

2. An exception is found in the functional theory of leadership
in which group task and maintenance roles are defined
independently of the professional or volunteer status of
the participants. In this view, leadership does not inhere
in one person, but instead it is a function that can be
performed by anyone who provides what the group process
requires. Typical of the extensive literature on this
practice theory is E. P. Hollander, Leadership Dynamics,
New York: The Free Press, 1978.

REFERENCES

Argyris, C. and D. Schon
  1974   Theory in Practice: Increasing Professional Effective-
          ness, San Francisco, California: Jossey-Bass.

Bates, F. L.
  1962   "Some Observations Concerning the Structural Aspects of
          Role Conflict," Pacific Sociological Review 5 (Fall):
          75-82.

Biddle, B. J.
  1979   Role Theory, New York: Academic Press.

Bolan, R. S.
  1980   "The Practitioner as Theorist," Journal of the American
          Planning Association, 46:3 (July): 261-74.

Bolan, R. S.
  1971   "The Social Relations of the Planner," Journal of the
          American Institute of Planners (November): 386-96.

Brager, George and Harry Specht
  1973   Community Organizing, New York: Columbia Unviersity
          Press.

Caiden, G. E.
  1969   Administrative Reform, Chicago, Illinois: Aldine.

Conrad, W. and W. Glen
  1976   The Effective Voluntary Board of Directors, Boulder,
          Colorado: National Center for Voluntary Action.

Emerson, R. M.
  1975   "Social Exchange Theory." In Alex Inkeles (ed.), Annual
          Review of Sociology, Palo Alto, California: Annual
          Reviews, Inc. I, pp. 335-362.

Fayence, M.
    1977   Citizen Participation in Planning, New York: Pergamon.

Feldstein, Donald
    1982   "Democratic Governance and Professional Role in Agency
            Policy." Unpublished paper.

Foa, E. B. and O. G. Foa
    1980   "Resource Theory: Interpersonal Behavior as Exchange."
            In Social Exchange: Advances in Theory and Research,
            editors K. J. Gergen, M. S. Greenberg, and R. H. Willis.
            New York: Plenum Press.

Forester, John
    1982   "Planning in the Face of Power," Journal of the American
            Planning Association (Winter): 67-80.

Gouldner, Alvin W.
    1963   "The Secrets of Organizations." In The Social Welfare
            Forum, 1963, New York: Columbia University Press:
            161-177.

Gross, B. M.
    1968   Organizations and Their Managing, New York: The Free
            Press.

Gross, Neal et al.
    1958   Explorations in Role Analysis, New York: John Wiley
            and Sons.

Gummer, Burton
    1980   "Organization Theory for Social Administration." In
            Leadership in Social Administration, editors Felice
            Perlmutter and Simon Slavin. Philsadelphia, Pa.:
            Temple University Press, 22-52.

Hasenfeld, Yeheskel
    1983   Human Service Organizations, Englewood Cliffs, N.J.:
            Prentice-Hall, Inc.

Homans, George C.
    1961   Social Behavior: It's Elementary Forms, New York:
            Harcourt, Brace & World.

Kahn, William
    1978   "On Working with the Agency Board: A Sometime Neglected
            Skills," Journal of Jewish Communal Service LIV:4
            (Summer): 309-313.

Katz, D. and R. L. Kahn
    1966   The Social Psychology of Organizations, New York:
            John Wiley and Sons.

Kiesler, S.
    1978   Interpersonal Processes in Groups and Individuals,
            Arlington Heights, Ill.: AHM Publishers.

Knight, B. M.
    1968   "The Professional and the Board," Canadian Welfare
            (July-August): 8-9, 16.

Kramer, Ralph M.
    1965   "Ideologies, Status and Power in Board-Executive
            Relationships," Social Work 10: 108-114.

Kramer, Ralph M.
    1981   Voluntary Agencies in the Welfare State, Berkeley,
            California: University of California Press.

Levy, Charles S.
    1982   Guide to Ethical Decisions and Actions for Social
            Service Administrators, New York: Haworth Press.

Marmor, T. R. and J. A. Marone
    1980   "Representing Consumer Interests: Imbalanced Markets,
            Health Planning and the HSAs," Milbank Memorial Fund
            Quarterly 58: 125-165.

Nettler, Gwynn
    1958-9 "Ideology and Welfare Policy," Social Problems 6:3,
            pp. 203-211.

O'Connell, Brian
    1976   Effective Leadership in Voluntary Organizations,
            New York: Association Press.

Robins, A. J. and C. Blackburn
    1974   "Governing Boards in Mental Health: Roles and
            Training Needs," Administration in Mental Health
            (Summer): 37-45.

Rosenthal, S. and J. Young
    1980   "The Governance of the Social Services." In Leadership
            in Social Administration, editors F. D. Perlmutter and
            Simon Slavin. Philadelphia, Pa.: Temple University
            Press.

Schoderbek, Peter P.
    1979   Volunteer and Staff Responsibilities, New York:
            United Way of America.

Senor, James M.
    1963   "Another Look at the Executive-Board Relationship,"
            Social Work 8:2 (April): 19-25.

Specht, Harry
  1983   "Professional Interpersonal Interaction." Unpublished
          manuscript.

Steckler, A. B. and W. T. Herzog
  1979   "How to Keep Your Mandated Citizen Board Out of Your
          Hair and Off Your Back," American Journal of Public
          Health 69:8 (August): 809-812.

Stein, Herman
  1961   "Some Observations on Board-Executive Relationships
          in Voluntary Agencies," Journal of Jewish Communal
          Service 38: 390-396.

Trecker, Harleigh
  1970   Citizen Boards at Work: New Challenges to Effective
          Action, New York: Association Press.

Turner, Ralph H.
  1968   "Role: Sociological Aspects." In D. L. Sills (ed.),
          International Encyclopedia of the Social Sciences,
          New York: MacMillan and Free Press, 552-557.

Unterman, I. and R. H. Davis
  1982   "The Strategy Gap in Not-For-Profits," Harvard Business
          Review 60:3 (May-June) 30-2, 34, 36, 40.

Weber, Joseph
  1976   Managing the Board of Directors, New York: Greater
          New York Fund.

Wilensky, H. L. and C. N. Lebeaux
  1965   Industrial Society and Social Welfare, New York:
          The Free Press.

Zald, Mayer N.
  1970   "Political Economy: A Framework for Comparative
          Analysis." In Power in Organizations, editor Mayer
          N. Zald. Nashville, Tenn.: Vanderbilt University
          Press: 221-261.

Zald, Mayer N.
  1969   "The Power and Functions of Boards of Directors: A
          Theoretical Synthesis," American Journal of Sociology
          75: 97-111.

VOLUNTARISM AND PROFESSIONALISM: QUESTIONS OF IDENTITY AND RELATIONSHIP

Charles Guzzetta
Hunter College of The City University of New York

Introduction

"Volunteers" and "voluntarism" are examples of a class of terms
used in the social services which share a curious quality. They
convey a sense of understanding and agreement which frequently
masques a total lack of either. Everyone is familiar with the
terms and assumes predictable feelings evoked by their use.
A common assumption is that interpretations of the writer or
speaker and reader or listener are consistent with each other,
or at least that the meaning is clear. Therein lies a problem.
While it is the assumption which is incorrect, resultant disagreement over intent often leads, not to examination of the
assumption, but to charges of betrayal or malfeasance. There
are many examples of this class of seductive but unfaithful
terms, including "confidentiality," "authority," and "self-
determination." All are wonderfully ambiguous and help create
a substantial literature which may enjoy popularity, but seldom
advances clarity.

Who is a "volunteer" or the "voluntary worker" and what is
"voluntarism"? Reason would suggest that they are the same, but

that is not likely to be the case. In the time since non-governmental services ceased to be considered "private" and became "voluntary," the distinctions have become truly subtle. "Public" and "voluntary" as applied to social agencies do not necessarily refer either to funding or to the mode of practice of agency personnel, but only to auspice. A government agency is a "public" agency, even if 80% of its workers are volunteers. An agency created and sponsored by a non-governmental body such as a religious order, is "voluntary" even if all the workers are paid and 80% of its funding comes from tax revenues. In short, the impressions created and responses produced by use of the terms "volunteer" and "voluntarism" may have little to do with what those terms have come to represent in the present-day delivery of social services.

Phase I: Volunteer as "unpaid"

It is common knowledge even among non-social workers that human service organizations in the United States proliferated in the wake of the Civil War and the growth of industrialization and urbanization, as well as massive immigration. The phenomenon of human service groups was not new; the Scots Charitable Society was founded in Boston in 1657 (Pumphrey and Pumphrey, 1961) and there is evidence to suggest an even earlier mutual aid group formed by Portugese Jews in New Amsterdam, a burial society whose consecrated property can still be seen in Manhattan. Volunteers worked in legislatively mandated programs of poor relief, following the provisions of the Elizabethan Poor Law of 1601 which placed responsibility for implementation of the poor laws upon unpaid townspeople who were appointed by the judiciary: they might be called "the involuntary volunteers."

One of the most frequently cited descriptions of early 19th century American society is deTocqueville's observation about the voluntary groups so readily organized for any purpose. While Europeans might expect the government to take necessary action, he noted, Americans do not hesitate to organize and collectively address whatever concerns or interests them.* Yet, all the activity of the preceding 200 years was little more than an introduction to the explosion of concern for human well-being which accelerated steadily during the second half of the

---

*"Americans of all ages, all conditions and all dispositions constantly form associations," he wrote. Their associations are "religious, moral, serious, futile, general or restricted, enormous or diminutive." Americans organize to build inns, "found hospitals, prisons and schools" and to accomplish any purpose, "they form a society" (Woodroofe, 1962, pp. 178-179).

19th century, until America's entry into the first World War.

The change in voluntarism was fundamental. Most of the early non-governmental volunteer activity centered around mutual aid and self-help groups. The post-Civil War period introduced a basic shift from voluntarism for personal protection or security to voluntarism on behalf of another group, unrelated except through bonds of compassion and concern.

Two conditions developed to make this shift possible. One was the growth of a leisure class in cities, influenced by strong revivals of Protestant notions of stewardship. The other, less frequently recognized, was the legal basis for the foundation of charitable trusts. Philanthropy and charity have always been viewed with ambivalence and many English laws which specifically forbad charity formed the basis for challenges to charitable bequests in the new Republic. It was argued that charitable bequests withdrew from circulation resources that should be redistributed every generation. That principle seemed confirmed by the Supreme Court in a decision written by Chief Justice John Marshall in 1819. It was not until 1844 that the Supreme Court, in the Girard Will Case, adopted a permissive posture with respect to the establishment of philanthropic trusts, which became the basis for so much volunteer activity thereafter.* With the growth of industrialization, the charitable organizations that attracted the devotion of volunteers represented both religious objectives and, increasingly, secular goals.**

---

*For an analysis of this change, see H. S. Miller, The Legal Foundations of American Philanthropy (Madison: The State Historical Society, 1961). In this brilliant essay, Miller traces the two major doctrines which finally were settled in Vidal vs. Girard's Executors. Perhaps one reason the earlier Marshall decision has not received more attention is that it was written in the incredible year which included Dartmouth College vs. Woodward, M'Culloch vs. Maryland and Sturges vs. Crownshield. The Virginia case was brought partly in a concern for a free economy which had led Virginia earlier to abolish, under Jefferson's leadership, primogenitare and entail, and partly in fear of the power of religious organizations.

**Education was a popular objective of such bequests. First, such bequests sought to provide Christian education for Indians; later for slaves and freemen; ultimately for all who were able to benefit. Even such secular uses were not entirely popular. One author referred to the "very system of private endowment of institutions of learning" as "vicious and demoralizing in the extreme degree." I. Ladoff, American Pauperism and the Abolition of Poverty (Chicago: Kerr, 1904).

As philanthropy expanded, it was necessary to employ paid workers to oversee the efficient use of the monies left in trust. The idea grew, as the bequests and number of volunteers grew, that system had to be imposed on the chaotic world of charity and voluntarism. Leading scholars and organizers called for "scientific charity as opposed to purely emotional philanthropy" (Warner, 1889).

Conflict between "volunteers" and the paid agents was not long in coming, and paced the service expansion. Preoccupation with matters of efficiency under the new doctrine of "scientific philanthropy" led the paid agents, soon to pronounce themselves "professionals," to attend to prevention of abuses of charities. Protective measures included devices for cost control and procedures for eligibility determination. The march toward scientific philanthropy was marked by the successful transplant from England to the United States of the Charitable Organization Society in 1877. Fairly soon, it became clear that the new methods required training of workers. As these training programs appeared near the turn of the century, the distinctions between "volunteer" and "professional" began to be as muddled as the arguments exalting the superiority of each.

In ordinary usage, "volunteer" means non-coercive. A "volunteer" may be subject to the same rules and discipline as any other worker, but the volunteers presumably selected the course freely. For example, "volunteer army" is no less an army, but it is not raised by conscription. The Marine Corps may want "a few good men," but in peacetime it must convince those men to volunteer, or do without them. This common distinction never really has applied to social service. Rather, "volunteer" meant "unpaid", although something of the status attached to performing a kindly act without compulsion still clung to the word. The volunteer was seen as the truly altruistic worker, whose activity was motivated entirely by a sense of service or stewardship, without consideration of recompense, particularly financial. On the other hand, the paid worker might be similarly impelled by generous altruistic motivation, but it was a motivation which the worker could not entirely afford, requiring some financial payment to augment the more distinctive spiritual rewards of service. Since income was not a consideration for volunteers, their work stemmed from goodness and "from humanitarian aims" unsullied by cash reward (Cohen, 1958).

Phase II: Volunteer as "untrained"

With the success of training programs after the turn of the century, the term "paid" was supplanted by "professional" to distinguish the paid agent, and another dimension was added to the difference between the "volunteer" and other workers. In a maneuver that was as brilliant as it was unplanned (and perhaps even unconscious), trained workers reversed the moral valence on the term "volunteer," forcing it to stand against the term "professional" rather than "paid." Formerly, "volunteer" had meant: generous, good, kindly, successful, responsible--Christian. With the shift, to be a "volunteer" took on additional meanings, less positive. Volunteers came to be seen as "do-gooders," to whom the social problems were a hobby or recreation; affluent people with nothing better to occupy them than to peep in on the miserable lives of the downtrodden and "inferior" people, in the sense captured by Nietzche's observation that "curiosity creeps into the homes of the poor disguised as pity."

Meanwhile, the paid agents, now increasingly trained, redefined themselves. Formerly, they had been seen, at least in part, as well-intentioned people who could not afford to provide social services without a financial offset. This placed them, with respect to the volunteers, in an only slightly better position than the recipients of the volunteers' largesse. In a way, the paid agents were the "good" poor, a step above "worthy," but several steps below "successful." Now, the paid agents, identifying themselves as "professional," sought to take on the respected attributes of the professional. Shifting attention away from the payment for work, they purported to be (in contrast to the volunteers) educated in the proper ways of providing service: scientific, serious, and embarked upon careers. The very moral advantages of volunteer service were applied to the term "professional."*

Thus, it was sought to neutralize the status advantages of affluence and influence. As the director of the first training program for social workers put it, in placing the wealthy in their "proper" position with respect to the oft-noted moral inferiority of the impoverished, "the errors of the poor as a class are not much more serious...than those of the rich. It is simply that the consequences are more serious" (Devine, 1914, pp. 77-78).

For half a century, the paid worker had been an adjunct to the volunteer, employed for the purpose of helping the volunteer achieve his moral mission. Now, the drive to professionalism by paid workers reversed their position with the volunteer and they used various devices to secure the advantage. The power and financial resources which had signified the inherent Protestant superiority of the volunteer came to be identified with the oppressor. The paid workers continued to be predominantly

---

*Originally, the word "professional" had defined the true amateur; one to whom the activity gave pleasure and required supreme effort and to whom the notion of "professing" for money was morally repugnant (Seeley, 1964).

Protestant, in contrast to the waves of poor Catholics and Jews inhabiting the urban ghettos, but there was a certain advantage in placing distance between themselves and the unpaid workers who, representing the affluent class, were seen more and more as being "part of the problem rather than part of the solution." It was held of volunteers that "in general they accepted the prevailing laissez-faire philosophy" (Cohen, 1958, p. 79) of the increasingly distrusted and hated industrialists. In the Charity Organization Society, the professionals, originally hired to serve the volunteers, now barred volunteers from any administrative responsibility related to material assistance (Mencher, 1959), effectively reversing their relative roles.

The change was remarkably swift--about one generation. For years, there had been close cooperation between volunteers and paid workers "in building the framework of organized welfare services" and the paid workers "never doubted the real or potential contribution of voluntarism" (Lubove, 1965, p. 160). The first training program was merely a summer institute which lasted for six weeks in 1898 (Pumphrey and Pumphrey, 1961). Within a short time, paid workers, seeking professional status, were viewing the spirit, impulse and activity of the volunteer with "suspicion and derision" (Mencher, 1959).

By 1915, the paid workers were prepared to be publicly anointed as professionals. Abraham Flexner, whose report a few years earlier had had a profound impact upon medical education and who was the foremost authority on professionalism, was invited to deliver the benediction. Instead, he announced that social work was not, in his judgment, a profession, a blow from which the collective psyche of social workers has never fully recovered.* The report did, however, help the paid workers to make a decision about goals. Following Flexner's advice to do something about

---

*Flexner was followed to the lectern by a young lawyer who had been active in the settlement house movement, Felix Frankfurter. In his address, Frankfurter stated that social work certainly was a profession, but it was too late--the psychic damage had been done. Of course, not all social workers had taken the move to professionalism seriously. Robert Woods wrote in 1905 that the characteristics of a profession were male, independent, intelligent, skilled and impersonal, while the "model" of the social worker was female, dependent, warm and not-too-bright. For seventy years, the literature has been full of studies by sociologists claiming that social work is not "yet" or "fully" a profession or is a "semi-profession"; with a parade of articles by social workers which say, in effect, "We are, we are, too."

the "lack of specificity" which "affects seriously the problem
of training social workers," the field moved toward a
definition of social casework which, ignoring the sage advice
of Mary Richmond in her celebrated 1917 book Social Diagnosis,
became increasingly intrapsychic.

There are many reasons for this shift. An obvious one is that
it would require specialized training, which was not considered
necessary for social action or social policy influence, where
the monied classes had all the advantages of power, position and
access to lawmakers. The move received a great boost in the
post-War atmosphere of hysteria which defined social action as
foreign and subversive.

In an ambivalence toward its own status which has become almost
a hallmark of the field, social workers followed the growing
trade union movement of hostility toward volunteers while
simultaneously rejecting identity as workers themselves and
seeking the special prerogatives of professional status. The
irony is that many of the foremost spokesmen for the working
poor were the most significant volunteers within social agencies,
while the paid agents remained, for the most part, hostile
toward the trade unionists' struggle.

All through the 1920's, the search for clarity of goal continued,
intimately tied to problems of relationships between voluntarism
and professionalism. Professionals protested that

> "even after much progress had been made in analyzing
> scientific methods of handling the various types of
> work, there was a persistence of the conception of
> the worker as merely a benevolent person 'doing good
> to the poor'" (Van Kleeck and Taylor, 1922).

Increasingly, "professional" was defined as casework or administration and social change was replaced by individual change.
The dual aspects of individual charitable work and social
action in which paid agents and volunteers had been united*
faded, with the social actionists no longer welcome in social
work and social work no longer interested in changing society as
a way of helping the oppressed. As Freidson was to point out

----

*Generally, the paid agents had been working in voluntary
 (non-public) welfare agencies with volunteers. These volunteers who were engaged in trying to change the conditions that
 led to social problems were most closely identified with the
 settlement house movement. Both served the same general
 population, but in a markedly different relationship to them
 and to each other.

rather delicately, social workers became more involved in performing "services which the layman not only did not himself ask
for, but the purpose of which he sometimes could not see."

Voluntarism's social change objectives became blunted, too,
and volunteers could no longer be sure that they were welcome
anywhere in social services, except as financial contributors.
Even that role was hotly debated in professional social worker
meetings. At the turn of the century, "volunteers were engaged
in public welfare as much as they were in private organizations"
(Mencher, 1959, p. 223); during the 1920's voluntarism was
becoming almost moribund in key areas. What had been "a
dynamic, progressive influence in American life" was becoming a
"substitute for social action" (Lubove, 1968, p. 2). There was
ecstatic praise for the "forward rank" of workers who sought to
"transform old-style philanthropy into genuine social thera-
peutics" (The New Republic, 1926), but the change also had its
detractors. Decrying the decline of social action and the
professionalization of the social services, Abraham Epstein
called it a "soulless" field of activity. "What has become
essential in modern social welfare work is not so much broad
understanding or social vision," he wrote, "but executive
ability and detailed technical skill." The field, he declared,
"has become too practical to be passionate...it has become
merely amiable" (Epstein, 1928, pp. 391-392).

Phase III: Volunteer as "non-public"

The Depression produced another change in the definition of
"voluntarism" and in the relations between volunteers and
professionals. The leading social worker in the public sector
was Harry Hopkins. Hopkins had been a settlement worker who
had, after receiving advanced training, worked in the private
welfare sector. From Frank Bane, Hopkins adopted the idea of
"public funds expended by public agencies" (Sherwood, 1948,
p. 47). In 1931, Hopkins spoke to the national meeting of
social workers and was induced to take a public stand that
opposed the distribution of relief through the private or
voluntary sector. Two years later, in setting up the Federal
Emergency Relief Agency, Hopkins endorsed the hiring of
experienced, skilled private charity workers by public relief
agencies (Charles, 1973, p. 32).

With this major shift in direction, "volunteer" came to mean
"non-public" (although not necessarily 'private'), as contrasted
with those whose payment for social services work came from tax
revenues.

The country always had provided various forms of poor relief
through an assortment of agencies, usually local, but in-

increasingly at the state level. However, these were generally agencies of last resort, the major burden of poor relief being provided through the well-organized voluntary sector. Public monies, when available for social services, was usually channelled through these agencies, whose workers were a mix of volunteers and paid agents or "professionals," as they now fashioned themselves. The public agencies principally used paid employees, who did not enjoy the same status as the private agency paid workers.

Hopkins' decision brought two important changes to the world of voluntarism. For one, it gave immediate employment to numbers of private agency employees whose sponsors had come to the end of their resources. The private money vanished quickly in the first year or two of the Depression. By 1933, the cities and states also were out of funds and the voluntary agencies had nowhere else to go for funds except the federal government and many of them were in principle opposed to federal intervention. Increasingly, the volunteers had nothing to distribute and the professionals had no programs to administer. Since the volunteers still had personal resources, the lack of work may have been the same for volunteers as for professionals, but to use Devine's observation, the consequences were different for each group.

A second effect of Hopkins' decision in hiring workers from private agencies was to change the status of the public relief worker. However distasteful it may have been for private agency professionals to work as mere public employees, they did not propose to surrender their status as professionals, no matter how illusory. The influx of paid, trained, experienced social workers from the voluntary sector imparted to the public relief agencies an identity heretofore unknown to them, although a certain stigma was to persist in its attachment to welfare department social workers for another three or four decades. As the federal government strained to reduce the disastrous impact of the Depression, it was pressed on both sides: on one, to use the power of the government directly with the economic and social problems and on the other, to rely on voluntarism as "the distinctly American method of collective action" (Lubove, 1968, p. 24). The attempt to reconcile these two points of view was passed into the laws of the nation in 1935: it was the Social Security Act (Lubove, 1968).

The changing relationship between volunteers and professionals was part of other social changes which had been transforming the nation since the 1890's. The wave of Christian reform zeal which had been an integral part of abolition and institutional reform, then of child-saving and social service organization, and finally culminated in Prohibition and suffrage for women ended with the disillusionment of a World War. Class privileges were swept away in Europe and the developing industrial class system in the United States came under assault, partly through the trade union movement.

With the decline of religious fervor and the attack on the excesses of wealth, along with a rising sense of self-interest by the immigrant poor in cities and native poor in the heartland, the status conferred by engaging in volunteer work began to evaporate. The rich began to seek new outlets for their impulses, outlets which would still confer a special positive value of moral superiority. And as paid professionals began to take control of the eleemosynary system, pushing volunteers into low-prestige activity and/or fund-raising, the population which comprised the volunteers also changed.

For many years, the ranks of voluntarism contained many men, often men of means. Singular workers such as Dix, Addams, Lathrop and others notwithstanding, many leaders and the workers in social welfare movements during the 19th century were men. The list of such volunteers in social welfare movements from corrections to mental illness, poverty to child welfare, education to abolition includes the most celebrated men of the century. Charles Loring Brace, Samuel Gridley Howe, Stanton Coit, John Augustus, Thomas Eddy, Thomas Gallaudet, Robert Hartley, S. Humphreys Gurteen, Franklin B. Sanborn, Clifford Beers-- it goes on and on. As status began to flow to the professional side of services and away from volunteers, so did the men. Voluntarism became a proper activity only for women. It is true that women in comfortable means had been well-represented among the direct service providers; but to a much greater extent than had been true before, only such positions on the lower rungs now were open to them. While men had been represented both in administration and direct service positions; they gravitated extensively to the first, coming to dominate policy in both the public and private, and volunteer and professional services. Where they continued to serve as unpaid volunteers, they did so with titles or names which set them apart from the mainstream of volunteers; they were called "philanthropists," "fund raisers," "board members" and the like. Moreover, women found that it could be difficult to move out of volunteer roles, while men had access not only to the administrative ladder, but to alternate careers. Once established in another career, they often were not identified with their origins in voluntarism. For example, Jane Addams won a Nobel Peace Prize, but is always associated with volunteer work in the settlement house movement; the political activity and significant successes of Julia Lathrop, Florence Kelley and Grace Abbott nevertheless tend to be overshadowed by their identification with voluntarism. On the other hand, many male settlement house workers who were their contemporaries moved out of the field after sometimes long associations but seldom later were identified with their work as social service volunteers; for example, Felix Frankfurter, Adolf A. Berle, Dean Acheson, Henry Morganthau, Jr. and Herbert Lehman.

Phase IV: Volunteer as "non-member"

By the time of World War II, another stage in the changing identifies of voluntarism and volunteers was well-established. It was to last until the massive efforts of the federal government in the mid-1960's to break the powerful, but ineffective monopoly of public welfare agencies and private social service agencies on human services. That futile effort did result in another identity for "volunteer," but it did not become as well established as the preceding three stages. After 1965, one aspect of voluntarism was the activity of "indigenous worker." A unique development on the federal level, although it had roots in the colonial and immigrant self-help groups, it was somehow out of place. "Indigenous worker" meant neither monied volunteers nor middle-class professionals, but the recipients of services themselves. Long before this emerging trend was able to be established as a new strain of volunteers, the national organization of social workers coopted it by a startling redefinition downward of "professional." After sixty years of battling to raise the standards required for official recognition as a "professional social worker"--the two-year master's degree had been adopted as the minimum standard in 1939--the National Association of Social Workers announced that it would henceforth admit holders of the baccalaureate degree to full professional standing. In 1974, the Council on Social Work Education began to accredit programs which awarded the B.S.W. degree. Further activity by both organizations to assure adequate "indigenous" activity and support has so far left in disarray both the public understanding of what is a "professional" in social services and precisely how to differentiate one from a "volunteer," except by a receipt of a salary.

The present ambiguity which shrouds the terms "volunteer" and "voluntarism" is largely a function of the historical changes briefly sketched here. The differing and often conflicting attitudes and moral values attached to the terms continue to provoke responses long after the original reasons for them have receded. Problems arise because individuals respond in emotional and highly personal ways to their private perceptions of "voluntarism" and "volunteers." Yet, one is seldom required to explain or even to examine the nature of the response or the reasons for it. Instead, there is a tendency to believe that one's response to the terms is not only appropriate, but that it is shared by most other people.

This matter would be less significant if voluntarism had declined or withered away. Had that happened, it could be regarded as a quaint historical phenomenon. That did not happen. Each time voluntarism was attacked, it demonstrated the vigor of the phoenix, even though its reappearance took a somewhat altered form. Even after the precipitous decline of post-World War II years, voluntarism revived in the 1960's, and the first years of the 1980's were witness to a federal commitment to restore voluntarism to the central role of actual service provider. As volunteers and professionals have been thrown together, intimacy does not appear to have created greater understanding. Old mythologies show little sign of losing vigor.

Current characteristics of volunteers and voluntarism

A recent review of the current literature on volunteers revealed extensive discussions of their work and proper roles in schools, mental health centers, hospitals, probation offices, correctional institutions, social welfare agencies, and telephone hot-line centers, to name a few examples (Gidron, 1982). The writer found that five reasons are widespread as explanations for the value and persistence of volunteers, and reflect the "current wisdom" surrounding the roles and activities of volunteers.

1. extension of agency service without enlargement of paid staff;
2. addition of a spontaneous, non-bureaucratic dimension to service;
3. provision of a link between agency and community;
4. promotion of client advocacy and representation; and,
5. advancement of the values and ideals of social work and democracy.

The list contained the results of the literature review: it didn't attempt a redefinition, but rather, a description of the present state. There is no shortage of examples to show the prevalence of the five ideas. Professionals have noted that volunteers do not reduce the work of paid workers, but the use of volunteers "expands the range and scope of agency service" (Hardcastle, 1971), and make it possible to "provide new services in innovative ways" (Reissman, 1965). Other claims for volunteers within the scope of the five-item list are that they provide "more individual attention than the impersonal, and often inflexible, state agency," especially where the social problems being addressed call for "a special degree of tact and understanding" (Woodroofe, 1962, p. 20). Similar advantages have been reported among British volunteers, including those of "economy, of freeing...manpower, of permitting more time to be spent on purely personal and friendly contacts than a salaried worker may rightly give" and harnessing the good will of individual local people (Slack, 1965, p. 32).

The general ambivalence toward volunteers, never far from the surface, would seem to have clearly tipped in favor of volunteers and voluntarism as morally superior but technically inferior in the provision of service.

A number of writers have sought to paint a more balanced portrait, noting that the present perception of volunteers results from "misunderstanding." Many volunteers, Schwartz noted, are "highly skilled" and not just "misguided do-gooders" (Schwartz, 1978). Yet, even this attempt at an even-handed description indicates the importance of volunteers for meeting social issues "in a free society." The clear implication in this assertion gives volunteers a morally elevated position only a few degrees removed from a statement in the House of Lords to the effect that volunteers counteract "the natural bias of the Welfare State towards totalitarianism" (Woodroofe, 1962, p. 21).

The idea that volunteers are not very technically proficient fits the presently dominant ideology that the practice of social work must be "scientific." This is, of course, a current strategy in the long war for professional status. It is a direct descendent of 19th century scientific philanthropy. In its present metamorphosis, the aggressive position on professionalism is that the only legitimate practice is that which can be justified by scientific study and "empirical evidence." This evidence upon which practice principles and procedures are to be based usually consists of observations and opinions which have been subjected to elaborate statistical manipulation. The evidence which is acceptable is that which can be counted. What cannot be counted is not "scientific." Since the sorts of roles into which volunteers have been moved preclude the sort of activity which lends itself to counting and statistical procedure (for example, activity requiring "tact" and "understanding," "goodwill," "friendly contacts," "advocacy" and upholding "ideals"), the work of volunteers is not "skilled" enough to be considered professional.

But ambivalence requires opposing views. If volunteers are disdained as unprofessional, they are still admired for their selfless, financially unrewarded work. They still enjoy the mystique of special power that goes with being financially independent in our Republic; that special quality of being truly "different" in the sense that F. Scott Fitzgerald meant it. The ambivalence is probably primarily on the side of paid workers. It is not uncommon for upwardly-yearning, middle-class, white collar workers to feel ambivalence toward those who may work beside them, often as diligently and as well; but by choice, and with the option of stopping, without significant

penalty. It is easy to understand why the ambivalence should be
so strong. An analogy that may illustrate the reactions may be
seen by moving the case one class down. The child of professional social workers may feel himself "poor" while attending
college. He realizes that he is sacrificing time which could
be used to earn income and his living circumstances may be
reduced. He may have difficulty understanding why the ghetto
residents who live near his small dormitory room see his "poverty"
as an affectation; an artificial and temporary circumstance
which will end in ultimate gain and in any event, may be
terminated at will.

As after World War I, the economics of social services have
changed in recent years. In the industrial nations, wages for
production workers and for social workers have increased
dramatically. However, the advancing wages of industrial
workers have been offset by increased productivity. This increase in productivity in the industrial sector has not been
matched by increased productivity in the social sector (Wagner,
1982). As a consequence, the cost of social services has risen
sharply in real terms, but even more sharply as a proportion of
the national economy.

The expense of social services began to create a situation
which provided the justification for a sharp adjustment. The
move in the United States from "demand side" to "supply side"
economic theory testifies, in large part, to public concern over
the cost of social services as a percentage of total government
spending. In the social services, "supply side" is translated,
in one way, as "reprivatization" of social welfare. The
vigorous expansion of the '60's ended by the time of the Ford
administration and actual contraction of services began in the
Carter administration. This curtailment became severe as the
Reagan administration reorganized federal priorities.

In an atmosphere of support for reprivatization of services and
planned contraction of the public sector, the work of volunteers
began to metamorphose again: another shift in the balance
between voluntarism and professionalism, between volunteers and
paid workers cannot be far off. Although his research centered
in West Germany, Wagner's findings could be expected to have a
similar or parallel image in the United States. That image is
one of enormous potential offset for government programs provided by the work of volunteers, whether or not reprivitization
succeeds extensively.

Of the changing and confusing currents which flow between and
around volunteerism and professionalism, little systematic
study has been done. Literature about the values of each have
tended to reflect assumptions and belief systems which are

presented in naked innocence of any substantive evidence to support them. One significant exception is a massive, eight-year research study conducted by Ralph Kramer, the results of which were published piecemeal throughout the duration of the work and in 1981, provided in complete and final form. Kramer compared voluntarism in Netherlands, Israel, United States and England. His conclusions present impressive evidence which tends to uphold certain popular beliefs and to refute others (Kramer, 1981).*

For example, the study addressed the belief that voluntarism provides a spontaneity and autonomy which is lost or severely diminished in public programs or where there is greater govern-ment accountability. This idea that "private-voluntary" programs become more rigid and less responsive to client need as they become more dependent upon public funds was not supported in the findings of the research.

Kramer noted that the voluntary sector, perhaps because it has been held less accountable for its activity than the public sector for use of tax revenues, has not been particularly successful in demonstrating any results--either good or bad--that have resulted from its activities. Rather than explain the outcomes of their activities, voluntary agencies have tended to emphasize specification of what those activities are. That is, the focus has been on process rather than conclusions. As voluntary agencies have become more reliant on public funding during the past twenty years, they have become increasingly accountable for the consequences of their activities. No significant loss of spontaneity nor creativity was found to result from this increased public accountability.

The idea that the use of volunteers provides more responsive, sensitive, client-oriented, community-related, non-bureaucratic, idealistic service was examined. Kramer found that the use of volunteers did not appear to increase these qualities of service, since volunteers generally have been kept from direct service

---

*To avoid the necessity of extensive footnotes, the discussion of Kramer's work will be stipulated to be based upon this book. Exceptions to this stipulation will be noted. Because most of the conclusions discussed here appear several times throughout the book, the reader is advised to take time to read the entire volume rather than to spot specific conclusions. It goes with-out saying, of course, that the study was not conducted entirely without an ideological premise, which is readily apparent in the final recommendations.

delivery and shunted into peripheral support roles, primarily fund-raising.* There seems to be a sufficiency of suggestions on recruiting and deploying volunteers in direct service roles, but only a modest number of examples of such activity actually taking place.

The function of volunteers and voluntary agencies in filling a "vanguard role" in social welfare was studied by Kramer. He described as the "vanguard role", the movement into innovative, independent, creative directions in providing improved service delivery. The study did not confirm the existence of such a role particular to volunteers. First of all, it found that small, flexible, voluntary programs do not remain either small or flexible for very long. If they survive, the programs grow, become bureaucratic, and narrow their function. It may be that this change is related to survival. Moreover, the initiative for innovation arises about twice as often from bureaucratic, paid, staff professionals as from volunteer workers, according to this study. This phenomenon was found to exist in agencies of all sizes and did not vary significantly with size of agency. It persisted in various ways. For example, the higher the proportion of professionals to volunteers, the more original programs were developed by an agency. The largest, most professionalized, most bureaucratic programs were found to be the most common leaders in program innovation and aggressive policy activity.

One of the more startling findings of the Kramer study was that professionals often "plant" new ideas among volunteers, who then press to try them out. Then, the professionals implement the innovations as a "response to demand," protecting themselves from charges of empire-building. The "spokesmen and advocates" for clients were found to appear more frequently among professionals than among volunteers, irrespective of agency function.

Kramer found "innovation" to be a grossly misused word, usually applied to modest, incremental, noncontroversial extensions of existing services, rather than to new programs or radical ways of delivering services. Even where voluntary agencies

---

*There have been notable exceptions, of course. One which was reported nearly 20 years ago was a program of the Association for Jewish Children of Philadelphia (Goldstein, 1966). This program functioned under a Director of Volunteers whose responsibilities included "constant direction" and oversight of "the absorption of [the] volunteers into the agency's operation." However, the Director of Volunteers was "not a social worker."

successfully implement truly innovative programs, their influence on the public sector was found to be minimal: either they die during implementation or, if successful, are not taken up by the public sector. If the new programs are not adopted, the voluntary agencies cannot be said to serve a "vanguard role" in social services, however worthy their intentions.

Despite the misconceptions about the role and functions of voluntarism and volunteers in social welfare agencies, there is virtually no articulate objection to them. Use of volunteers has been found to be almost universally endorsed,* but there is great disagreement about what they should do in agencies. Kramer found two basic positions. The first follows the historical line of stewardship and personal caring; the second follows the line of mutual help and policy influence, what has been called "socio-political" work. It is the former which is closer to the American model.

This excellent study provides a basis for a much better under-standing of the nature of voluntarism in our society. It has become available at a crucial time. If it is true that collabora-tive work between volunteers and professionals has been marred by lack of knowledge and suspicion, Kramer's work will be in-valuable in helping create a common ground for understanding, as well as a reliable foundation upon which to extend the research and understanding.

Summary and conclusions

Questions around which the relationships between volunteers/ voluntarism and paid workers/professionalism have moved over the past century in this country, have changed every thirty years or so.

The first arose after 1877, when the COS was introduced into American social welfare: the focus was pay and the result was the control of the provision of direct social service by paid workers rather than by volunteers (although volunteers retained control of policy-setting). The second arose after 1905, when the first School of Civics and Philanthropy was established: the focus was special training and the result was the domination of the provision of direct social services by trained workers

---

*The exceptions found by Kramer were objections by clinical workers, who may have felt that their jobs were threatened, and certain feminist groups who object to voluntary work as a form of exploitation of women. There is no record of their objection to volunteers who are men.

rather than by untrained volunteers (although volunteers and untrained workers continued to represent the larger group of
workers).

The third arose after 1934, when the federal commitment to social
welfare began:* the focus was auspice and the result was the
assumption of broad policy-setting for social services by the
public sector rather than the voluntary sector (although the
voluntary sector continued to command the services of most of the
professional social workers).

The current stage arose after 1974, when the leading social work
membership organizations redefined professionalism for the
purpose of rapid expansion and pre-emption of all positions of
social service provision by paid, social work-educated professionals, both in the public and the voluntary sectors: the
focus was extension and consolidation of power and control. It
is too early to assess clearly the ultimate result.

The relationship among service providers remain ambiguous. In
seeking to examine them, and how they are developing, it is
necessary always to be clear about what categories are being
compared. At present, four major categories exist among social
service providers: (1) paid workers with undergraduate social
work education; (2) paid workers with graduate social work
education; (3) paid workers without social work education, and
with or without education in another profession or discipline;
and, (4) unpaid workers. Only the fourth category represents
volunteers.

Precise identification of voluntarism with respect to program
(rather than worker identification) is considerably more complex.
However, the withdrawal of financial support by governmental
units from the federal to the local level, should the trend
continue, will bring a painful clarity in fiscal terms.

The current shifts in relationship between volunteers/
voluntarism and paid workers/professionalism are somewhat
clouded by the bitterness and acrimony of struggles among the
professionals. If these are not resolved, other questions may
be rendered moot, as professional social work could decline
rapidly to be replaced by some other group. If the professionals
resolve their differences and again struggle collectively to
eliminate or completely control volunteers, the final outcome of

---

*Previous federal programs, even the massive and impressive
 Freedman's Bureau notwithstanding, this was the first true
 federal commitment on a continuing basis.

such a struggle may not be predicted with certainty. However, volunteers in social service have seen the emergence and decline of many professions and pursuits during the last several hundred years and always survived intact. What is certain is that the price for the present movement to alter the relationship between voluntarism/volunteers and professionalism/paid workers is likely to be paid, as usual, by those most affected and least consulted: the recipients of social services.

REFERENCES

Charles, Searle F.
   1963   <u>Minister of Relief</u>, Syracuse: University Press.

Cohen, Nathan
   1958   <u>Social Work in the American Tradition</u>, New York: Holt, Rinehart and Winston.

Devine, Edward T.
   1914   <u>The Practice of Charity</u>, New York: Dodd, Mead.

Epstein, Abraham
   1928   "The Soullessness of Present-day Social Work," <u>Current History</u>, June.

Fox, Daniel M.
   1967   <u>The Discovery of Abundance</u>, Ithaca: Cornell.

Freidson, Eliot
   1959   "Specialties without Roots: the Utilization of New Services." <u>Human Organization</u>, Fall: 112-116.

"From Social Work to Social Science," <u>The New Republic</u>, June 2, 1926.

Gidron, Benjamin
   1982   "Teaching Social Workers to Utilize Volunteers in their Practice." Unpublished paper presented at Congress of the International Association of Schools of Social Work, Brighton. August 24, 1982.

Goldstein, Harriet
   1966   "Supplementary Services by Volunteers in a Casework Agency," <u>Social Welfare Forum</u>, Columbia: NCSW.

Hardcastle, David
   1971   "The Indigeneous Nonprofessional in the Social Service Bureaucracy," <u>Social Work</u> 16: April.

Kramer, Ralph
   1981   <u>Voluntary Agencies in the Welfare State</u>. Berkeley: Calif.

Ladoff, Isador
  1904   American Pauperism and the Abolition of Poverty,
         Chicago, Ill.: Karn.

Lubove, Roy
  1965   The Professional Altruist, Cambridge: Harvard.

Lubove, Roy
  1968   The Struggle for Social Security 1900-1935, Cambridge:
         Harvard.

Mencher, Samuel
  1959   "The Future of Voluntaryism in American Social Welfare,"
         in Issues in American Social Work, Alfred Kahn (ed.),
         New York: Columbia.

Miller, Howard S.
  1961   The Legal Foundation of American Philanthropy
         1776-1844, Madison: The State Historical Society of
         Wisconsin.

Reissman, Frank
  1965   "The 'Helper' Therapy Principle," Social Work 10:
         April.

Schwartz, Florence S.
  1978   "The Professional Staff and the Direct Service
         Volunteer: Issues and Problems," Journal of Jewish
         Communal Service, March.

Seeley, John
  1964   "Professional Perplexities: Priests or Prostitutes,"
         Occasional Paper of the Center for the Study of Demo-
         cratic Institutions, Santa Barbara, January 15.

Sherwood, Robert E.
  1948   Roosevelt and Hopkins, New York: Grosset & Dunlap.

Slack, Kathleen M.
  1965   "Voluntary Effort," in Trends in Social Welfare,
         James Farndale (ed.), Oxford: Pergamon Press.

Van Kleeck, Mary and Graham Taylor
  1922   "The Professional Organization of Social Work,"
         The Annals 51.

Wagner, Antonin
  1982   "On Decentralization, Privatization and Depro-
         fessionalization: Is Small Always Beautiful?"
         Paper presented at Congress of International Association
         of Schools of Social Work, Brighton, August 25.

Warner, Amos G.
    1889   "Scientific Charity," <u>Popular Scientific Monthly</u> 39.

Woodroofe, Kathleen
    1962   <u>From Charity to Social Work</u>, London: Routledge &
            Kegan Paul.

Woods, Robert
    1905   "Social Work: A New Profession," <u>International Journal
            of Ethics</u> 16.

TRENDS AND CHANGES IN THE VOLUNTEER WORLD

Eva Schindler-Rainman

Organization and Community Consultant
Los Angeles, California

"May you be cursed to live in interesting times," is an old Chinese proverb. Those of us who move in the world of voluntarism have indeed been so "cursed." For the vast and rapid social changes are radically altering the world we have known and are also affecting the world of voluntarism. Voluntarism has an exciting and important past, and an even more promising, multi-faceted, creative future.

The 1980's and the 1990's will be challenging periods for volunteers, and staff working with volunteers, and for the systems with volunteer opportunities. The changes that are occurring are rapid and complex in the national and the international arenas. It is a time of transition which makes it possible to be creative, non-traditional, energetic, bound by nothing but human limitations, turfdoms, lack of vision and resistance to change. Indeed transition may be the key concept that characterizes where the volunteer world has been and where it is going. This is the period of the post-industrial society, the service society, or the Third Wave, as Alvin Toffler (1980) has said. It is a time of change, challenge and explosion.

The profile of the volunteer has also changed during the last thirty years. Today a volunteer might be any person, from three years of age to 103, who gives time, energy, skills or knowledge voluntarily to a chosen cause or activity without monetary profit. Volunteers come from all religious, racial, ethnic and lifestyle backgrounds. There is beginning to be an increasing number of handicapped people who volunteer. The vast majority of Americans are available to volunteer in their states, their cities and neighborhoods to help improve the quality of life in a vast variety of ways. The fact that so many people are available does not necessarily mean that recruitment methods have been reviewed or revised. To recruit and to motivate this rapidly expanding population requires of us that we think of them in new ways. Toward this end, this writer suggests the following categories as indicators of how and where they

225

may serve.

1. <u>Direct helpers</u>: These are people who give a direct service to others. This may be done on a one to one or one to group basis. Included here are such services such as tutoring, driving sick people to appointments, helping clients in an Internal Revenue office, shopping for the elderly and taking care of stray animals.

2. <u>Decision makers</u>: He or she is the Board member, an administrative volunteer, the volunteer who makes policy. Anyone can learn to be a decision making volunteer, and more persons from diverse backgrounds are being sought out to serve on Boards of Trustees, Commissions, and Committees.

3. <u>The connector or linker</u>: This is the volunteer whose major job it is to connect persons to available services, or providers of services to potential consumers. This may include persons who connect clients and patients to public health clinics and centers, or perhaps the person who connects adult volunteers to the school system.

4. <u>Cause of social action volunteers</u>: These people volunteer to work for a particular cause, like the Heart Association, Amnesty International, the local Rape Hotline, the National Organization for Women, and many more. Basically we have here people who are highly motivated to work for a movement, a social problem or a system which holds special interest for personal, social or political reasons. There may indeed be two kinds of cause or social action volunteers--those who advocate, and those who work directly with causing change to happen. The change agent volunteer, for example, might be a person who wants to change the mission or structure of an organization and may work to implement such change as a member of the Board of Directors. An advocate volunteer is one who advocates particular positions, be they political, economic, or in the health and welfare arenas.

5. <u>The monitor volunteer</u>: This is the volunteer who is specifically recruited to monitor programs and functions and to make sure that they are being operated in accordance with accepted standards, policies and the law. For instance, in some localities volunteers have been recruited to work in nursing and old age homes, both as program participants and as persons who make sure that the patients receive all the necessary services. Indeed, there has been some legislation requiring monitor volunteers as part of the program personnel.

There are also persons to whom volunteering is therapeutically prescribed, and who volunteer as part of a mental health program that will help them become reactivated or resocialized. In addition, there are people whose major function it is to do fund raising and/or research.

George Gallup Jr. (1980) has stated that volunteerism is important in a democratic society, implemented through the voluntary efforts of an estimated sixty million volunteers and thousands of voluntary organizations.

Volunteer influence and power is on the increase, and the volunteer world, or "Third Sector," is a viable, important, strong force in American society today. It is also growing and becoming a force in other countries around the world. Indeed the above categories barely begin to suggest the many functions which may be carried out by volunteers. The social trends and consequent implications for change noted in the next section will indicate some of the causes for the explosion of volunteer opportunities.

CHANGING - OLDER - NEWER - POPULATIONS

Our society is becoming older, and there is an end of the youth culture. The median age of the population is approximately thirty; therefore more volunteers will be available in the older age ranges, and also more of these people will be in need of services. The society is becoming more varied with an increasing number of immigrants from different countries and cultures: Hispanic, Asian and Polynesian to name a few.

The availability of these new populations makes it imperative to find creative new methods to recruit and tap into the motivations of such persons to volunteer. It is estimated that 82% of the population is willing to work on a variety of issues, but it will be necessary to change in order to involve both the new and the older populations.

This trend offers challenges of change, including: the need to develop methods to tap into intergenerational and intercultural wisdom; to develop culturally suited involvement methods; to develop community-wide resource skills banks, and centers where persons can let it be known that they wish to volunteer and can be helped to get connected; to develop "touch and go" exploration opportunities for potential volunteers before they decide whether and where they wish to put their energy and time; also to develop volunteer personnel policies and records that make the volunteer work place as humane and productive as possible; to develop new volunteer jobs, and some of a more temporary nature than in the past. Also, schools of Social Work and other professional schools must include courses and field work practice for students so as professionals they will be more knowledgeable and skillful in working with older and new volunteer populations.

DOING MORE WITH LESS

It has become very clear that as Federal human service budgets shrink, and as the tax revolt gains momentum, there are important implications for the volunteer world. "Smaller can be beautiful," but it is an uncongenial idea when at the same time there are increased expectations to meet more needs of more sophisticated constituents; and also in a society where more extensive and complex integrations of wisdom and technology require higher levels of skill and interdisciplinary competence. To respond to this crisis of opportunity, it is clear that volunteer power is needed. In California, for example, when Proposition 13 was passed and decreased tax revenues, volunteers moved in to help libraries, schools, hospitals and other institutions to continue some services that might not have been available at all. The late Eduard C. Lindeman (1961) said, "Volunteers are what hold democracy together," and he asked about the consequences if all the volunteers in the United States went on strike. It became very clear that much of the work of both private and governmental systems would stop if that occurred.

The challenge of doing more with less includes mobilization of volunteer energy, exchanging and sharing of resources, merging of overlapping activities

227

and services, finding new sources of funds, voluntary reduction of overhead costs, discovering new ways to deliver old services, and moving toward collaboration and interdependence of disparate systems, services and groups, utilizing the reciprocal and complementary resources available in more creative ways. Human service teams that cut across professional and volunteer lines are other developments that will be helpful in providing better services. Courses in limited resource management can be offered to social work and other human service professional persons.

CONCERN ABOUT HUMAN UNDERUTILIZATION

The field of human resource development is prominent in the business work place. Human resource development must become part of the volunteer world also. It is time to develop better volunteer working conditions and contracts, better opportunities for older people, for the physically and/or mentally ill, for people with language or other educational limitations, and persons with a range of values and lifestyles. Modern before and on-the-job educational programs for volunteers must be developed as well as better processes for recognizing volunteer contributions.

CHANGING VALUES

This is and will continue to be a time of changing values, moving from an emphasis on conformity to an acceptance of pluralism and the beauty of difference; from an emphasis on quantity to one on quality, or demassification; from an emphasis on rootedness to one of mobility; from an emphasis on long term commitments to an appreciation of temporariness and very short commitments; from an acceptance of authority to one of confrontation; from success being upward mobility to a more situational definition of success, namely that success is anything that helps actualize a person; from little or no focus on mental or physical qualities of life to a heavy emphasis on both of these.

The challenges here include development of more temporary volunteer opportunities; development of means to utilize differences in new and better ways; increasing the discussion and therefore the understanding of value and lifestyle differences; the need to emphasize alternative plans, job descriptions and ways of work; the need to learn the skills of conflict utilization and resolution, the art of creative compromise and the development of flex-time, part-time and job sharing in the volunteer world. It is important for human service professionals to become familiar with some of the literature and practices of the corporate work place. Many of these participatory ways of work can be adapted in the Volunteer Agency field.

CORPORATE SECTOR SOCIAL RESPONSIBILITY

During the past few years, the corporate world has become increasingly involved and interested in the volunteer world. Many large and some small companies have a management person in charge of Community Relations or Volunteer Relations, and it is their responsibility to see that employees have opportunities to volunteer in the community. Such volunteer service becomes part of the employee's personnel record. An organization known as Involvement Corps has been active for the past several years in helping corporations develop volunteer programs for their employees.

Many corporations, in addition to human resources have financial resources available. The corporate world feels it is of great importance that the private sector remain viable and indeed become increasingly more potent, important and visible.

Challenges here include the need for non-profit organizations to learn about and connect with the corporate world; to develop relationships with officers of corporations who have been designated as community liaison persons; to invite corporate persons to participate in agency activities; to discover which corporations have grants and funds available for the non-profit sector; to learn approaches and skills in working with the corporate sector.

There are some national organizations active in this area. The Independent Sector, a relatively new national organization, is focusing on examining the roles of philanthropy volunteers and independent institutions in this society, in relation to other sectors, including the corporate sector.

Also active on the national scene, and bridging some communication gaps between the voluntary and corporate sectors is an organization known as Volunteer, the National Center for Citizen Involvement. Through the Association of Voluntary Action Scholars and the Association of Volunteer Administrators social workers and other professional persons can learn and contribute productively.

It seems now that voluntarism will continue to grow and flourish because of the efforts and the interests of the government, non-profit and corporate sectors together and separately.

CHANGING TECHNOLOGY AND COMMUNICATION RESOURCES

Rapid change in socio-technical systems is affecting the volunteer world. There has been complex and fast development in computer technology, including home computers, and computer conferencing across great distances. Increasingly this technology is becoming available to organizations and institutions. Cable television, video and audio tape advances, word processing, telephone lectures and conferences make it possible for human beings to communicate in a variety of ways. Indeed, these developments provide the opportunities for people to get together to plan and provide services in new ways, in spite of shortages, high costs and shrinking budgets.

Challenges include increasing the knowledge about and skill in utilization of the new technologies; involving persons who are knowledgeable in these areas on decision making bodies as volunteers; developing more sophistication about costs and trade-offs in relation to the utilization of these new technologies; helping train people in the use of new ways of work and new machines.

THE SCIENCE OF FUTURING

There is an increased concern about and emphasis on future planning. Realistic future planning becomes imperative as projections of human, material and environmental utilization become more product, measurement and budget oriented. There is increasing emphasis on planning with diminishing resources and

229

developing survival skills in the forecasting of new programs and services.

The challenges include the need to learn realistic and useful future planning methods; to involve persons as consultants who can help with futuring and realistic views of what the future will be, so far as that is possible; to involve persons from all levels of the system or systems in future planning activities; to collaborate with other groups to increase human, material and environmental resources.

Perhaps the biggest challenge in future planning is to find ways to combine the resources of insiders, outsiders, volunteers and staff in the process itself.

From the above trends, changes and challenges can be derived the fact that the human service, corporate, governmental and volunteer world will have to continue to change. It will continue to be necessary to develop new opportunities, places and spaces for volunteers to serve. Also, it is incumbent on professional schools to update and enlarge the education of persons going into volunteer administration. Volunteers must have important roles in all sectors of the community including recreation, the arts, health, religion, education, business, politics, the media and human services of all kinds. The social action emphasis of citizen involvement will increase, and it will be important for volunteers to affect such areas as patient rights, neighborhood quality of life and others. Volunteers will continue to be strong social change agents in this country, and so it should be in a democratic society.

REFERENCES

Adams, James Luther
1976 On Being Human Religiously, Boston: Beacon Press.

Alston, Pat
1981 "Changing Face of the Volunteer," an interview with Dr. Eva Schindler-Rainman, Santa Monica Evening Outlook, March 12.

Cleveland, Harlan and Alexander King
1980 "The Renewable Way of Life," The Futurist, Vol. XIV, No. 2, Washington, D.C.: April.

Falconer, Merry
1980 "Long Range Planning: Strategy that Works," Leadership, Washington, D.C.: March.

Fox, Robert, Ronald Lippitt, and Eva Schindler-Rainman
1976 The Humanized Future: Some New Images, San Diego, Calif.: University Associates.

Gallup, George Jr.
1980 "Volunteerism: America's Best Hope for the Future," Voluntary Action Leadership, Washington, D.C.: Fall.

Lindeman, Eduard C.
1961 The Meaning of Adult Education, Montreal: Harvest House.

Lippitt, Ronald
　1981　"A Crisis of Opportunity?", Ann Arbor, Michigan.

O'Connell, Brian
　1981　"The Independent Sector and Voluntary Action," The Social Welfare
　　　　Forum 1980, New York: Columbia University Press.

Schindler-Rainman, Eva
　1979　"New Challenges for Nonprofit Agency Boards and Staff," Channels,
　　　　New York: 31(10): October.

Schindler-Rainman, Eva and Ronald Lippitt
　1977　The Volunteer Community: Creative Use of Human Resources, 2nd edition,
　　　　San Diego, Calif.: University Associates.

Schindler-Rainman, Eva and Ronald Lippitt
　1980　Building the Collaborative Community: Mobilizing Citizens for Action,
　　　　Riverside, Calif.: University of California Extension.

Schindler-Rainman, Eva
　1982　Transitioning: Strategies for The Volunteer World. Vancouver,
　　　　British Columbia, Canada: Voluntary Action Resource Centre.

Toffler, Alvin
　1980　The Third Wave, New York: Morrow, Williams, and Company.

Contributors

Davis, King E., Ph.D. Professor, School of Social Work, Norfolk
    State University, Norfolk, Virginia.

Guzzetta, Charles, Ed.D. Professor, School of Social Work,
    Hunter College of the City University of New York,
    New York, N. Y.

Haeuser, Adrienne Ahlgren, M.S. Associate Professor and Director
    of Region V Resource Center for Children and Youth
    Services, School of Social Welfare, University of
    Wisconsin at Milwaukee, Milwaukee, Wisconsin.

Hermann-Keeling, Evie, M.A. Parents Anonymous of Connecticut, Inc.

Herington, Winnifred, M.S.W. Associate Dean, Faculty of Social
    Work, University of Toronto, Toronto, Canada.

Kramer, Ralph M., D.S.W. Professor, School of Social Welfare,
    University of California at Berkeley, Berkeley, Calif.

Lowy, Louis, Ph.D. Professor, School of Social Work, Boston
    University, Boston, Massachusetts.

McGrath, Susan, M.S.W., Association of Junior Leagues, Inc.,
    New York, N. Y.

Orr, Sally Y., M.S.W. Director of Public Policy, Association of
    Junior Leagues, Inc., New York, N. Y.

Perlmutter, Felice Davidson, Ph.D. Professor, Chairperson of the
    Administration and Planning Track, School of Social
    Administration, Temple University, Philadelphia, Pa.

Phillips, Michael H., D.S.W. Professor, School of Social Work,
    Fordham University, New York, N. Y.

Pincus, Cynthia S., Ph.D. Assistant Clinical Professor, Department
    of Psychiatry in Social Work, Yale University School of
    Medicine, New Haven, Conn.

Potter-Efron, Patricia S., B.A.   Director of Family Treatment,
        Buffalo Memorial Adolescent Chemical Dependence
        Treatment Center, Mondovi, Wisconsin.

Potter-Efron, Ronald T., Ph.D.   Assistant Professor, Department
        of Social Work, University of Wisconsin-Eau Claire,
        Eau Claire, Wisconsin.

Raiff, Norma Radol, Ph.D.   Director of Research and Evaluation,
        Mon Valley Community Mental Health Center, Monessen, Pa.

Reisch, Michael, Ph.D.   Assistant Professor, School of Social
        Work and Community Planning, University of Maryland
        at Baltimore, Maryland.

Schindler-Rainman, Eva, D.S.W. Organizational Consultant, Private
        Practice, Los Angeles, California.

Schwartz, Florence S., Ed.D. Associate Professor, School of
        Social Work, Hunter College of the City University of
        New York, New York, N.Y.

Seguin, Mary M., D.S.W.   Professor, School of Social Welfare,
        University of California at Los Angeles, California.

Seidel, Deborah L., Executive Director, Association of Junior
        Leagues, New York, N. Y.

Sieder, Violet M., Ph.D. Professor Emerita, Heller School,
        Brandeis University, Waltham, Massachusetts.

Shore, Barbara K., Ph.D.   Professor, School of Social Work,
        University of Pittsburgh, Pittsburgh, Pennsylvania.

Weil, Marie, D.S.W.   Assistant Professor, School of Social Work,
        University of Southern California, Los Angeles, Calif.

Wenocur, Stanley, D.S.W.   Associate Professor, School of Social
        Work and Community Planning, University of Maryland
        at Baltimore, Baltimore, Maryland.